Dreaming of Harvestar

THE GREAT COW RACE

VOLUME TWO:
THE GREAT COW RACE

JEFF SMITH

CARTOON BOOKS
COLUMBUS, OHIO

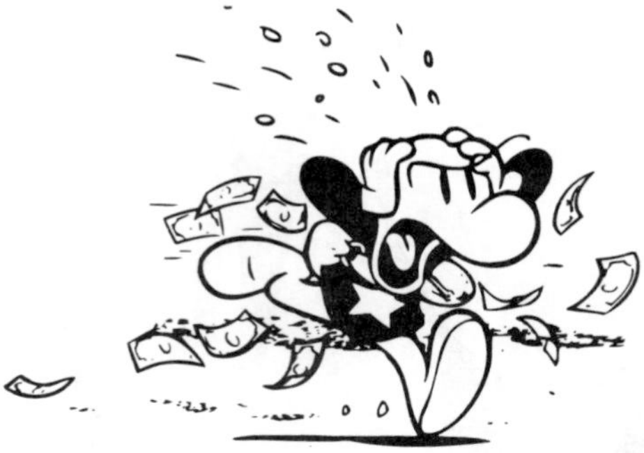

THIS BOOK IS
FOR
DAN ROOT

Acknowledgements: The Harvestar Family Crest designed by Charles Vess, and color airbrush on dustjacket by David Reed.

Other books by Jeff Smith: *BONE Volume One: Out From Boneville*

For information write:
Cartoon Books
P.O. Box 16973
Columbus, OH 43216

First Edition

Softcover ISBN: 0-9636609-5-0
Hardcover ISBN: 0-9636609-8-5

Library of Congress Catalog Card Number: 95-071607

10 9 8 7 6 5 4 3 2

Printed in Canada

AFTER BEING RUN OUT OF BONEVILLE, THE THREE BONE COUSINS, FONE BONE, PHONEY BONE, AND SMILEY BONE, ARE SEPARATED AND LOST IN A VAST UNCHARTED DESERT.

ONE BY ONE, THEY FIND THEIR WAY INTO A DEEP, FORESTED VALLEY FILLED WITH WONDERFUL AND TERRIFYING CREATURES...

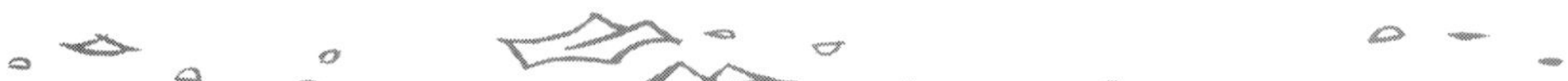

9

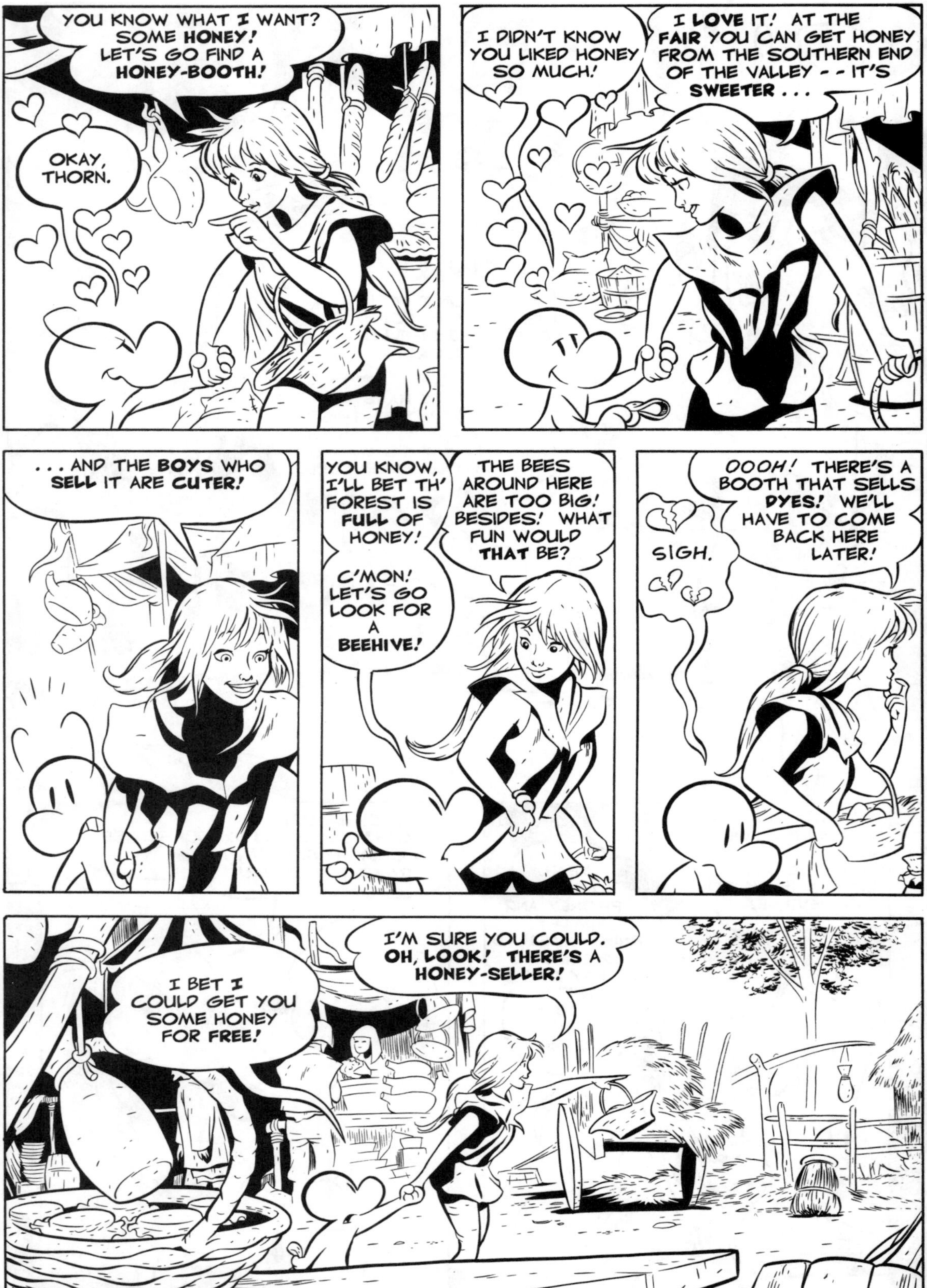

YOU KNOW WHAT I WANT? SOME HONEY! LET'S GO FIND A HONEY-BOOTH!
OKAY, THORN.
I DIDN'T KNOW YOU LIKED HONEY SO MUCH!
I LOVE IT! AT THE FAIR YOU CAN GET HONEY FROM THE SOUTHERN END OF THE VALLEY - - IT'S SWEETER . . .
. . . AND THE BOYS WHO SELL IT ARE CUTER!
YOU KNOW, I'LL BET TH' FOREST IS FULL OF HONEY!
C'MON! LET'S GO LOOK FOR A BEEHIVE!
THE BEES AROUND HERE ARE TOO BIG! BESIDES! WHAT FUN WOULD THAT BE?
SIGH.
OOOH! THERE'S A BOOTH THAT SELLS DYES! WE'LL HAVE TO COME BACK HERE LATER!
I BET I COULD GET YOU SOME HONEY FOR FREE!
I'M SURE YOU COULD. OH, LOOK! THERE'S A HONEY-SELLER!

12

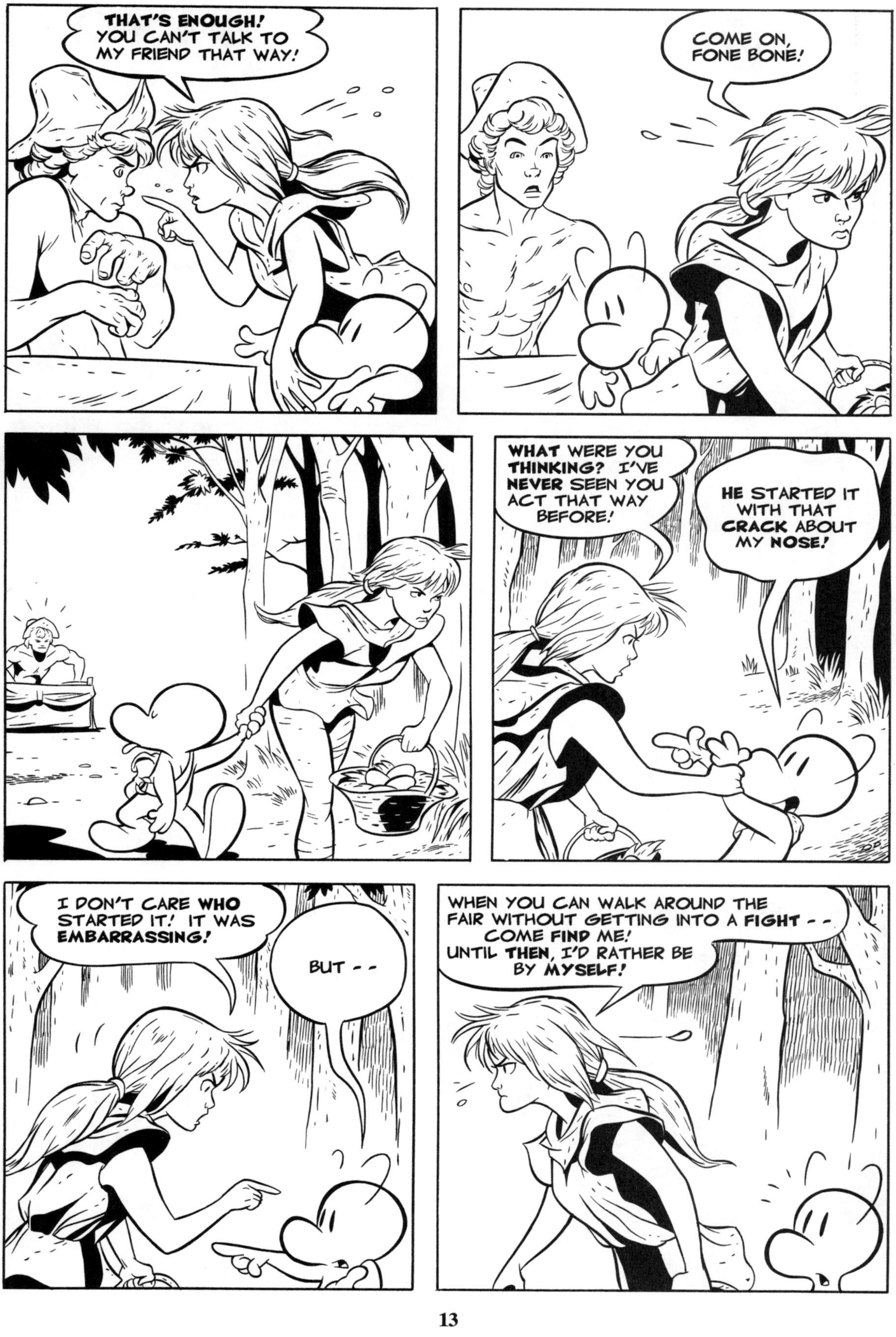
THAT'S ENOUGH! YOU CAN'T TALK TO MY FRIEND THAT WAY!
COME ON, FONE BONE!
WHAT WERE YOU THINKING? I'VE NEVER SEEN YOU ACT THAT WAY BEFORE!
HE STARTED IT WITH THAT CRACK ABOUT MY NOSE!
I DON'T CARE WHO STARTED IT! IT WAS EMBARRASSING!
BUT - -
WHEN YOU CAN WALK AROUND THE FAIR WITHOUT GETTING INTO A FIGHT - - COME FIND ME! UNTIL THEN, I'D RATHER BE BY MYSELF!

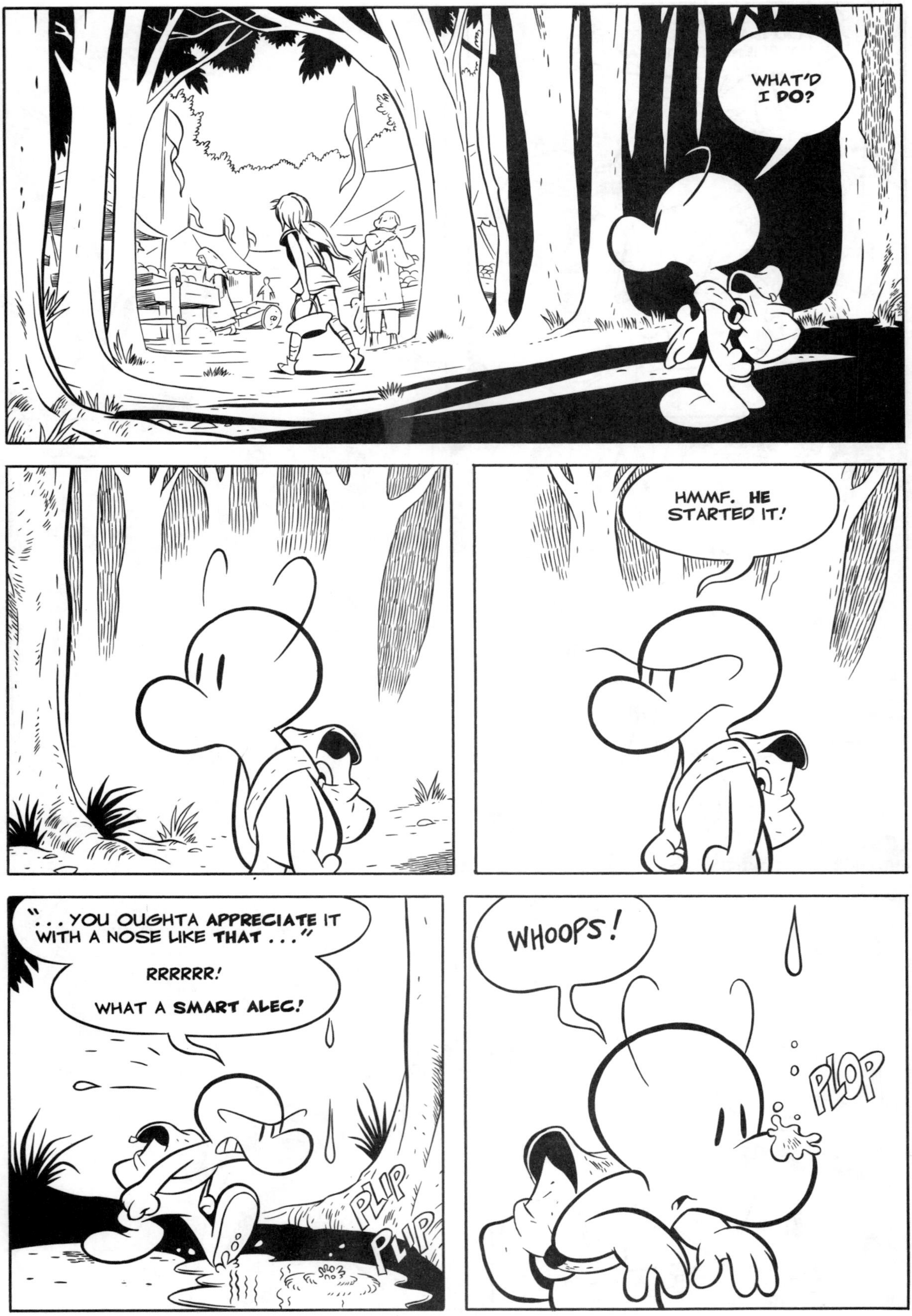
WHAT'D I DO?
HMMF. HE STARTED IT!
"...YOU OUGHTA APPRECIATE IT WITH A NOSE LIKE THAT..."
RRRRRR!
WHAT A SMART ALEC!
PLIP
PLIP
WHOOPS!
PLOP

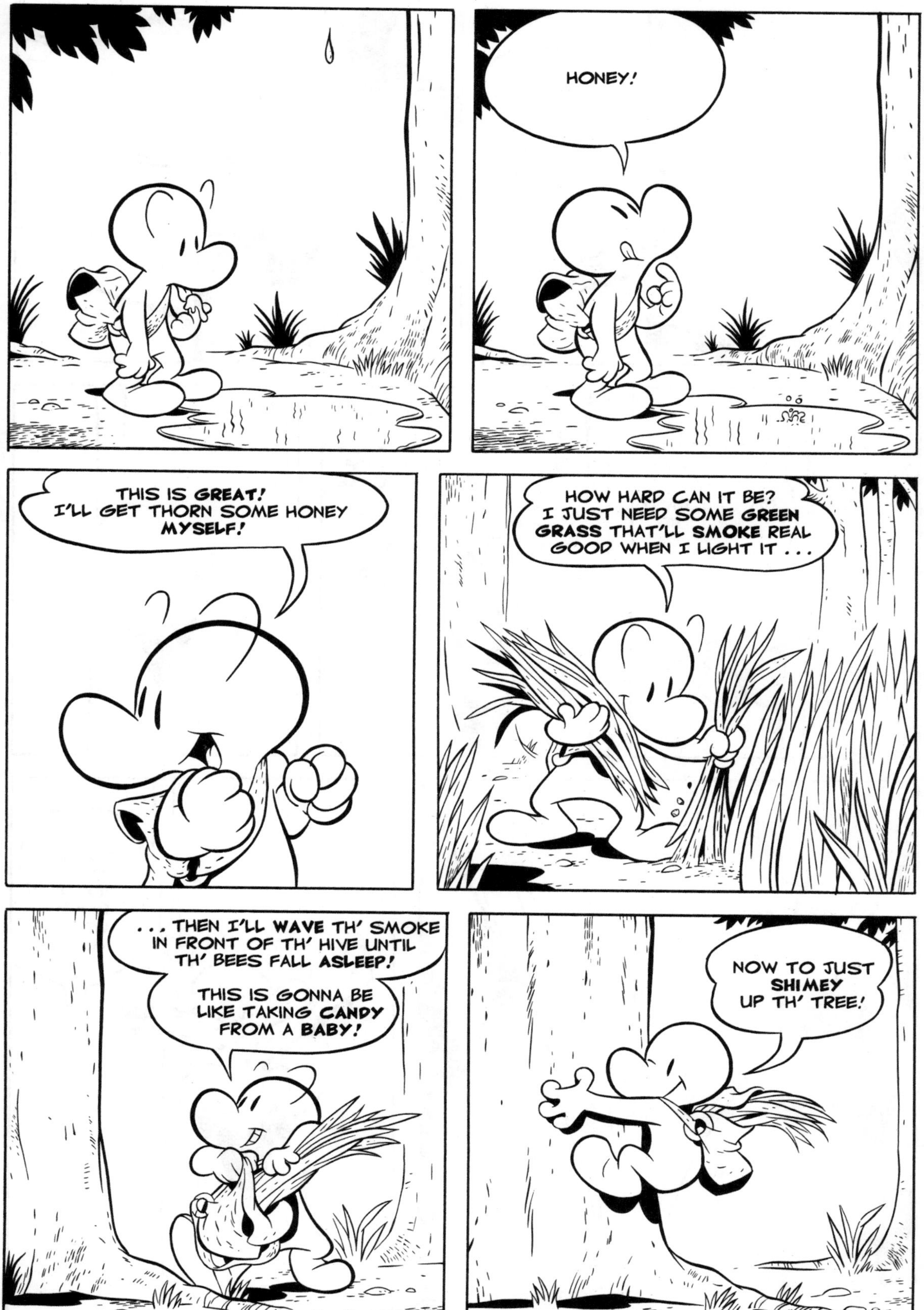
HONEY!
THIS IS GREAT! I'LL GET THORN SOME HONEY MYSELF!
HOW HARD CAN IT BE? I JUST NEED SOME GREEN GRASS THAT'LL SMOKE REAL GOOD WHEN I LIGHT IT . . .
. . . THEN I'LL WAVE TH' SMOKE IN FRONT OF TH' HIVE UNTIL TH' BEES FALL ASLEEP!
THIS IS GONNA BE LIKE TAKING CANDY FROM A BABY!
NOW TO JUST SHIMEY UP TH' TREE!

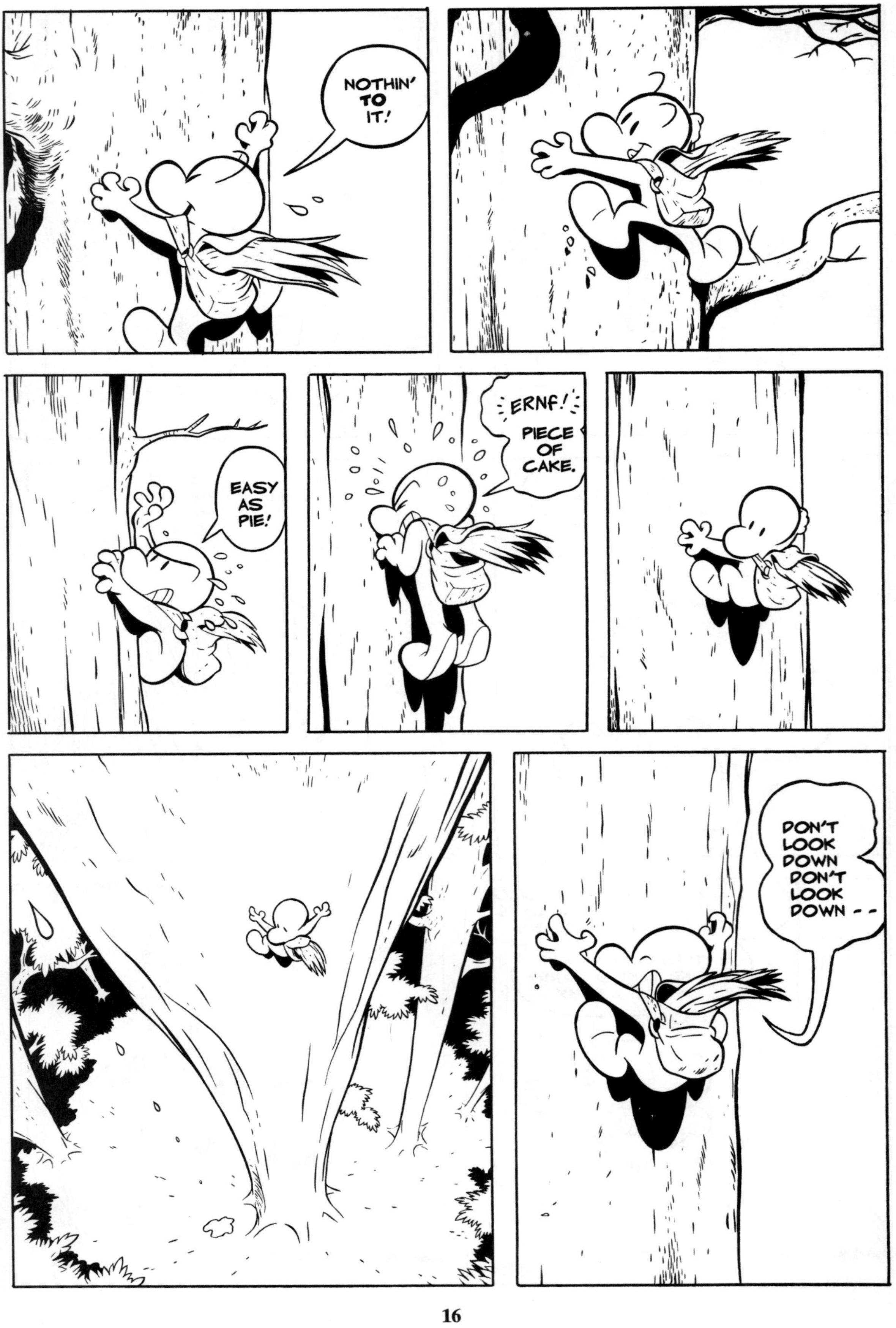
NOTHIN' TO IT!
EASY AS PIE!
ERNF!
PIECE OF CAKE.
DON'T LOOK DOWN DON'T LOOK DOWN - -

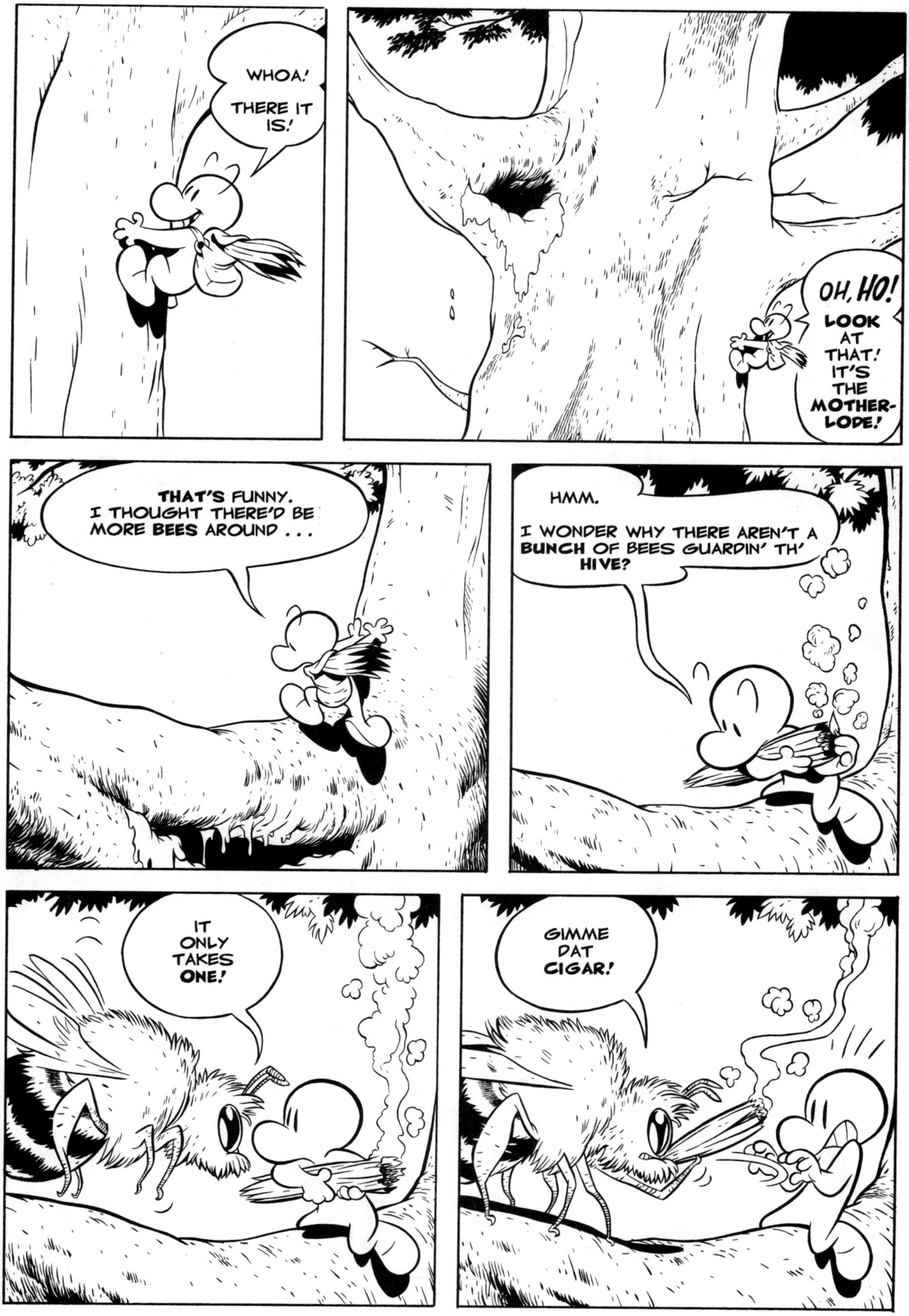
WHOA! THERE IT IS!
OH, HO! LOOK AT THAT! IT'S THE MOTHER-LODE!
THAT'S FUNNY. I THOUGHT THERE'D BE MORE BEES AROUND . . .
HMM.
I WONDER WHY THERE AREN'T A BUNCH OF BEES GUARDIN' TH' HIVE?
IT ONLY TAKES ONE!
GIMME DAT CIGAR!

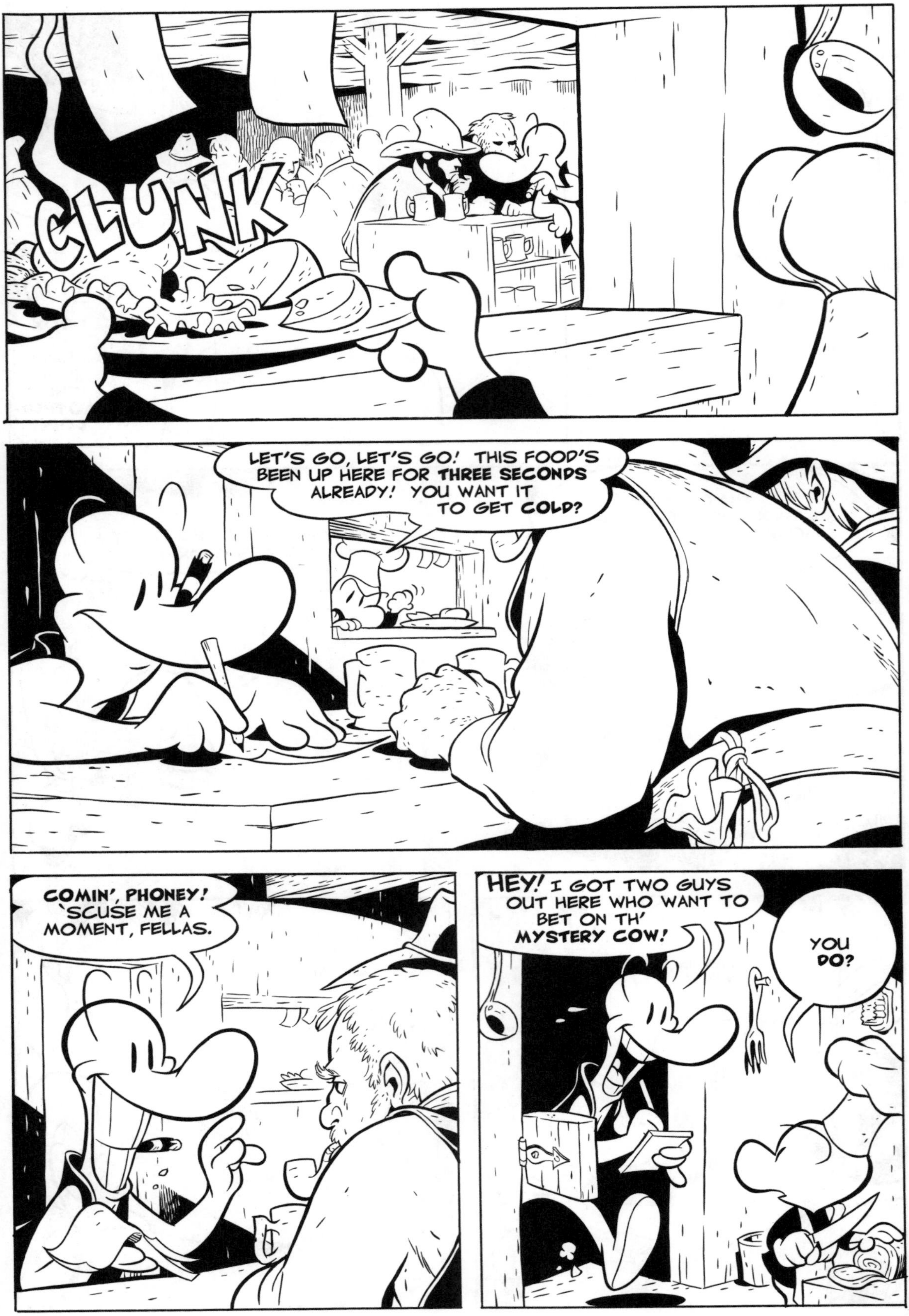
CLUNK
LET'S GO, LET'S GO! THIS FOOD'S BEEN UP HERE FOR THREE SECONDS ALREADY! YOU WANT IT TO GET COLD?
COMIN', PHONEY! 'SCUSE ME A MOMENT, FELLAS.
HEY! I GOT TWO GUYS OUT HERE WHO WANT TO BET ON TH' MYSTERY COW!
YOU DO?

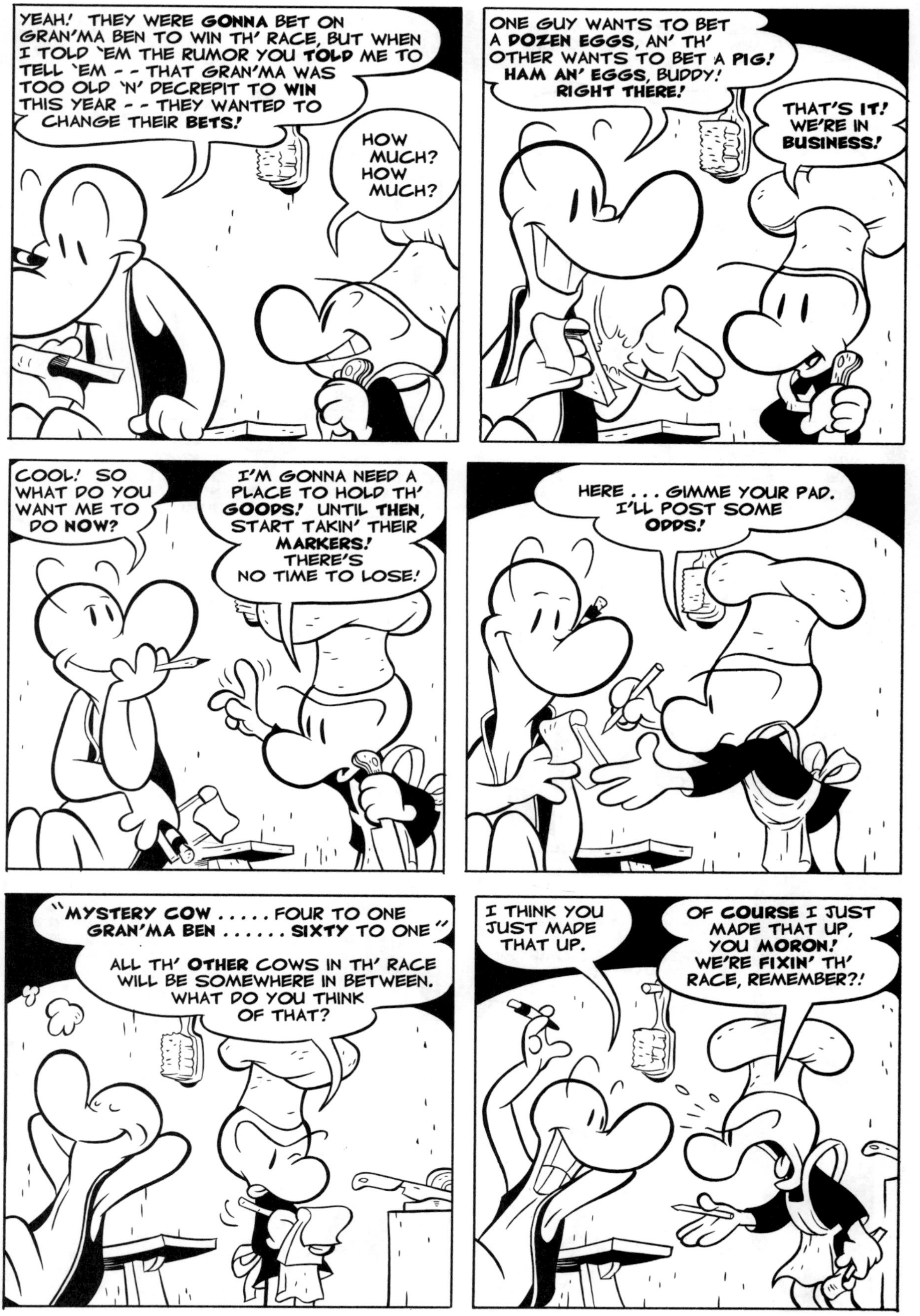
YEAH! THEY WERE GONNA BET ON GRAN'MA BEN TO WIN TH' RACE, BUT WHEN I TOLD 'EM THE RUMOR YOU TOLD ME TO TELL 'EM -- THAT GRAN'MA WAS TOO OLD 'N' DECREPIT TO WIN THIS YEAR -- THEY WANTED TO CHANGE THEIR BETS!
HOW MUCH? HOW MUCH?
ONE GUY WANTS TO BET A DOZEN EGGS, AN' TH' OTHER WANTS TO BET A PIG! HAM AN' EGGS, BUDDY! RIGHT THERE!
THAT'S IT! WE'RE IN BUSINESS!
COOL! SO WHAT DO YOU WANT ME TO DO NOW?
I'M GONNA NEED A PLACE TO HOLD TH' GOODS! UNTIL THEN, START TAKIN' THEIR MARKERS! THERE'S NO TIME TO LOSE!
HERE . . . GIMME YOUR PAD. I'LL POST SOME ODDS!
"MYSTERY COW ..... FOUR TO ONE GRAN'MA BEN ...... SIXTY TO ONE"
ALL TH' OTHER COWS IN TH' RACE WILL BE SOMEWHERE IN BETWEEN. WHAT DO YOU THINK OF THAT?
I THINK YOU JUST MADE THAT UP.
OF COURSE I JUST MADE THAT UP, YOU MORON! WE'RE FIXIN' TH' RACE, REMEMBER?!

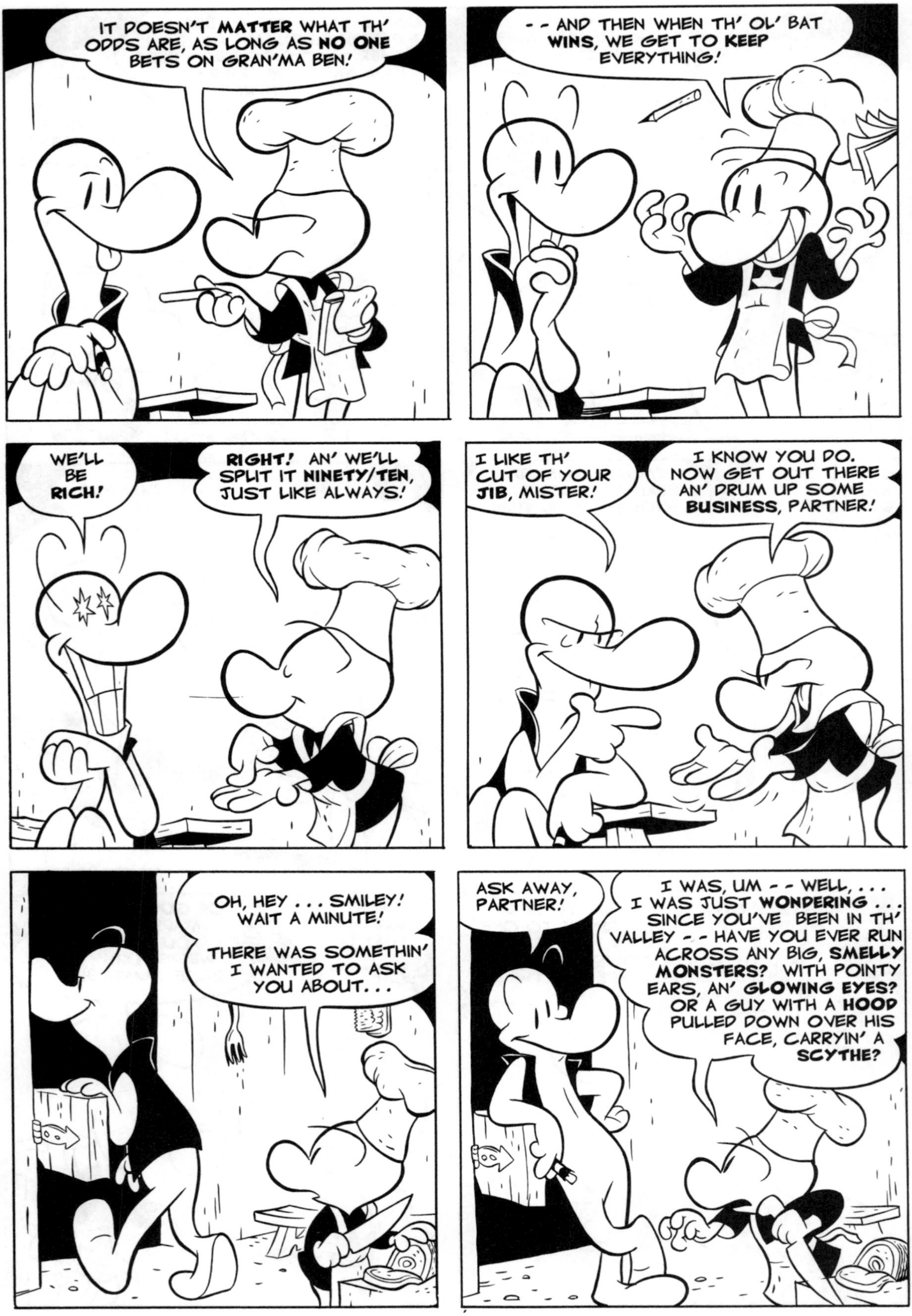
IT DOESN'T MATTER WHAT TH' ODDS ARE, AS LONG AS NO ONE BETS ON GRAN'MA BEN!
- - AND THEN WHEN TH' OL' BAT WINS, WE GET TO KEEP EVERYTHING!
WE'LL BE RICH!
RIGHT! AN' WE'LL SPLIT IT NINETY/TEN, JUST LIKE ALWAYS!
I LIKE TH' CUT OF YOUR JIB, MISTER!
I KNOW YOU DO. NOW GET OUT THERE AN' DRUM UP SOME BUSINESS, PARTNER!
OH, HEY . . . SMILEY! WAIT A MINUTE!
THERE WAS SOMETHIN' I WANTED TO ASK YOU ABOUT. . .
ASK AWAY, PARTNER!
I WAS, UM - - WELL, . . . I WAS JUST WONDERING . . . SINCE YOU'VE BEEN IN TH' VALLEY - - HAVE YOU EVER RUN ACROSS ANY BIG, SMELLY MONSTERS? WITH POINTY EARS, AN' GLOWING EYES? OR A GUY WITH A HOOD PULLED DOWN OVER HIS FACE, CARRYIN' A SCYTHE?

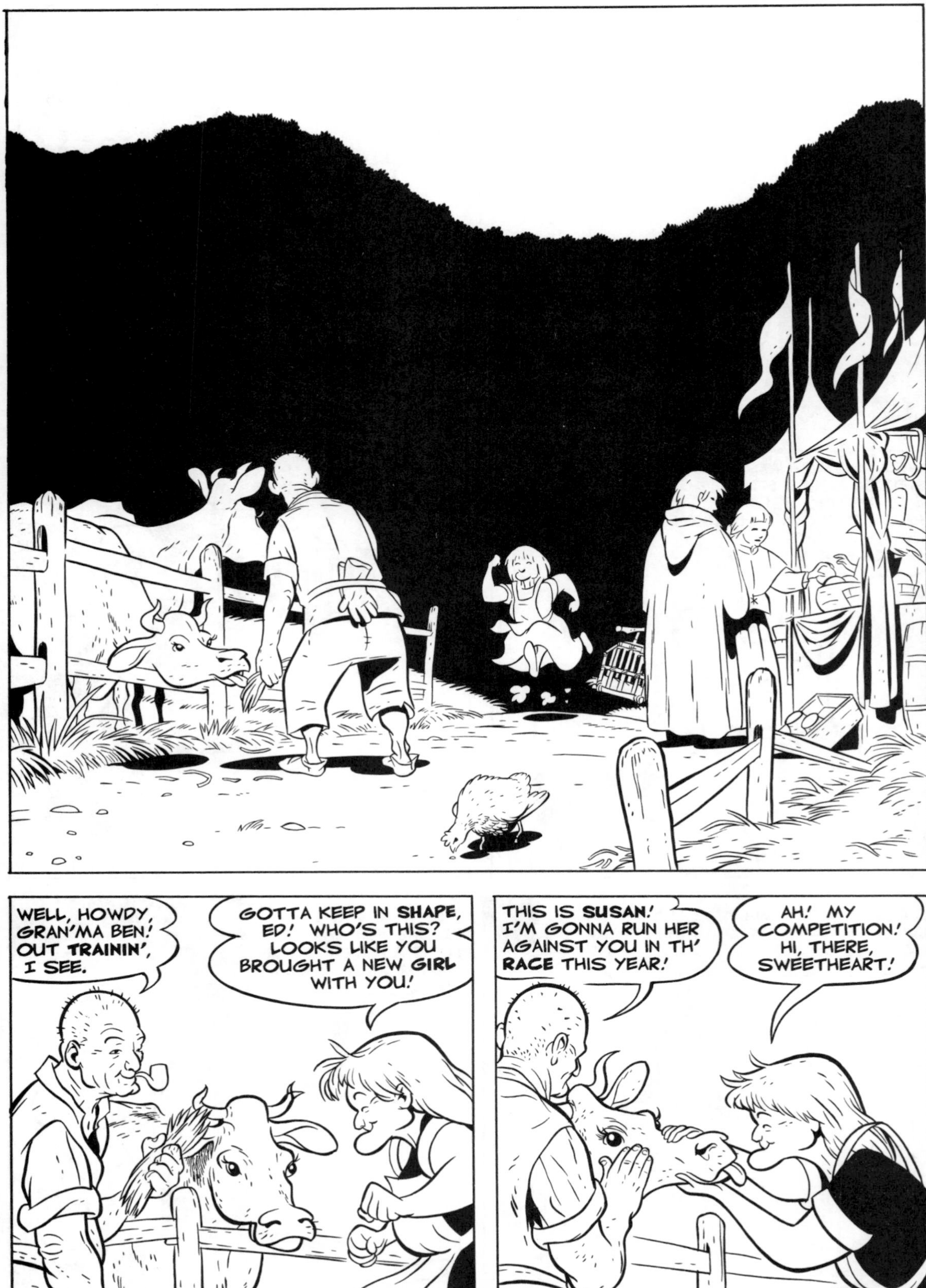
WELL, HOWDY, GRAN'MA BEN! OUT TRAININ', I SEE.
GOTTA KEEP IN SHAPE, ED! WHO'S THIS? LOOKS LIKE YOU BROUGHT A NEW GIRL WITH YOU!
THIS IS SUSAN! I'M GONNA RUN HER AGAINST YOU IN TH' RACE THIS YEAR!
AH! MY COMPETITION! HI, THERE, SWEETHEART!

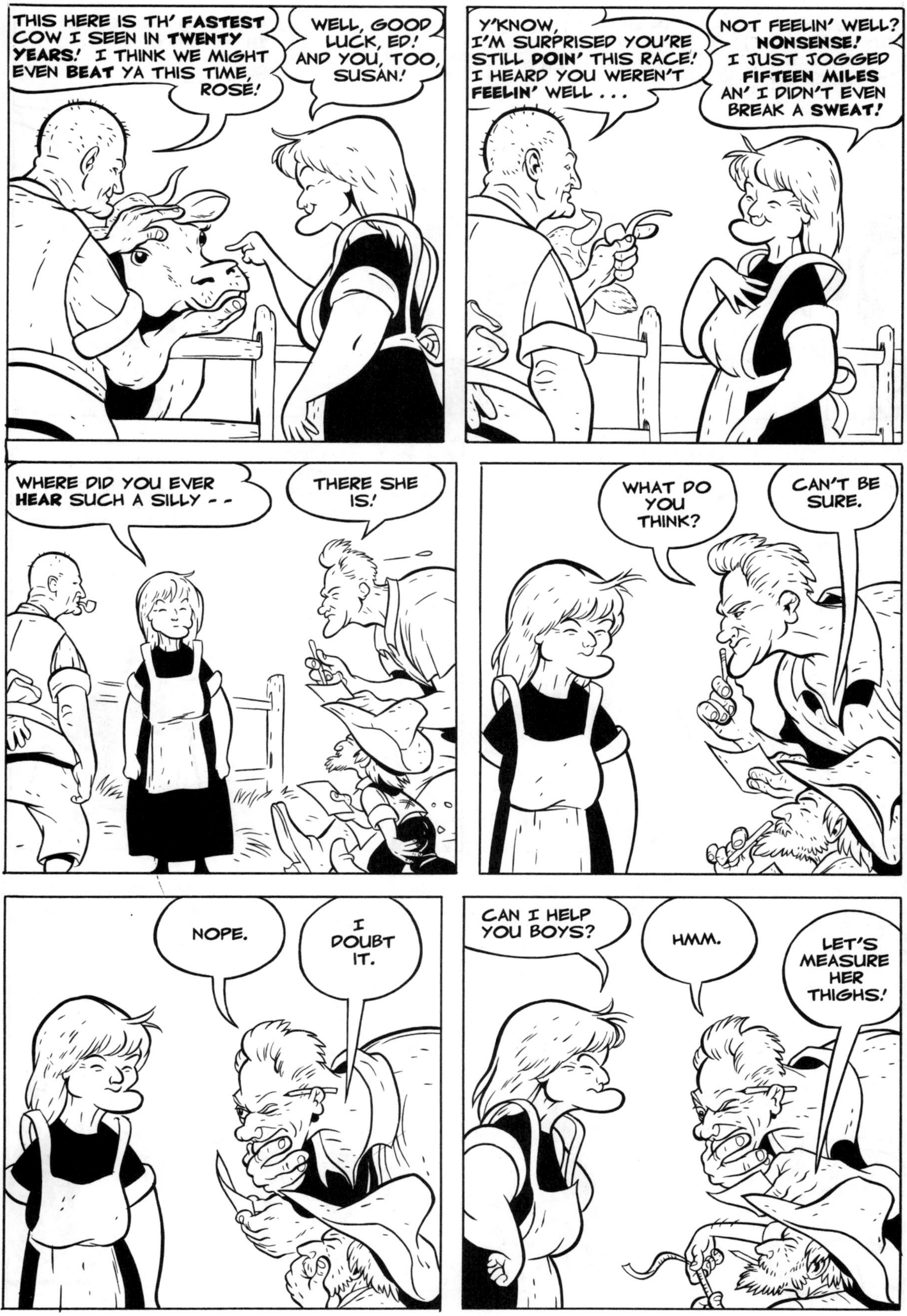
THIS HERE IS TH' FASTEST COW I SEEN IN TWENTY YEARS! I THINK WE MIGHT EVEN BEAT YA THIS TIME, ROSE!
WELL, GOOD LUCK, ED! AND YOU, TOO, SUSAN!
Y'KNOW, I'M SURPRISED YOU'RE STILL DOIN' THIS RACE! I HEARD YOU WEREN'T FEELIN' WELL . . .
NOT FEELIN' WELL? NONSENSE! I JUST JOGGED FIFTEEN MILES AN' I DIDN'T EVEN BREAK A SWEAT!
WHERE DID YOU EVER HEAR SUCH A SILLY - -
THERE SHE IS!
WHAT DO YOU THINK?
CAN'T BE SURE.
NOPE.
I DOUBT IT.
CAN I HELP YOU BOYS?
HMM.
LET'S MEASURE HER THIGHS!

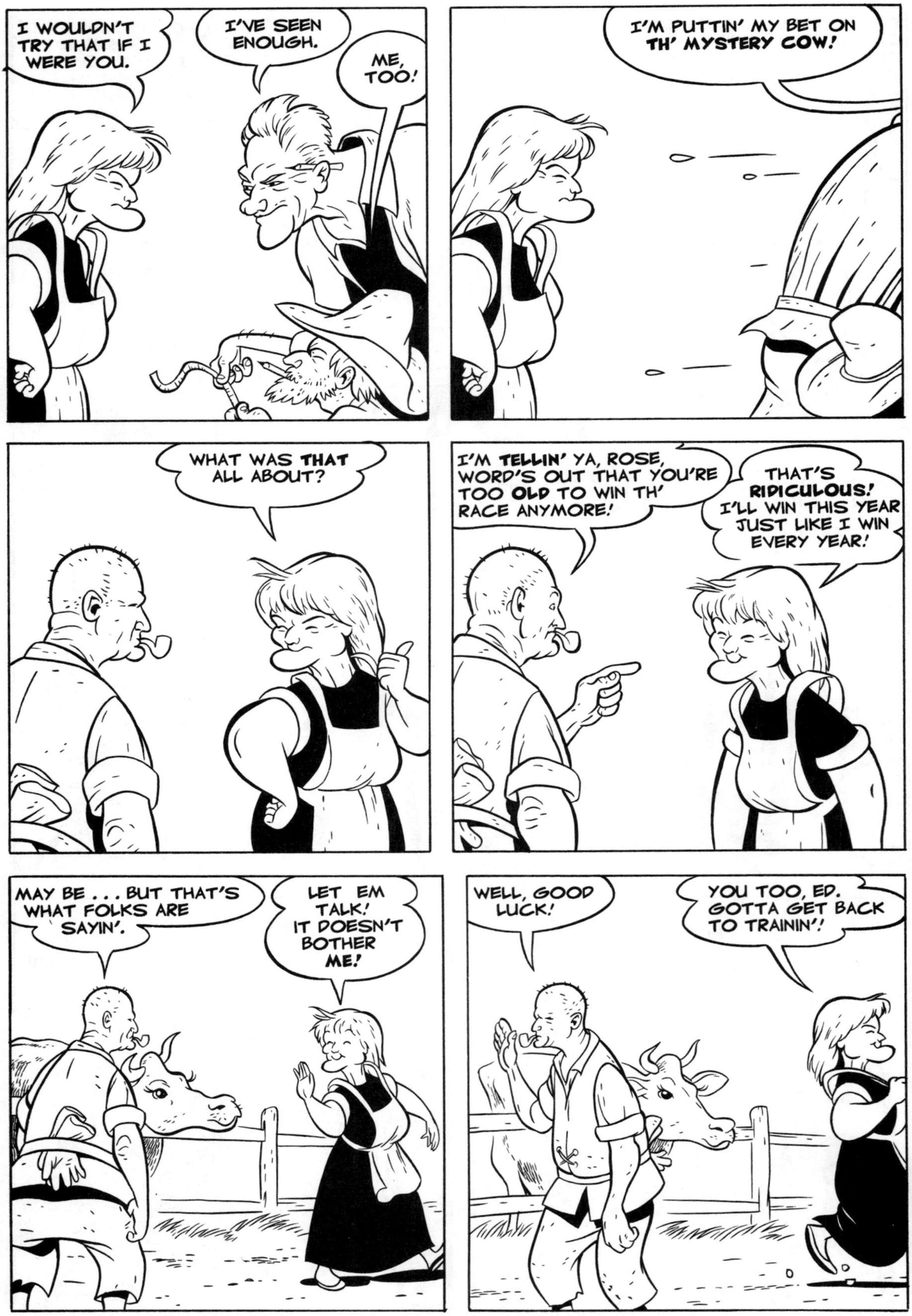
I WOULDN'T TRY THAT IF I WERE YOU.
I'VE SEEN ENOUGH.
ME, TOO!
I'M PUTTIN' MY BET ON TH' MYSTERY COW!
WHAT WAS THAT ALL ABOUT?
I'M TELLIN' YA, ROSE, WORD'S OUT THAT YOU'RE TOO OLD TO WIN TH' RACE ANYMORE!
THAT'S RIDICULOUS! I'LL WIN THIS YEAR JUST LIKE I WIN EVERY YEAR!
MAY BE . . . BUT THAT'S WHAT FOLKS ARE SAYIN'.
LET EM TALK! IT DOESN'T BOTHER ME!
WELL, GOOD LUCK!
YOU TOO, ED. GOTTA GET BACK TO TRAININ'!

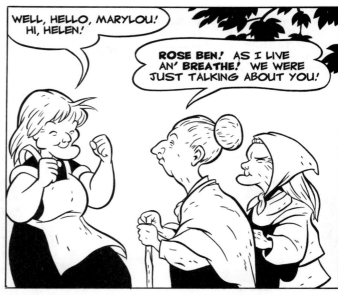

WELL, HELLO, MARYLOU! HI, HELEN!

ROSE BEN! AS I LIVE AN' BREATHE! WE WERE JUST TALKING ABOUT YOU!

WE WERE JUST SAYING THAT WE WEREN'T GOING TO BET ON YOU THIS YEAR!

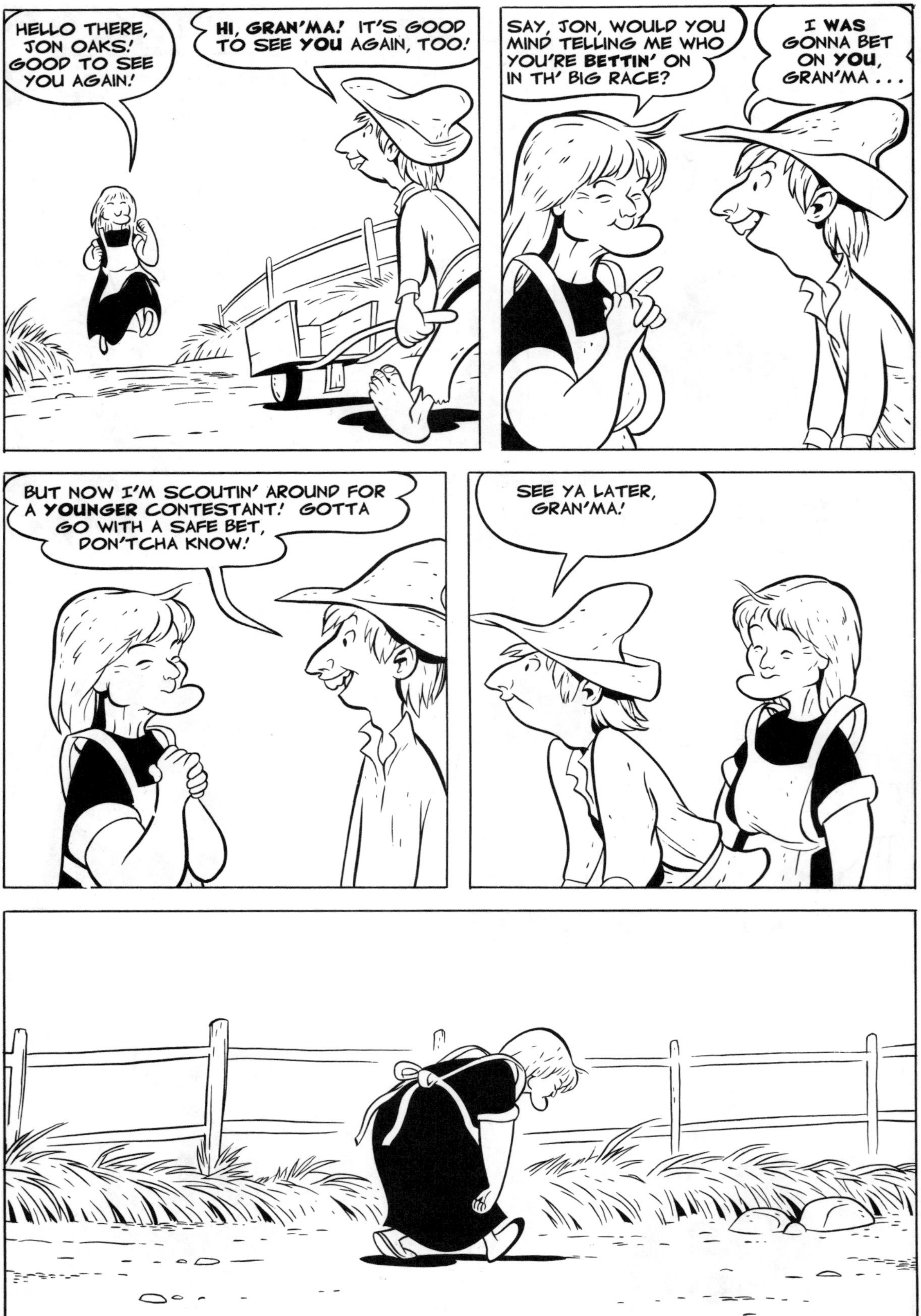
HELLO THERE, JON OAKS! GOOD TO SEE YOU AGAIN!
HI, GRAN'MA! IT'S GOOD TO SEE YOU AGAIN, TOO!
SAY, JON, WOULD YOU MIND TELLING ME WHO YOU'RE BETTIN' ON IN TH' BIG RACE?
I WAS GONNA BET ON YOU, GRAN'MA . . .
BUT NOW I'M SCOUTIN' AROUND FOR A YOUNGER CONTESTANT! GOTTA GO WITH A SAFE BET, DON'TCHA KNOW!
SEE YA LATER, GRAN'MA!

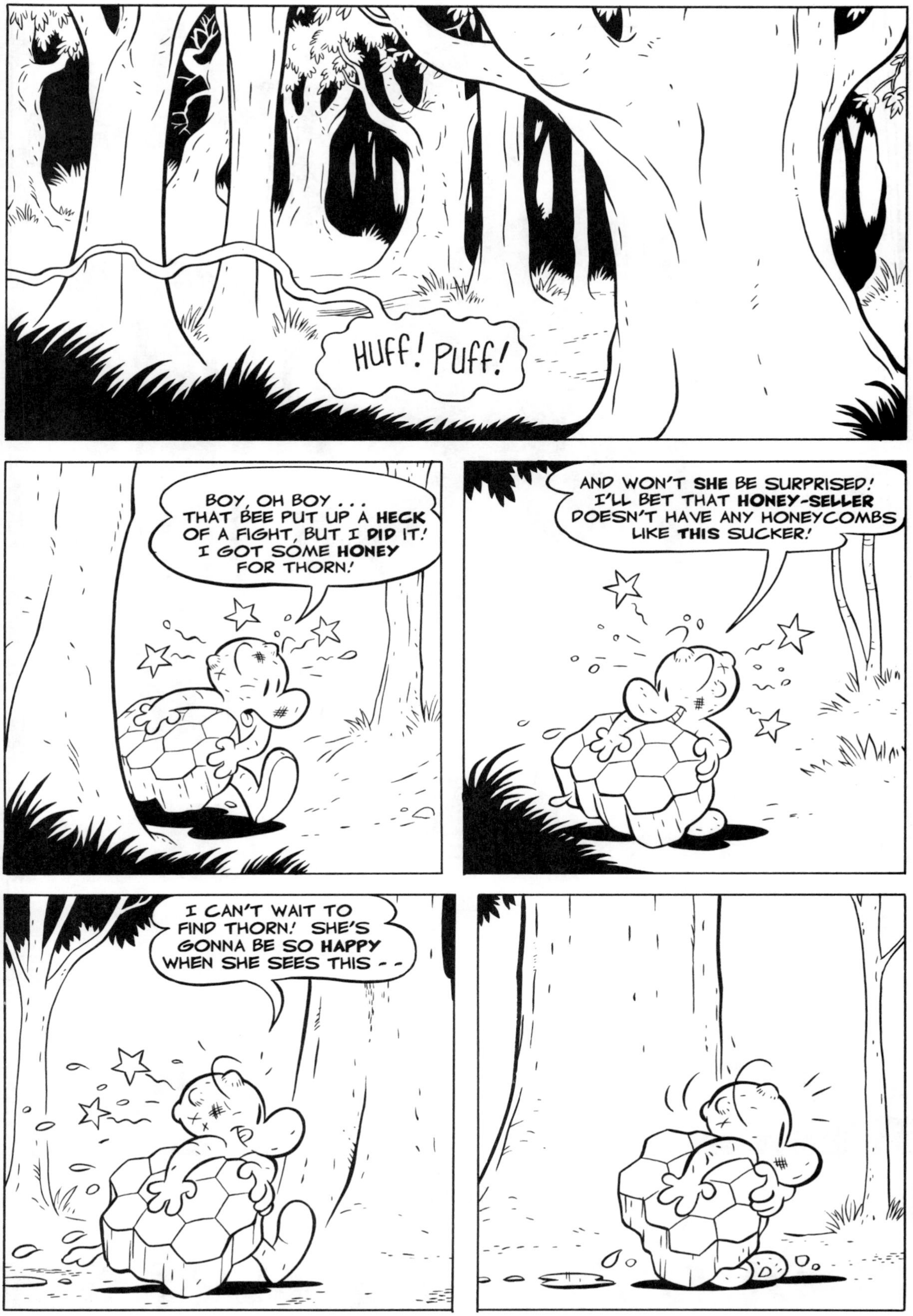
HUFF! PUFF!
BOY, OH BOY . . . THAT BEE PUT UP A HECK OF A FIGHT, BUT I DID IT! I GOT SOME HONEY FOR THORN!
AND WON'T SHE BE SURPRISED! I'LL BET THAT HONEY-SELLER DOESN'T HAVE ANY HONEYCOMBS LIKE THIS SUCKER!
I CAN'T WAIT TO FIND THORN! SHE'S GONNA BE SO HAPPY WHEN SHE SEES THIS - -

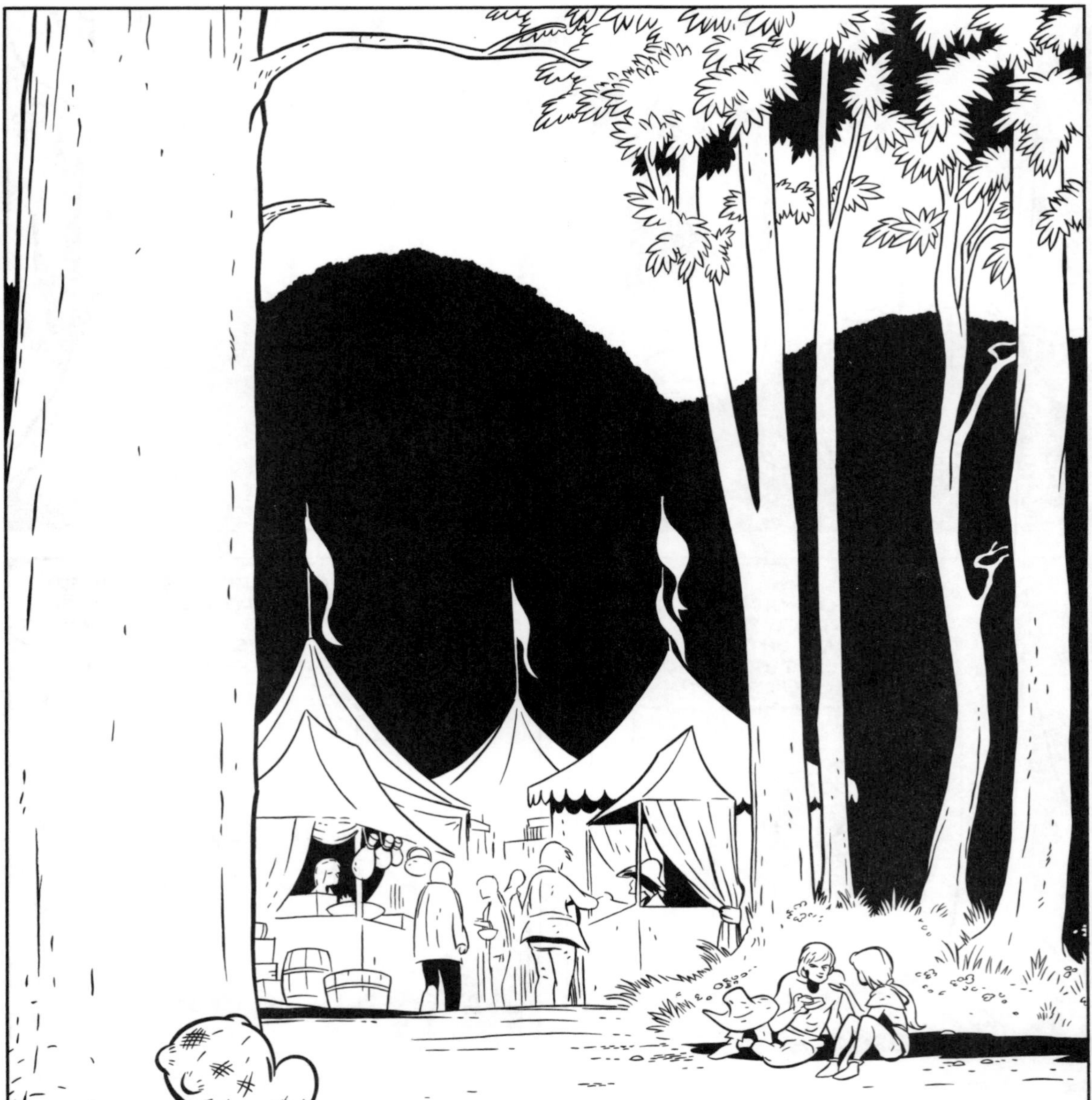

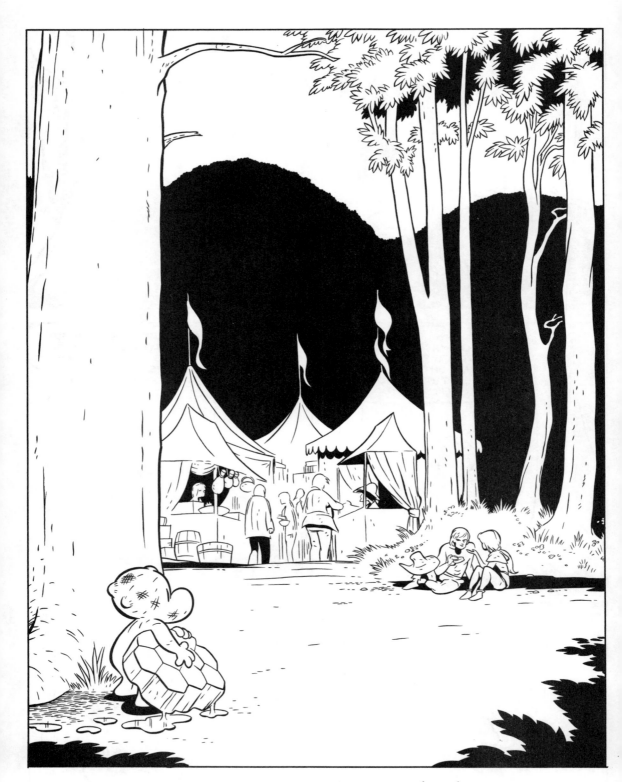

Next: THE MAP

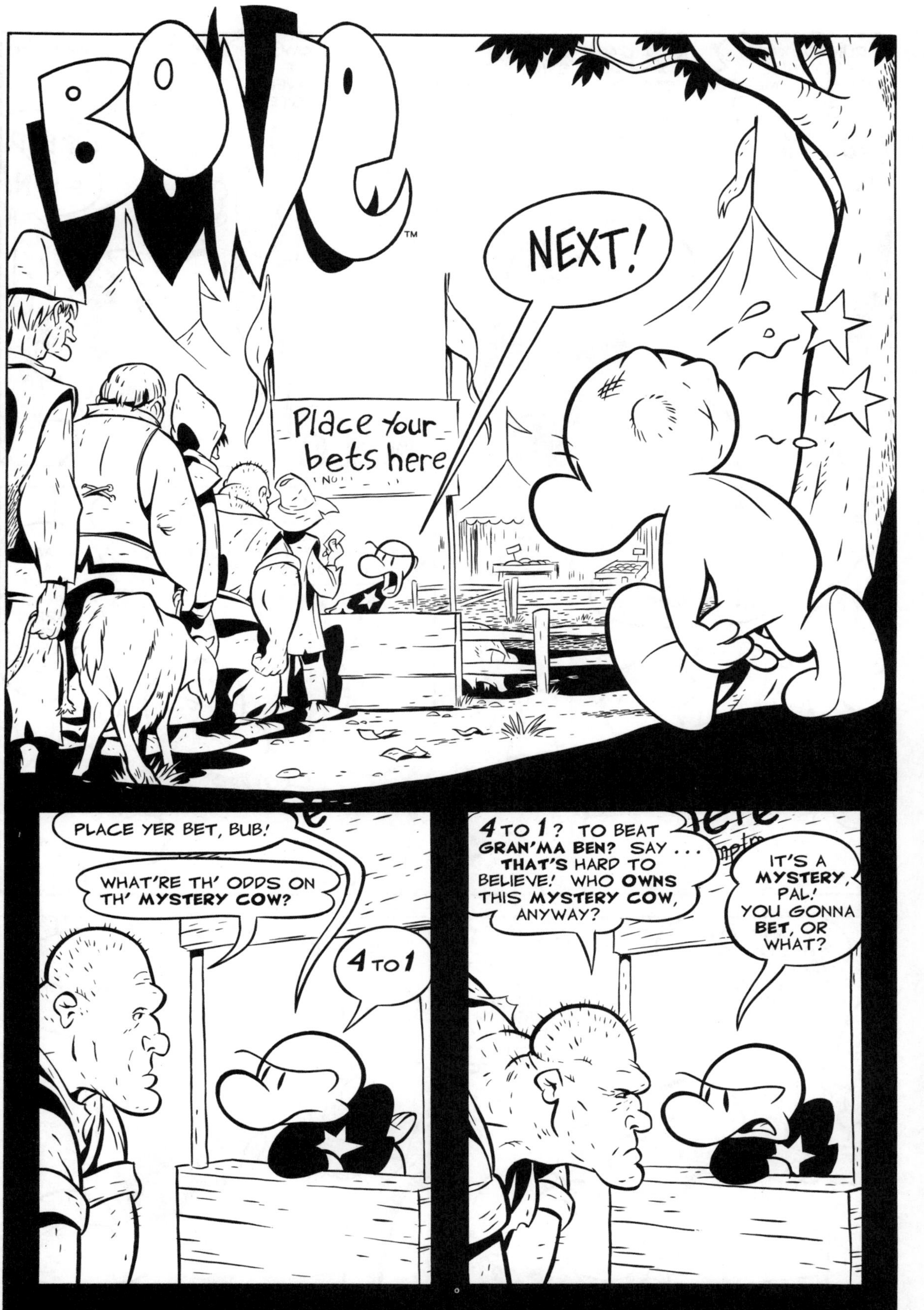
BONE™
Place your bets here
NEXT!
PLACE YER BET, BUB!
WHAT'RE TH' ODDS ON TH' MYSTERY COW?
4 TO 1
4 TO 1? TO BEAT GRAN'MA BEN? SAY... THAT'S HARD TO BELIEVE! WHO OWNS THIS MYSTERY COW, ANYWAY?
IT'S A MYSTERY, PAL! YOU GONNA BET, OR WHAT?

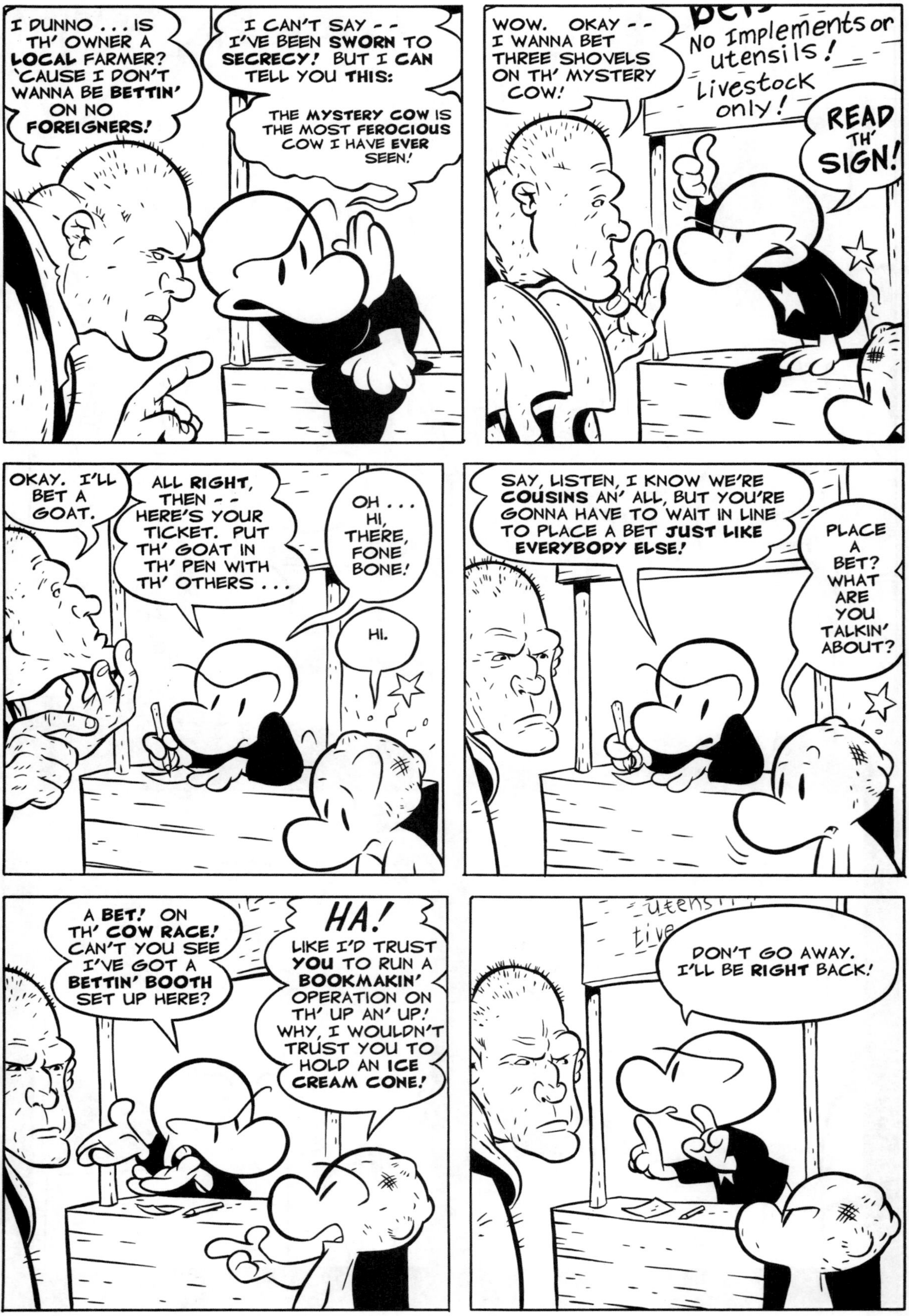
I DUNNO . . . IS TH' OWNER A LOCAL FARMER? 'CAUSE I DON'T WANNA BE BETTIN' ON NO FOREIGNERS!
I CAN'T SAY - - I'VE BEEN SWORN TO SECRECY! BUT I CAN TELL YOU THIS:
THE MYSTERY COW IS THE MOST FEROCIOUS COW I HAVE EVER SEEN!
WOW. OKAY - - I WANNA BET THREE SHOVELS ON TH' MYSTERY COW!
No Implements or utensils!
Livestock only!
READ TH' SIGN!
OKAY. I'LL BET A GOAT.
ALL RIGHT, THEN - - HERE'S YOUR TICKET. PUT TH' GOAT IN TH' PEN WITH TH' OTHERS . . .
OH . . . HI, THERE, FONE BONE!
HI.
SAY, LISTEN, I KNOW WE'RE COUSINS AN' ALL, BUT YOU'RE GONNA HAVE TO WAIT IN LINE TO PLACE A BET JUST LIKE EVERYBODY ELSE!
PLACE A BET? WHAT ARE YOU TALKIN' ABOUT?
A BET! ON TH' COW RACE! CAN'T YOU SEE I'VE GOT A BETTIN' BOOTH SET UP HERE?
HA!
LIKE I'D TRUST YOU TO RUN A BOOKMAKIN' OPERATION ON TH' UP AN' UP! WHY, I WOULDN'T TRUST YOU TO HOLD AN ICE CREAM CONE!
DON'T GO AWAY. I'LL BE RIGHT BACK!

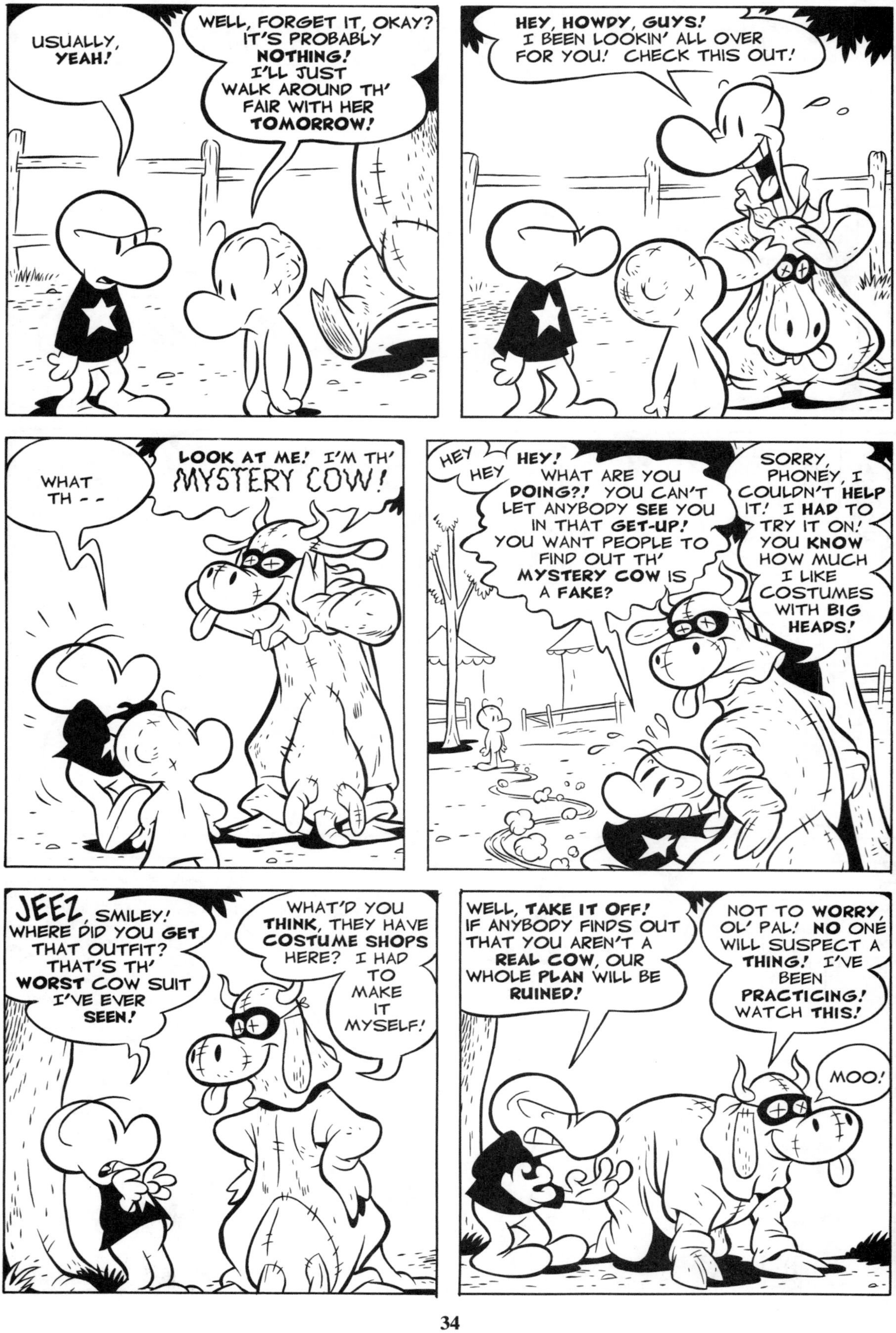

USUALLY, YEAH!
WELL, FORGET IT, OKAY? IT'S PROBABLY NOTHING! I'LL JUST WALK AROUND TH' FAIR WITH HER TOMORROW!
HEY, HOWDY, GUYS! I BEEN LOOKIN' ALL OVER FOR YOU! CHECK THIS OUT!
WHAT TH --
LOOK AT ME! I'M TH' MYSTERY COW!
HEY HEY
HEY! WHAT ARE YOU DOING?! YOU CAN'T LET ANYBODY SEE YOU IN THAT GET-UP! YOU WANT PEOPLE TO FIND OUT TH' MYSTERY COW IS A FAKE?
SORRY, PHONEY, I COULDN'T HELP IT! I HAD TO TRY IT ON! YOU KNOW HOW MUCH I LIKE COSTUMES WITH BIG HEADS!
JEEZ, SMILEY! WHERE DID YOU GET THAT OUTFIT? THAT'S TH' WORST COW SUIT I'VE EVER SEEN!
WHAT'D YOU THINK, THEY HAVE COSTUME SHOPS HERE? I HAD TO MAKE IT MYSELF!
WELL, TAKE IT OFF! IF ANYBODY FINDS OUT THAT YOU AREN'T A REAL COW, OUR WHOLE PLAN WILL BE RUINED!
NOT TO WORRY, OL' PAL! NO ONE WILL SUSPECT A THING! I'VE BEEN PRACTICING! WATCH THIS!
MOO!

36

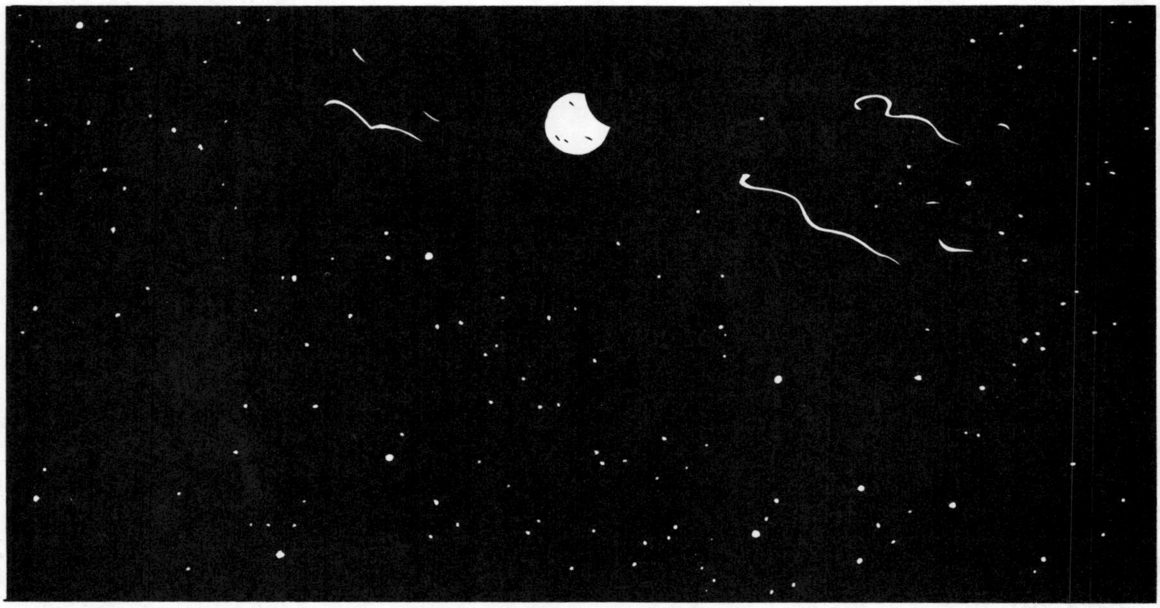

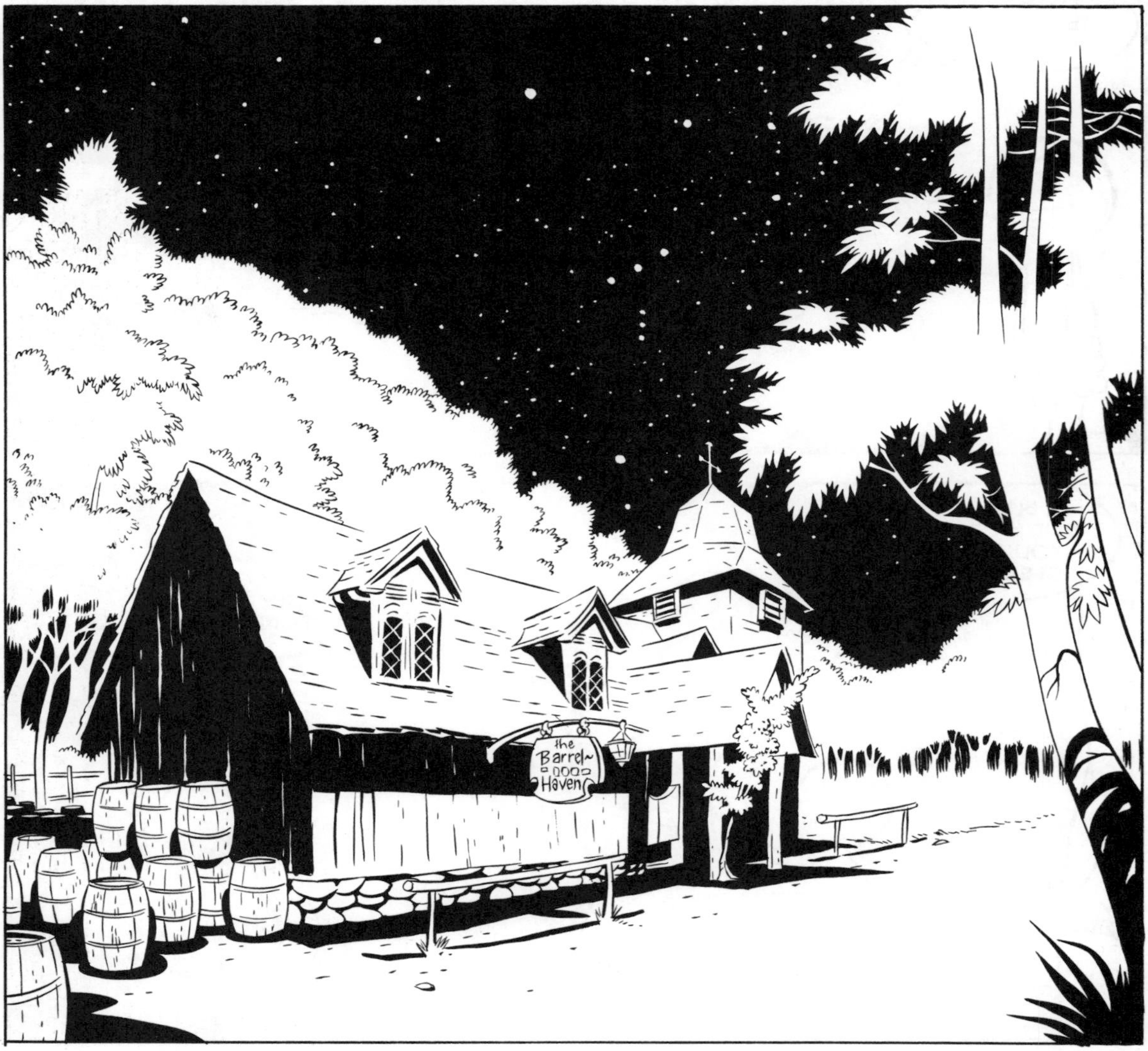
the
Barrel
Haven

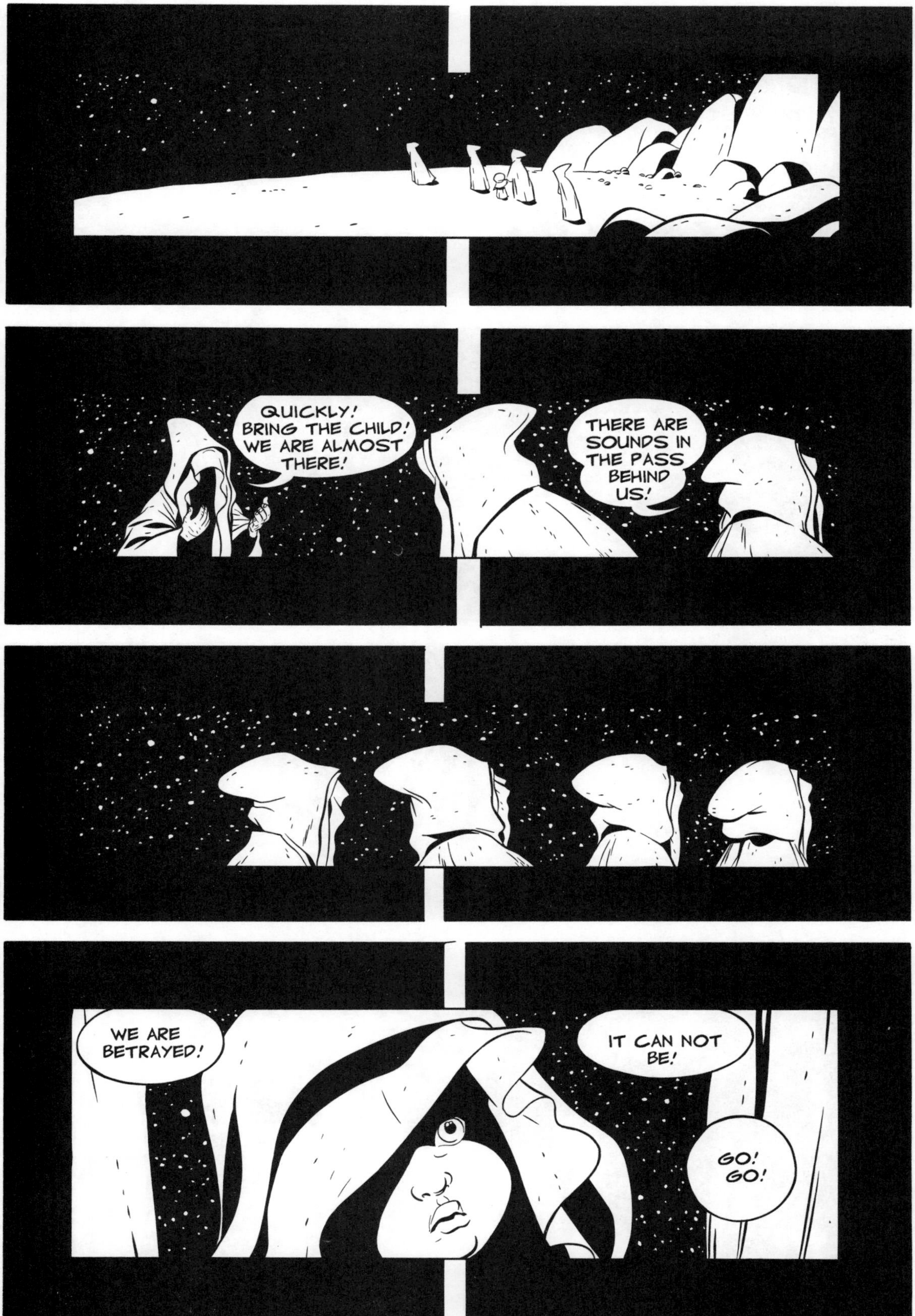
QUICKLY! BRING THE CHILD! WE ARE ALMOST THERE!
THERE ARE SOUNDS IN THE PASS BEHIND US!
WE ARE BETRAYED!
IT CAN NOT BE!
GO! GO!

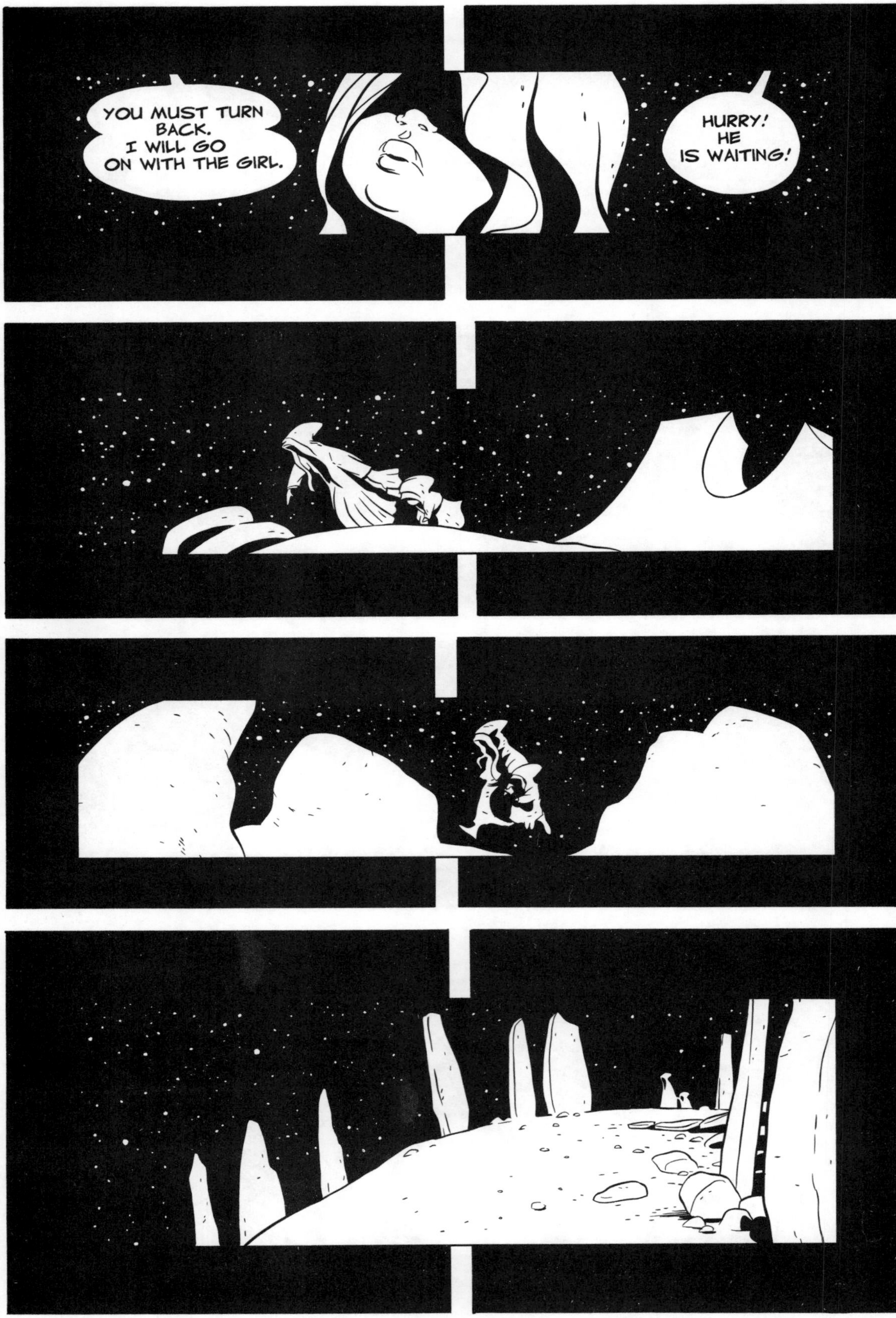
YOU MUST TURN BACK. I WILL GO ON WITH THE GIRL.
HURRY! HE IS WAITING!

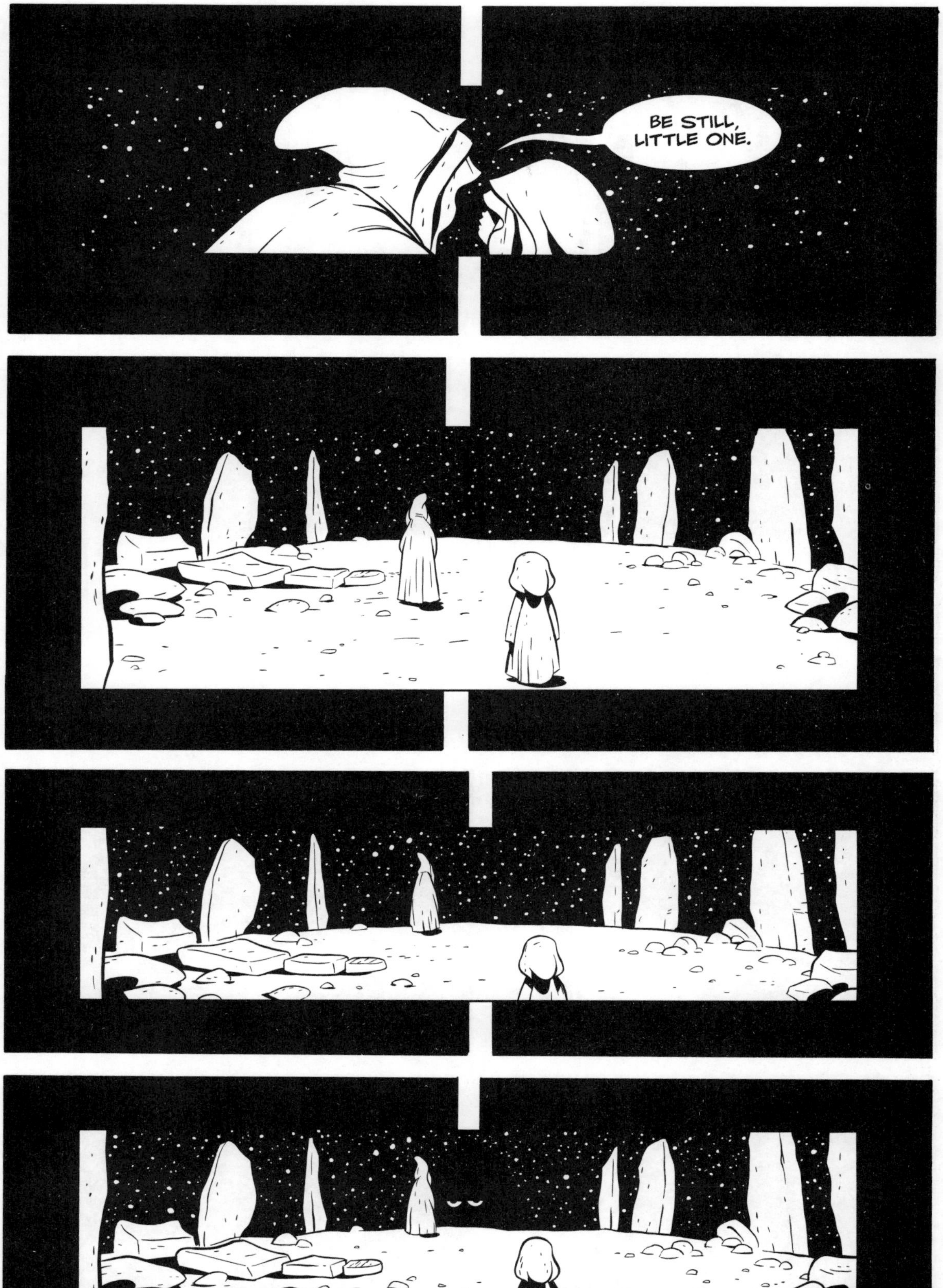
BE STILL, LITTLE ONE.

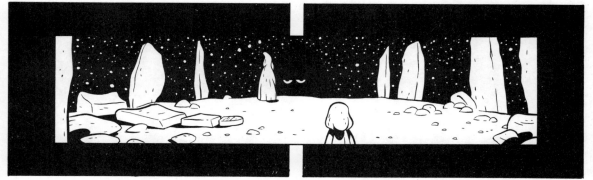

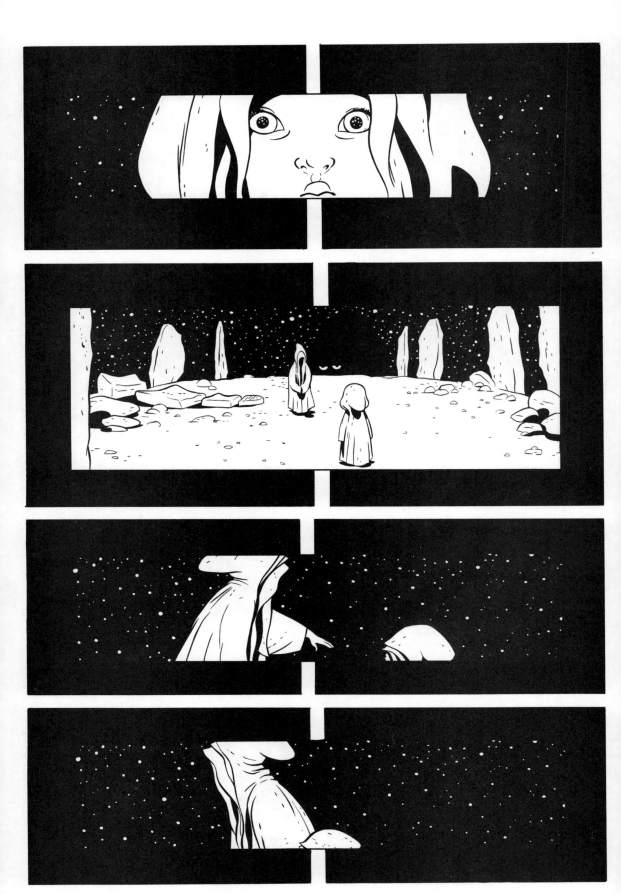

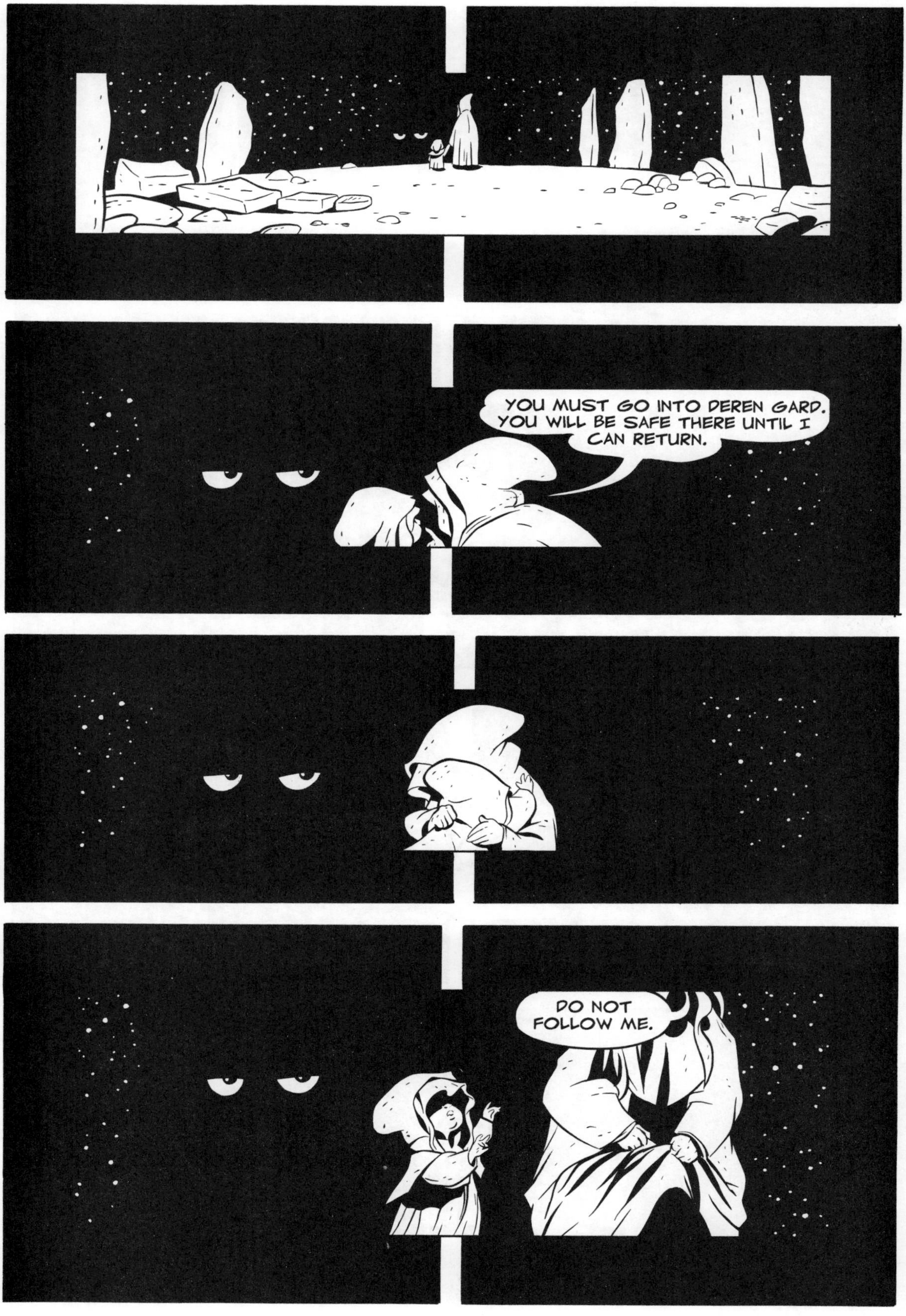
YOU MUST GO INTO DEREN GARD. YOU WILL BE SAFE THERE UNTIL I CAN RETURN.
DO NOT FOLLOW ME.

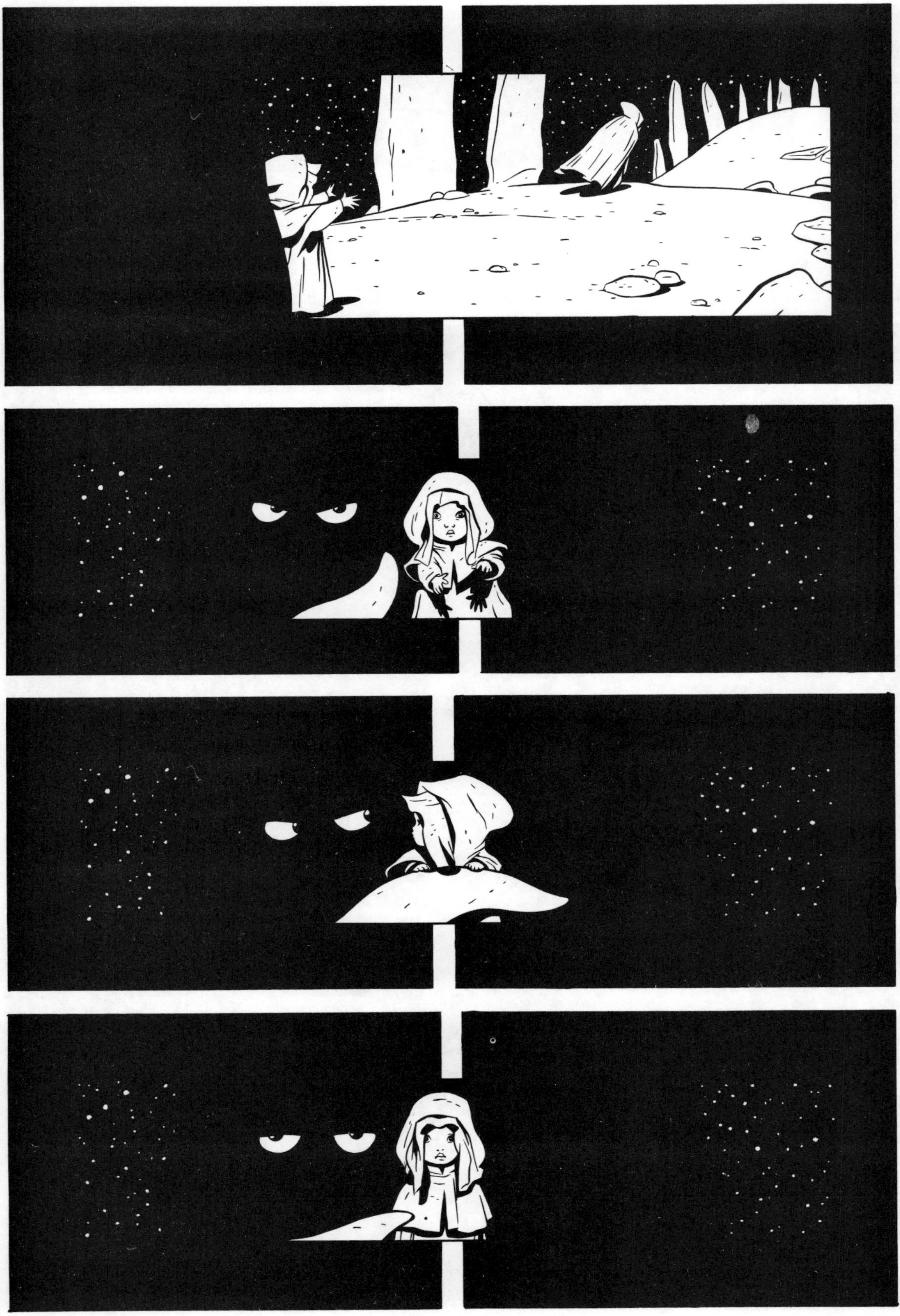

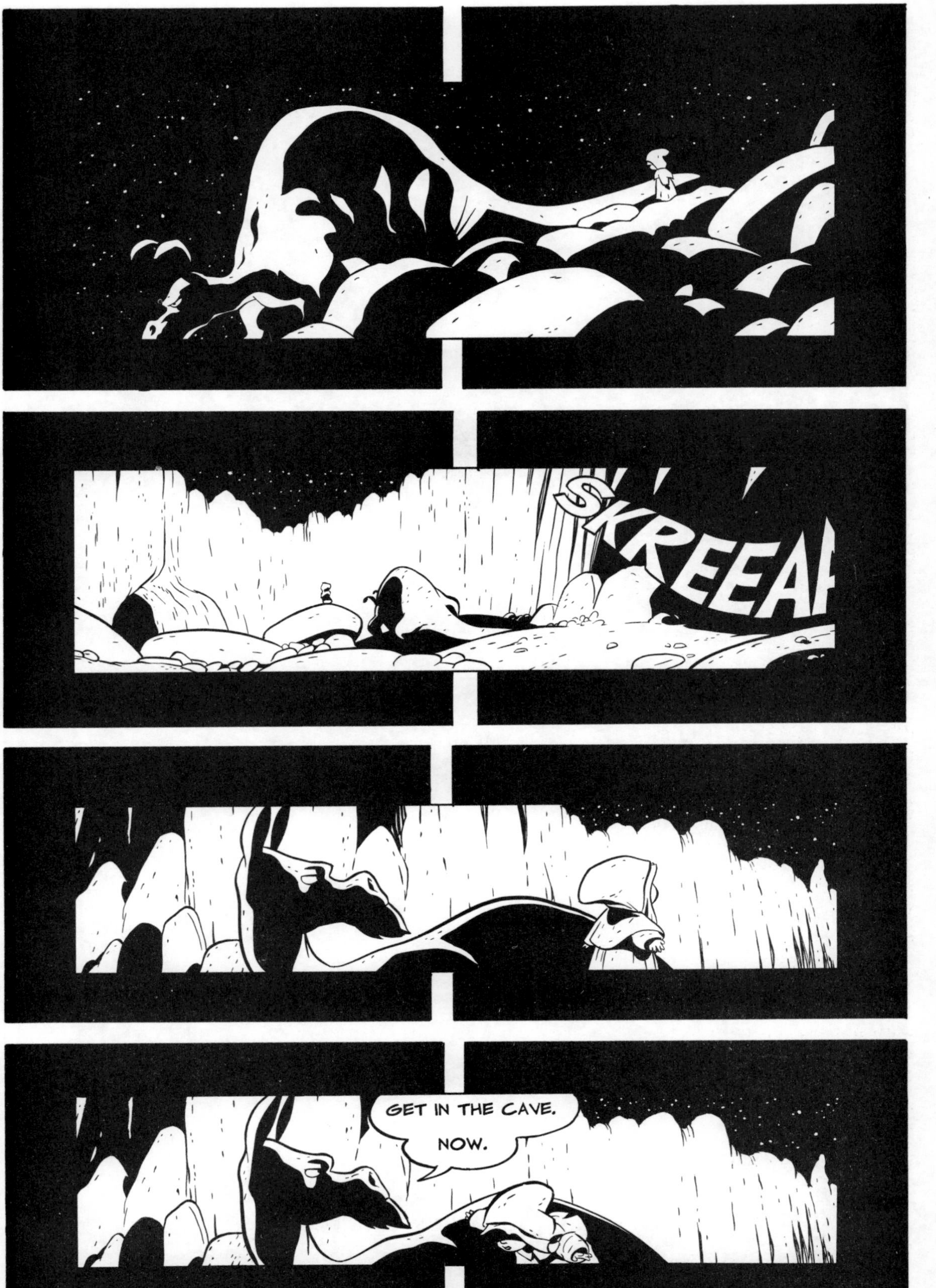
SKREEAR
GET IN THE CAVE.
NOW.

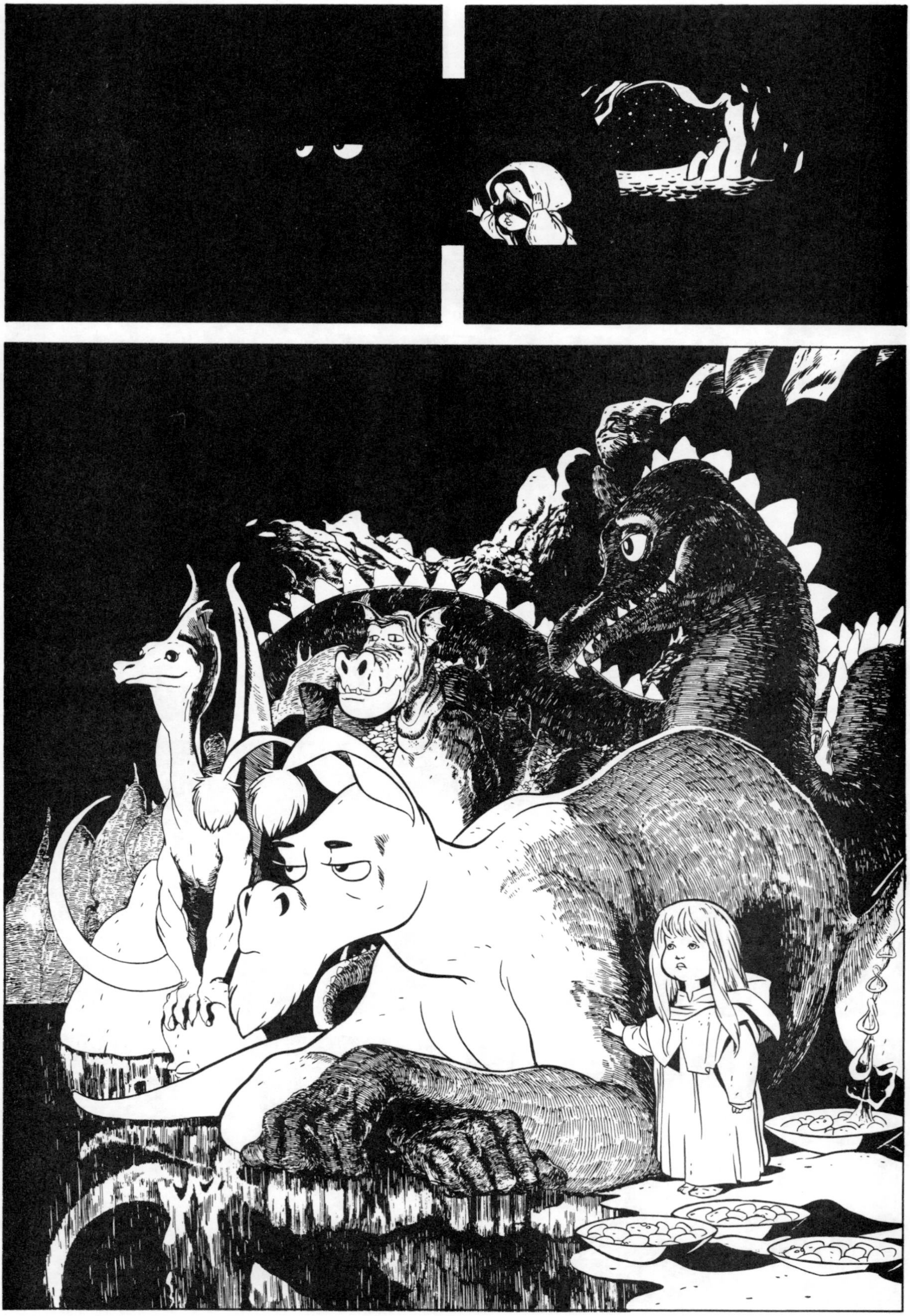

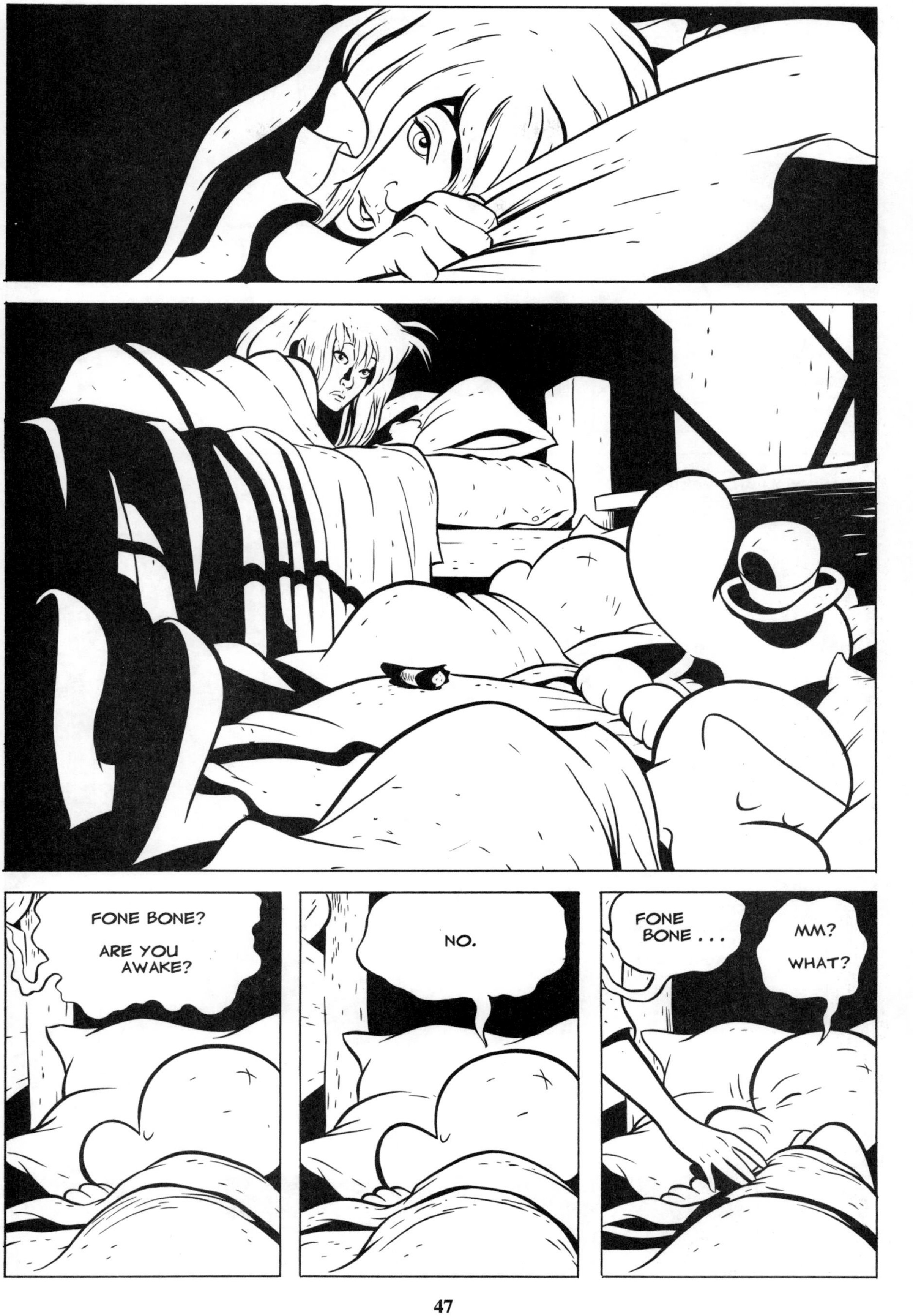
FONE BONE?
ARE YOU AWAKE?
NO.
FONE BONE . . .
MM?
WHAT?

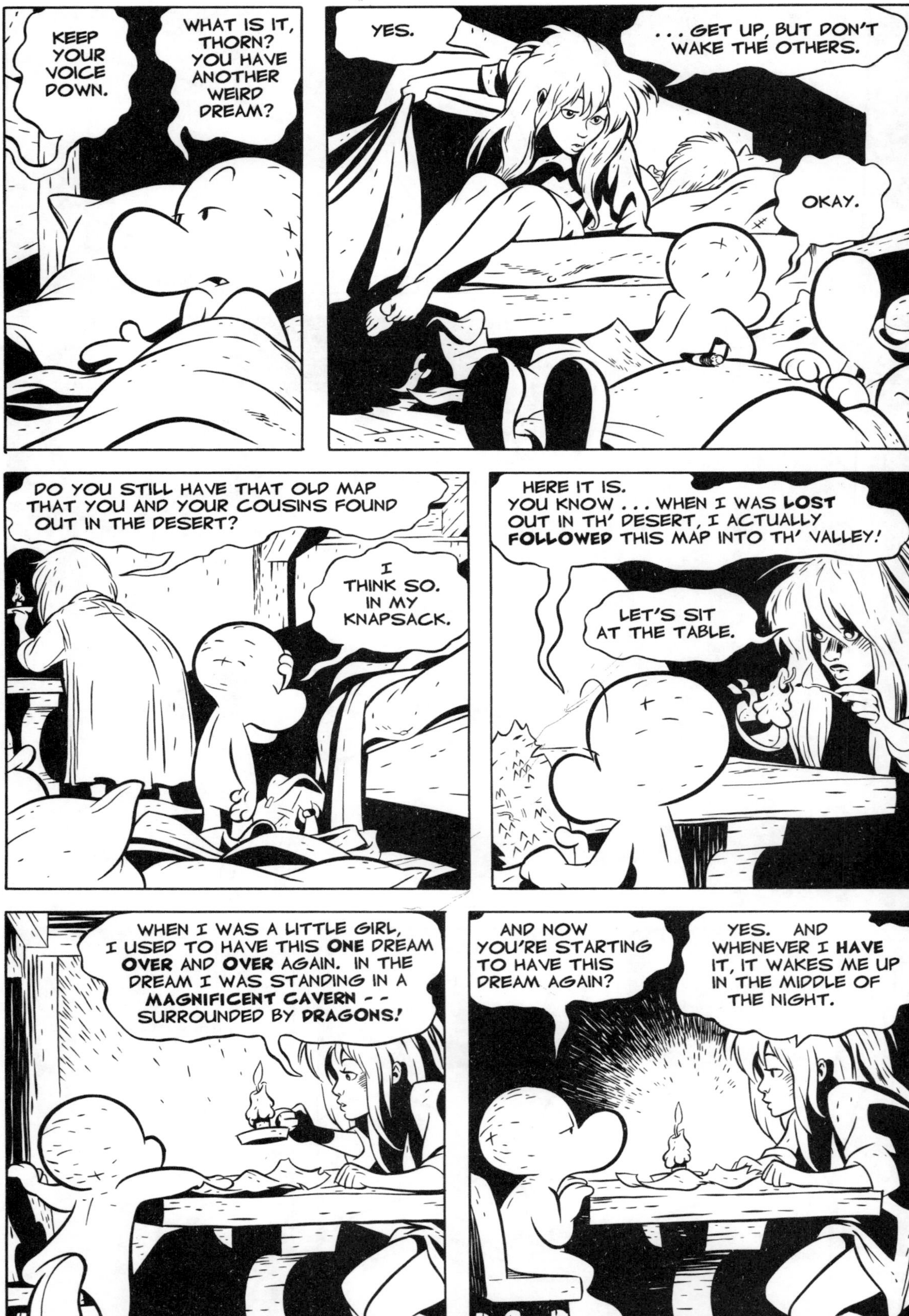
KEEP YOUR VOICE DOWN.
WHAT IS IT, THORN? YOU HAVE ANOTHER WEIRD DREAM?
YES.
. . . GET UP, BUT DON'T WAKE THE OTHERS.
OKAY.
DO YOU STILL HAVE THAT OLD MAP THAT YOU AND YOUR COUSINS FOUND OUT IN THE DESERT?
I THINK SO. IN MY KNAPSACK.
HERE IT IS. YOU KNOW . . . WHEN I WAS LOST OUT IN TH' DESERT, I ACTUALLY FOLLOWED THIS MAP INTO TH' VALLEY!
LET'S SIT AT THE TABLE.
WHEN I WAS A LITTLE GIRL, I USED TO HAVE THIS ONE DREAM OVER AND OVER AGAIN. IN THE DREAM I WAS STANDING IN A MAGNIFICENT CAVERN - - SURROUNDED BY DRAGONS!
AND NOW YOU'RE STARTING TO HAVE THIS DREAM AGAIN?
YES. AND WHENEVER I HAVE IT, IT WAKES ME UP IN THE MIDDLE OF THE NIGHT.

HAVE YOU TOLD GRAN'MA BEN ABOUT THE DREAMS?

I DID WHEN I WAS LITTLE. SHE USED TO TELL ME NOT TO BE AFRAID BECAUSE DRAGONS DON'T REALLY **EXIST!**

YAWN!

HMM. **THAT'S** STRANGE. **GRAN'MA KNOWS** ABOUT DRAGONS!

RIGHT, BUT I DIDN'T **KNOW** THAT THEN. AND YOU SAW THE WAY SHE AND THE GREAT RED DRAGON WERE **ACTING** THE OTHER DAY! THOSE TWO **KNOW** SOMETHING THAT WE **DON'T!**

YOU THINK IT HAS SOMETHING TO DO WITH THIS MAP?

ALL **I** KNOW IS I STOPPED HAVING THAT DREAM **YEARS** AGO -- UNTIL **YOU** SHOWED UP AND PULLED THAT MAP OUT OF YOUR KNAPSACK!

EVER SINCE THEN THE DREAMS HAVE BEEN BACK -- AND THEY'RE MORE **VIVID** AND **REAL** THAN **EVER BEFORE!**

I STILL DON'T UNDERSTAND WHY **SEEING** THIS OL' MAP WOULD TRIGGER TH' **DREAMS.**

I THINK I DO ...

... I **DREW** THAT MAP!

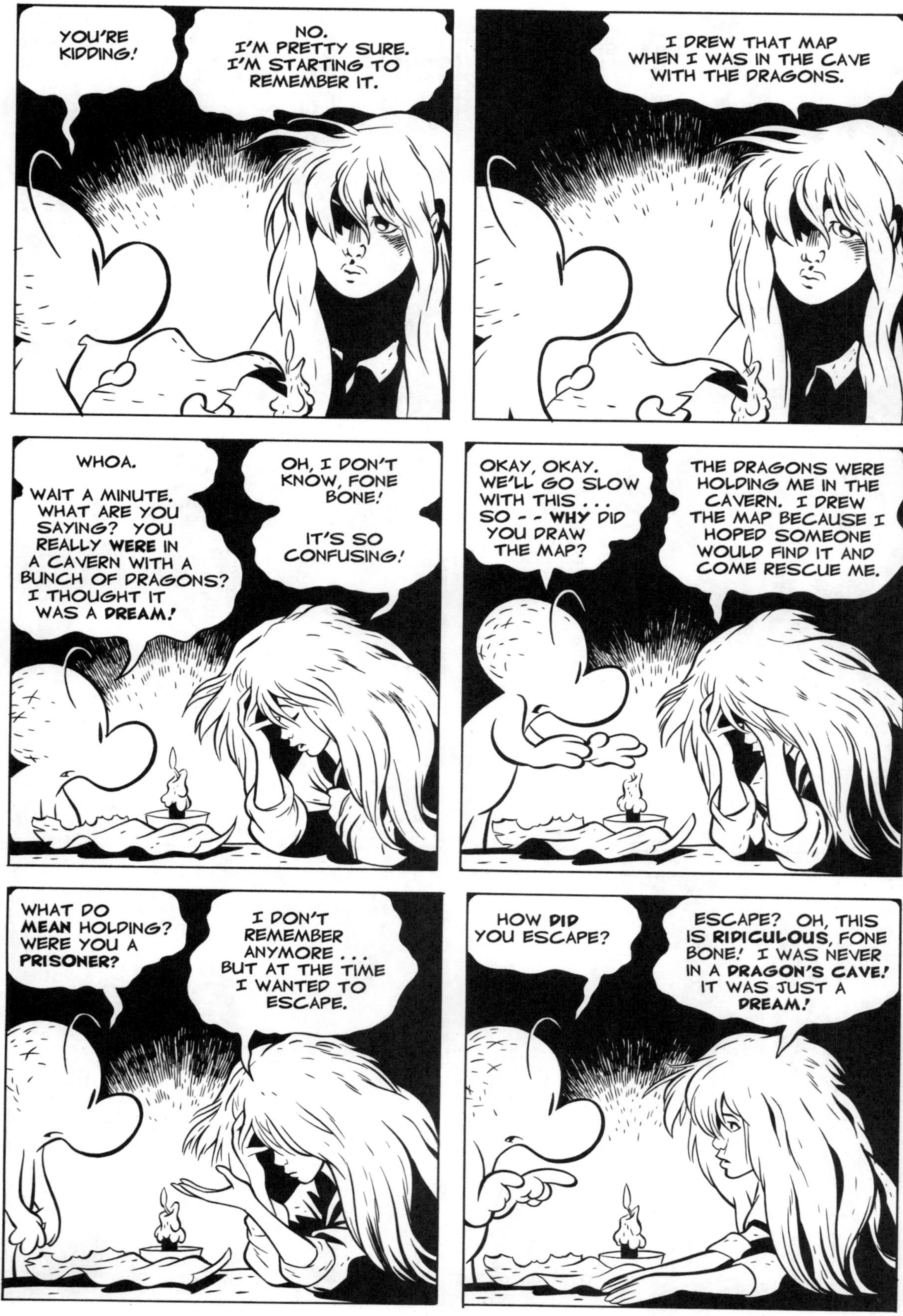
YOU'RE KIDDING!
NO. I'M PRETTY SURE. I'M STARTING TO REMEMBER IT.
I DREW THAT MAP WHEN I WAS IN THE CAVE WITH THE DRAGONS.
WHOA.
WAIT A MINUTE. WHAT ARE YOU SAYING? YOU REALLY WERE IN A CAVERN WITH A BUNCH OF DRAGONS? I THOUGHT IT WAS A DREAM!
OH, I DON'T KNOW, FONE BONE!
IT'S SO CONFUSING!
OKAY, OKAY. WE'LL GO SLOW WITH THIS . . . SO - - WHY DID YOU DRAW THE MAP?
THE DRAGONS WERE HOLDING ME IN THE CAVERN. I DREW THE MAP BECAUSE I HOPED SOMEONE WOULD FIND IT AND COME RESCUE ME.
WHAT DO MEAN HOLDING? WERE YOU A PRISONER?
I DON'T REMEMBER ANYMORE . . . BUT AT THE TIME I WANTED TO ESCAPE.
HOW DID YOU ESCAPE?
ESCAPE? OH, THIS IS RIDICULOUS, FONE BONE! I WAS NEVER IN A DRAGON'S CAVE! IT WAS JUST A DREAM!

... IF IT WASN'T FOR THAT MAP, I'D **SWEAR** I'D BEEN WITH GRAN'MA BEN SINCE THE DAY I WAS BORN.

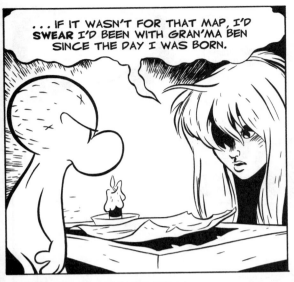

WELL, **THERE'S** TH' MAP! I SAY WE WAKE GRAN'MA UP AND **SHOW** IT TO HER!

NO. LET'S WAIT UNTIL AFTER THE RACE. SHE'S GOT ENOUGH TO WORRY ABOUT RIGHT NOW.

LET'S KEEP THE MAP A SECRET FOR NOW ... JUST BETWEEN YOU AND ME, OKAY?

OKAY. IF THAT'S WHAT YOU WANT.

GOOD. LET'S GO BACK TO BED.

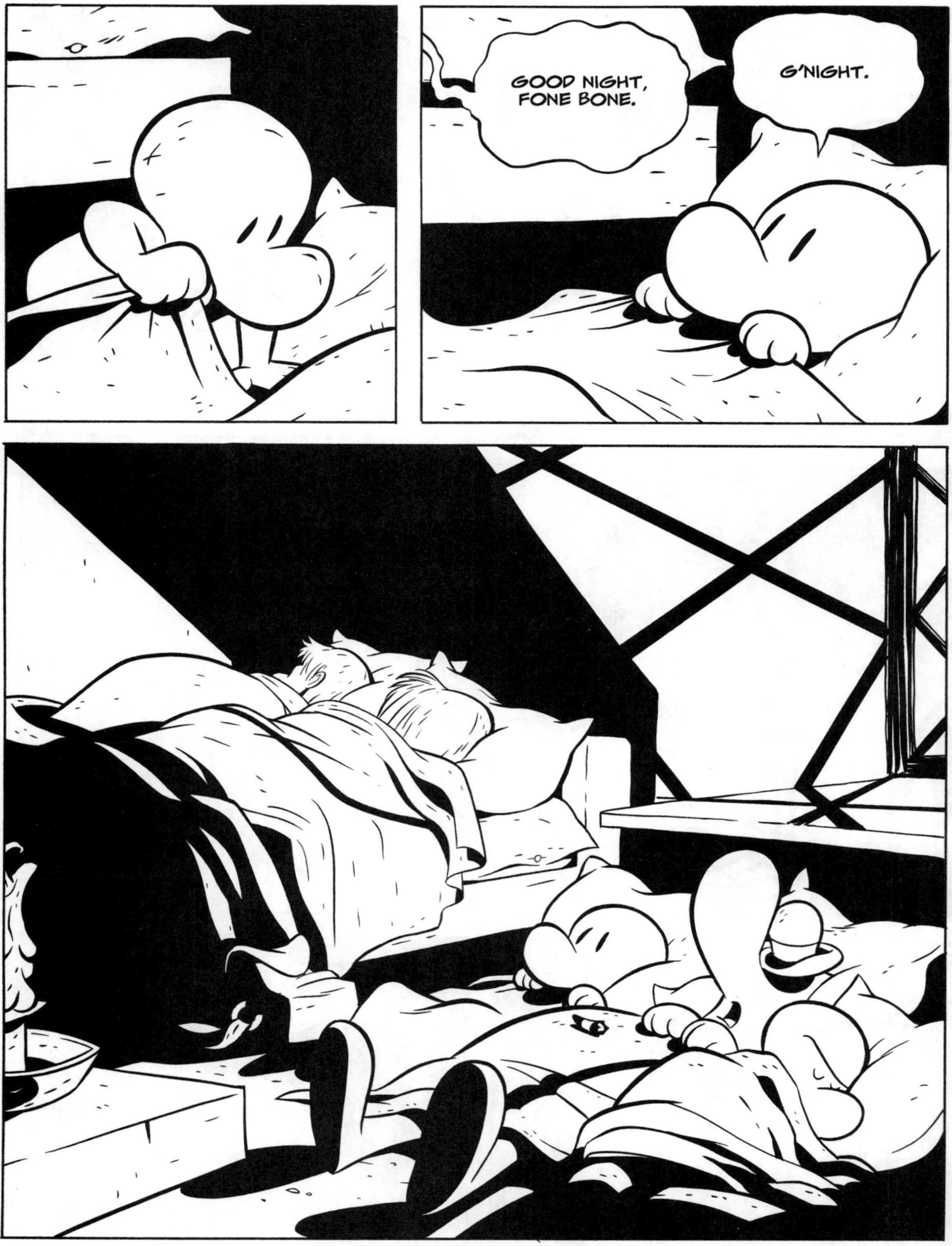
GOOD NIGHT, FONE BONE.
G'NIGHT.
NEXT: THE MYSTERY COW!

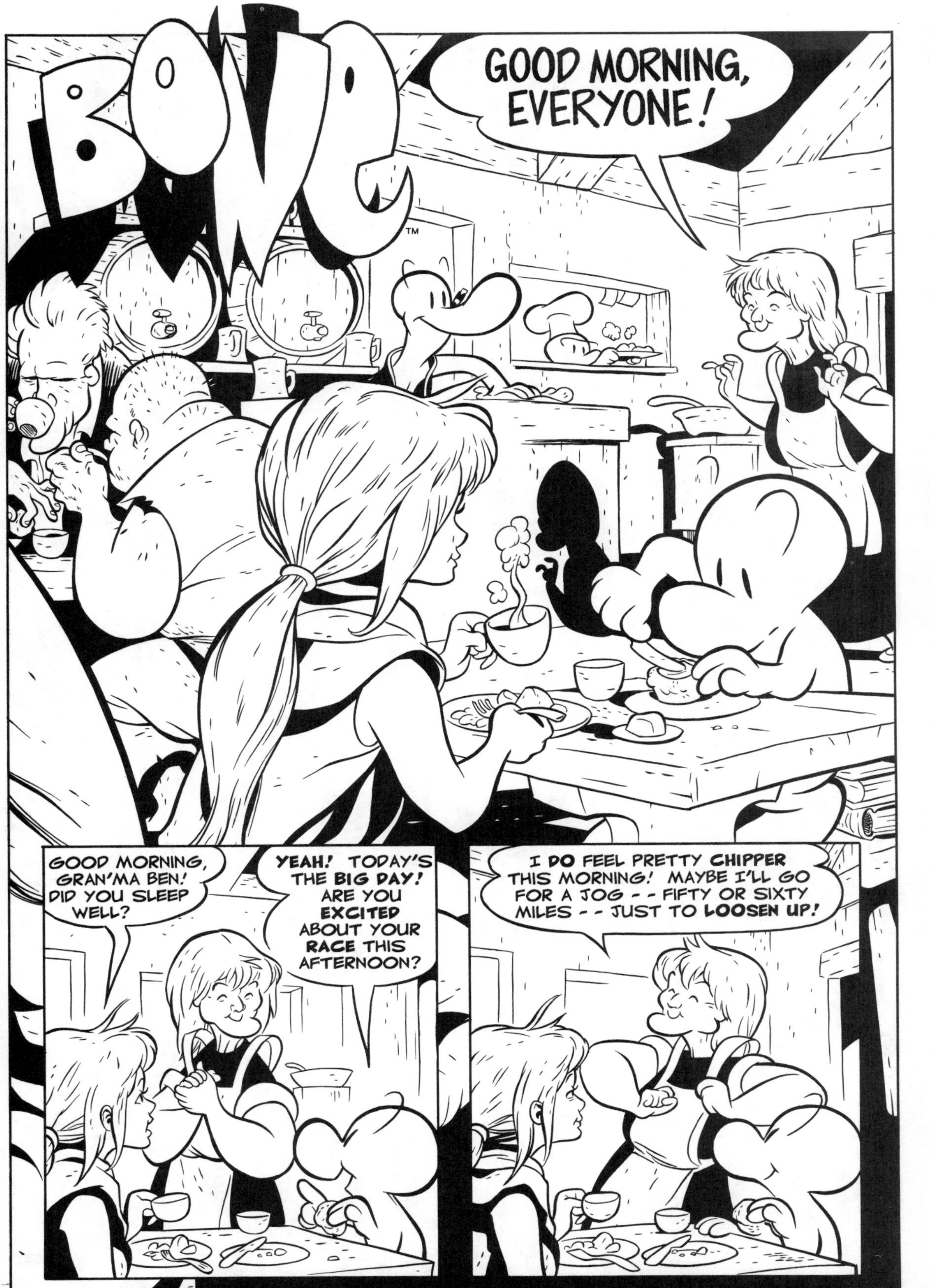
BONE™
GOOD MORNING, EVERYONE!
GOOD MORNING, GRAN'MA BEN! DID YOU SLEEP WELL?
YEAH! TODAY'S THE BIG DAY! ARE YOU EXCITED ABOUT YOUR RACE THIS AFTERNOON?
I DO FEEL PRETTY CHIPPER THIS MORNING! MAYBE I'LL GO FOR A JOG - - FIFTY OR SIXTY MILES - - JUST TO LOOSEN UP!

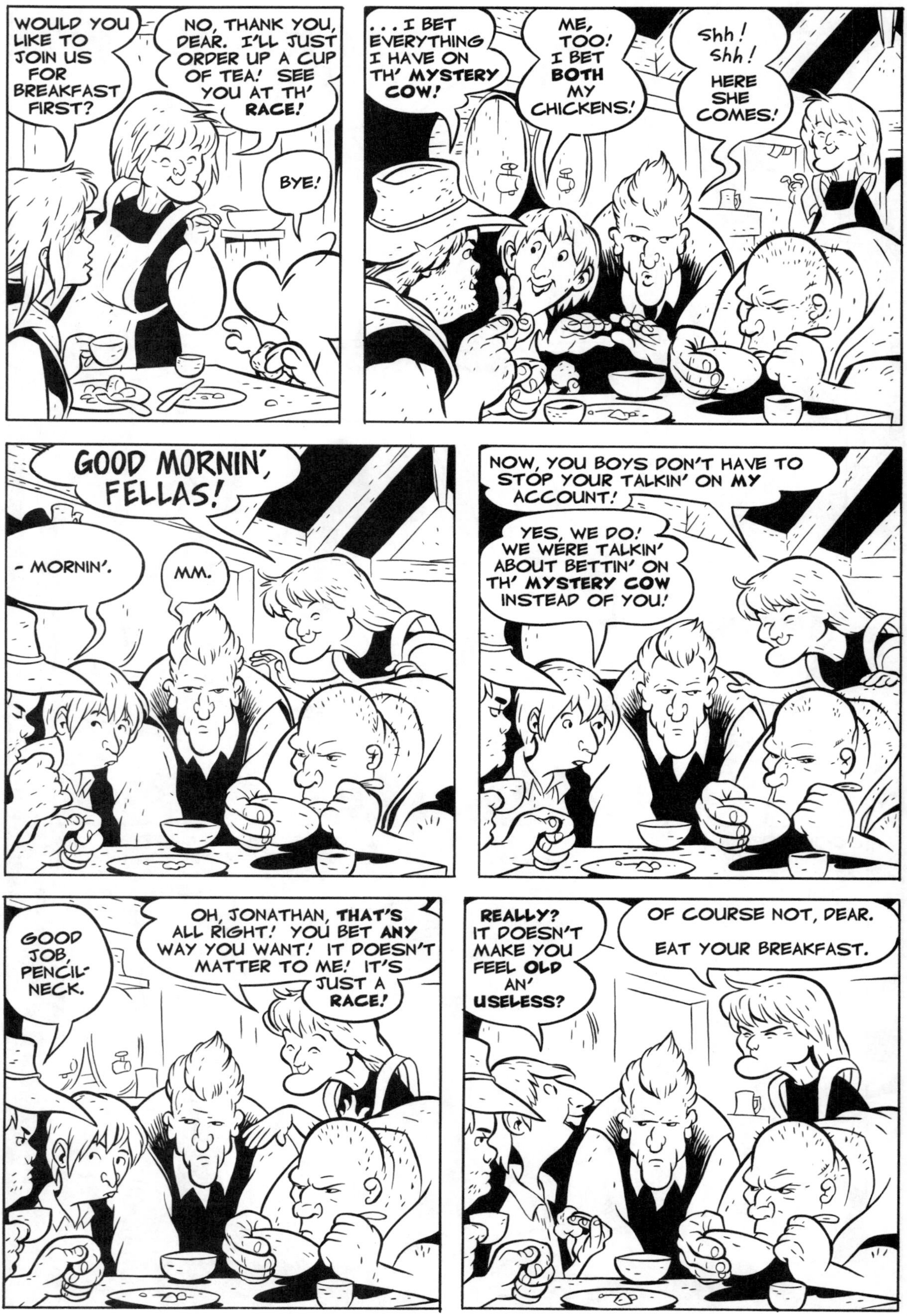
WOULD YOU LIKE TO JOIN US FOR BREAKFAST FIRST?
NO, THANK YOU, DEAR. I'LL JUST ORDER UP A CUP OF TEA! SEE YOU AT TH' RACE!
BYE!
. . . I BET EVERYTHING I HAVE ON TH' MYSTERY COW!
ME, TOO! I BET BOTH MY CHICKENS!
Shh! Shh! HERE SHE COMES!
GOOD MORNIN', FELLAS!
- MORNIN'.
MM.
NOW, YOU BOYS DON'T HAVE TO STOP YOUR TALKIN' ON MY ACCOUNT!
YES, WE DO! WE WERE TALKIN' ABOUT BETTIN' ON TH' MYSTERY COW INSTEAD OF YOU!
GOOD JOB, PENCIL-NECK.
OH, JONATHAN, THAT'S ALL RIGHT! YOU BET ANY WAY YOU WANT! IT DOESN'T MATTER TO ME! IT'S JUST A RACE!
REALLY? IT DOESN'T MAKE YOU FEEL OLD AN' USELESS?
OF COURSE NOT, DEAR.
EAT YOUR BREAKFAST.

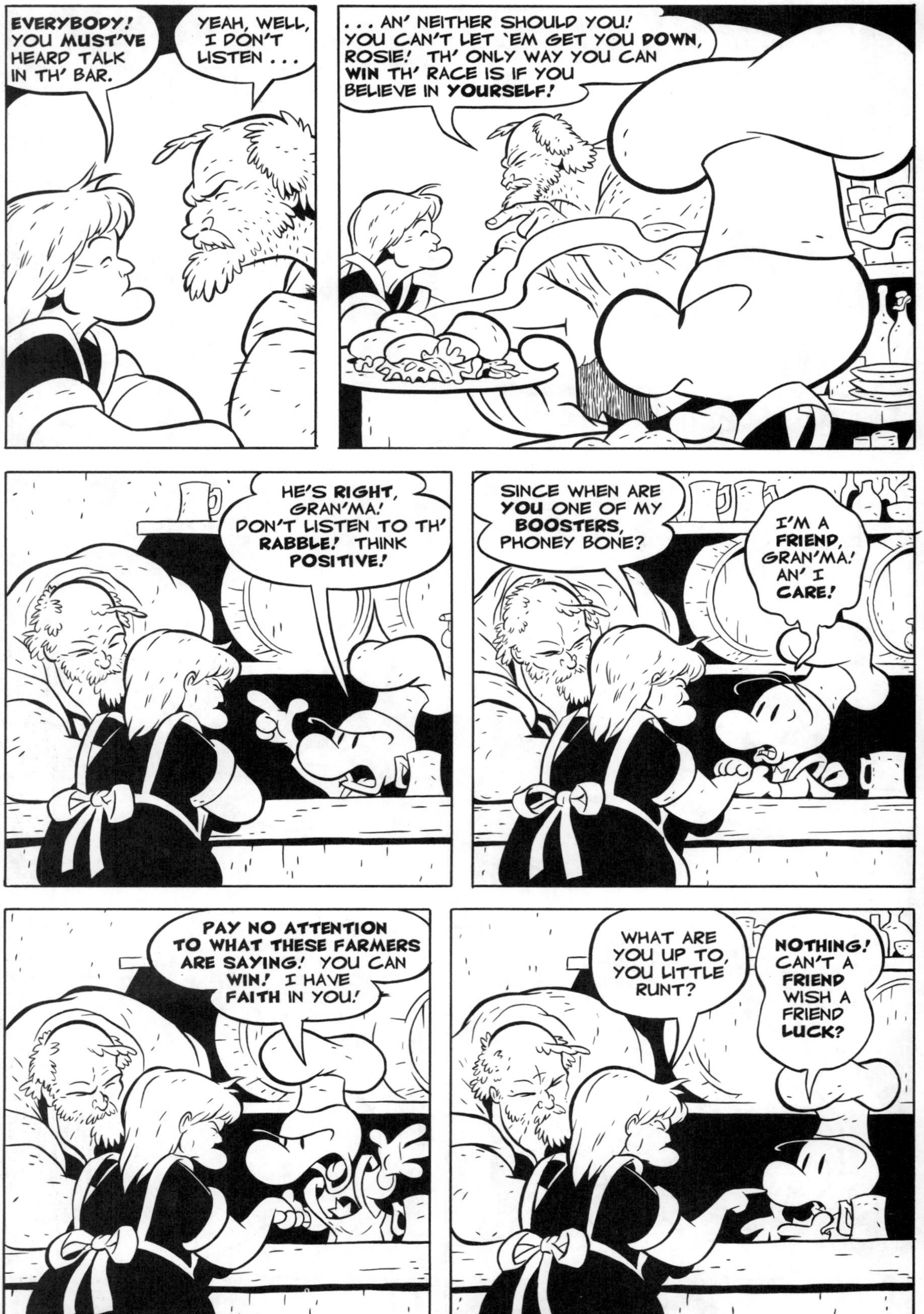
EVERYBODY! YOU MUST'VE HEARD TALK IN TH' BAR.
YEAH, WELL, I DON'T LISTEN . . .
. . . AN' NEITHER SHOULD YOU! YOU CAN'T LET 'EM GET YOU DOWN, ROSIE! TH' ONLY WAY YOU CAN WIN TH' RACE IS IF YOU BELIEVE IN YOURSELF!
HE'S RIGHT, GRAN'MA! DON'T LISTEN TO TH' RABBLE! THINK POSITIVE!
SINCE WHEN ARE YOU ONE OF MY BOOSTERS, PHONEY BONE?
I'M A FRIEND, GRAN'MA! AN' I CARE!
PAY NO ATTENTION TO WHAT THESE FARMERS ARE SAYING! YOU CAN WIN! I HAVE FAITH IN YOU!
WHAT ARE YOU UP TO, YOU LITTLE RUNT?
NOTHING! CAN'T A FRIEND WISH A FRIEND LUCK?

HORSE-KNOBBIES!

LUCIUS, DEAR . . . I'LL BE IN MY ROOM UNTIL TH' RACE STARTS. BRING ME THAT TEA WHEN YOU GET A CHANCE.

POOR OL' SAP! SHE'S GONNA GET CREAMED THIS AFTERNOON! IF YA WANT MY ADVICE, YOU'RE BETTER OFF BETTIN' ON TH' MYSTERY COW!

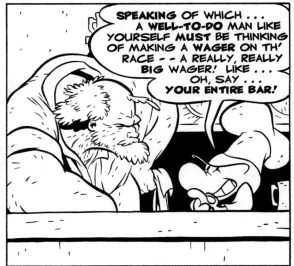

SPEAKING OF WHICH . . . A WELL-TO-DO MAN LIKE YOURSELF MUST BE THINKING OF MAKING A WAGER ON TH' RACE -- A REALLY, REALLY BIG WAGER! LIKE . . . OH, SAY . . . YOUR ENTIRE BAR!

. . . BUT THERE'S NO RUSH! WHEN YOU'RE READY TO BET -- YOU KNOW WHERE TO FIND ME! I'LL BE TAKING BETS RIGHT UP TO THE STARTING BELL! THINK ABOUT IT!

HMM.

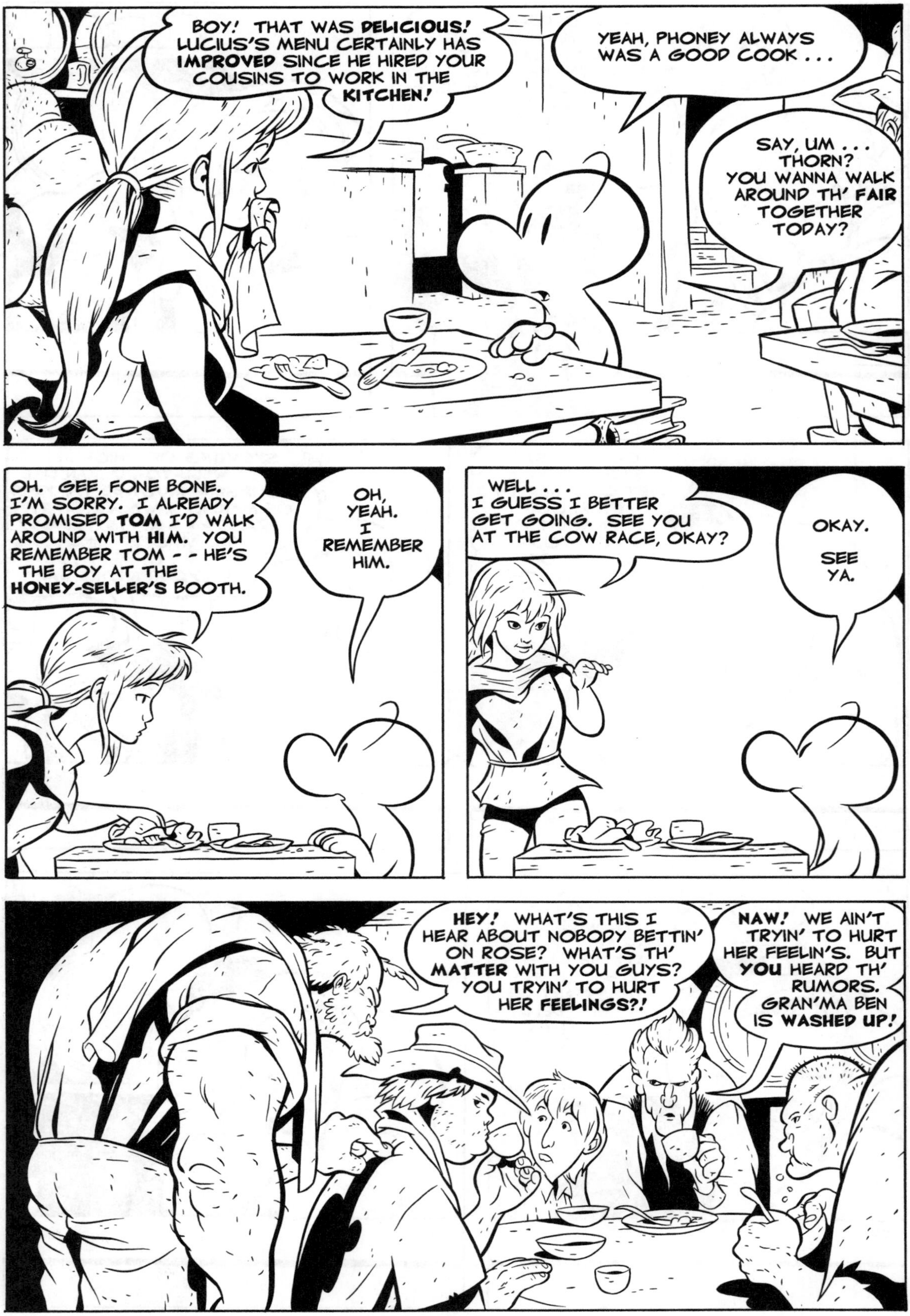
BOY! THAT WAS DELICIOUS! LUCIUS'S MENU CERTAINLY HAS IMPROVED SINCE HE HIRED YOUR COUSINS TO WORK IN THE KITCHEN!
YEAH, PHONEY ALWAYS WAS A GOOD COOK . . .
SAY, UM . . . THORN? YOU WANNA WALK AROUND TH' FAIR TOGETHER TODAY?
OH. GEE, FONE BONE. I'M SORRY. I ALREADY PROMISED TOM I'D WALK AROUND WITH HIM. YOU REMEMBER TOM - - HE'S THE BOY AT THE HONEY-SELLER'S BOOTH.
OH, YEAH. I REMEMBER HIM.
WELL . . . I GUESS I BETTER GET GOING. SEE YOU AT THE COW RACE, OKAY?
OKAY.
SEE YA.
HEY! WHAT'S THIS I HEAR ABOUT NOBODY BETTIN' ON ROSE? WHAT'S TH' MATTER WITH YOU GUYS? YOU TRYIN' TO HURT HER FEELINGS?!
NAW! WE AIN'T TRYIN' TO HURT HER FEELIN'S. BUT YOU HEARD TH' RUMORS. GRAN'MA BEN IS WASHED UP!

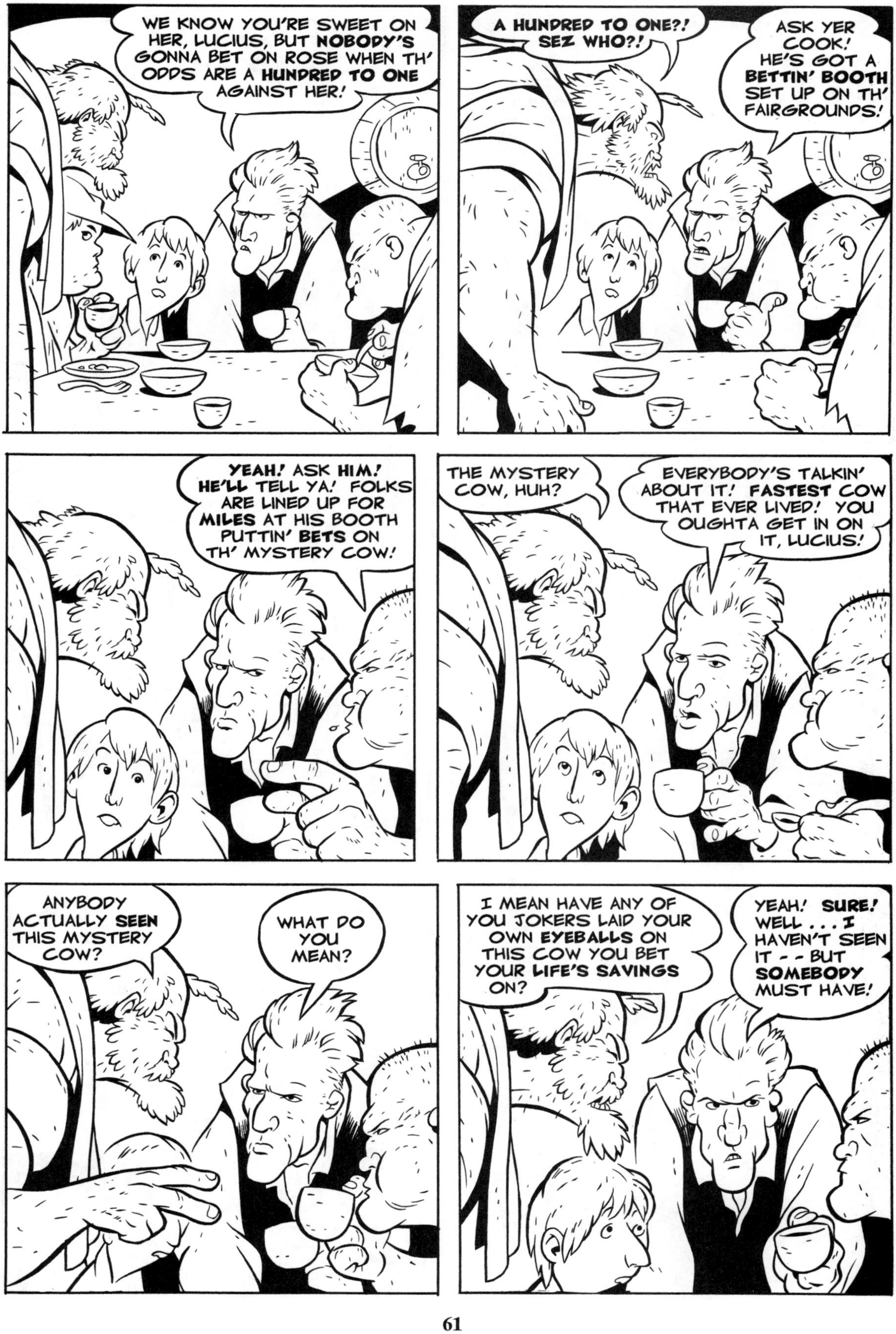

WE KNOW YOU'RE SWEET ON HER, LUCIUS, BUT NOBODY'S GONNA BET ON ROSE WHEN TH' ODDS ARE A HUNDRED TO ONE AGAINST HER!
A HUNDRED TO ONE?! SEZ WHO?!
ASK YER COOK! HE'S GOT A BETTIN' BOOTH SET UP ON TH' FAIRGROUNDS!
YEAH! ASK HIM! HE'LL TELL YA! FOLKS ARE LINED UP FOR MILES AT HIS BOOTH PUTTIN' BETS ON TH' MYSTERY COW!
THE MYSTERY COW, HUH?
EVERYBODY'S TALKIN' ABOUT IT! FASTEST COW THAT EVER LIVED! YOU OUGHTA GET IN ON IT, LUCIUS!
ANYBODY ACTUALLY SEEN THIS MYSTERY COW?
WHAT DO YOU MEAN?
I MEAN HAVE ANY OF YOU JOKERS LAID YOUR OWN EYEBALLS ON THIS COW YOU BET YOUR LIFE'S SAVINGS ON?
YEAH! SURE! WELL . . . I HAVEN'T SEEN IT - - BUT SOMEBODY MUST HAVE!

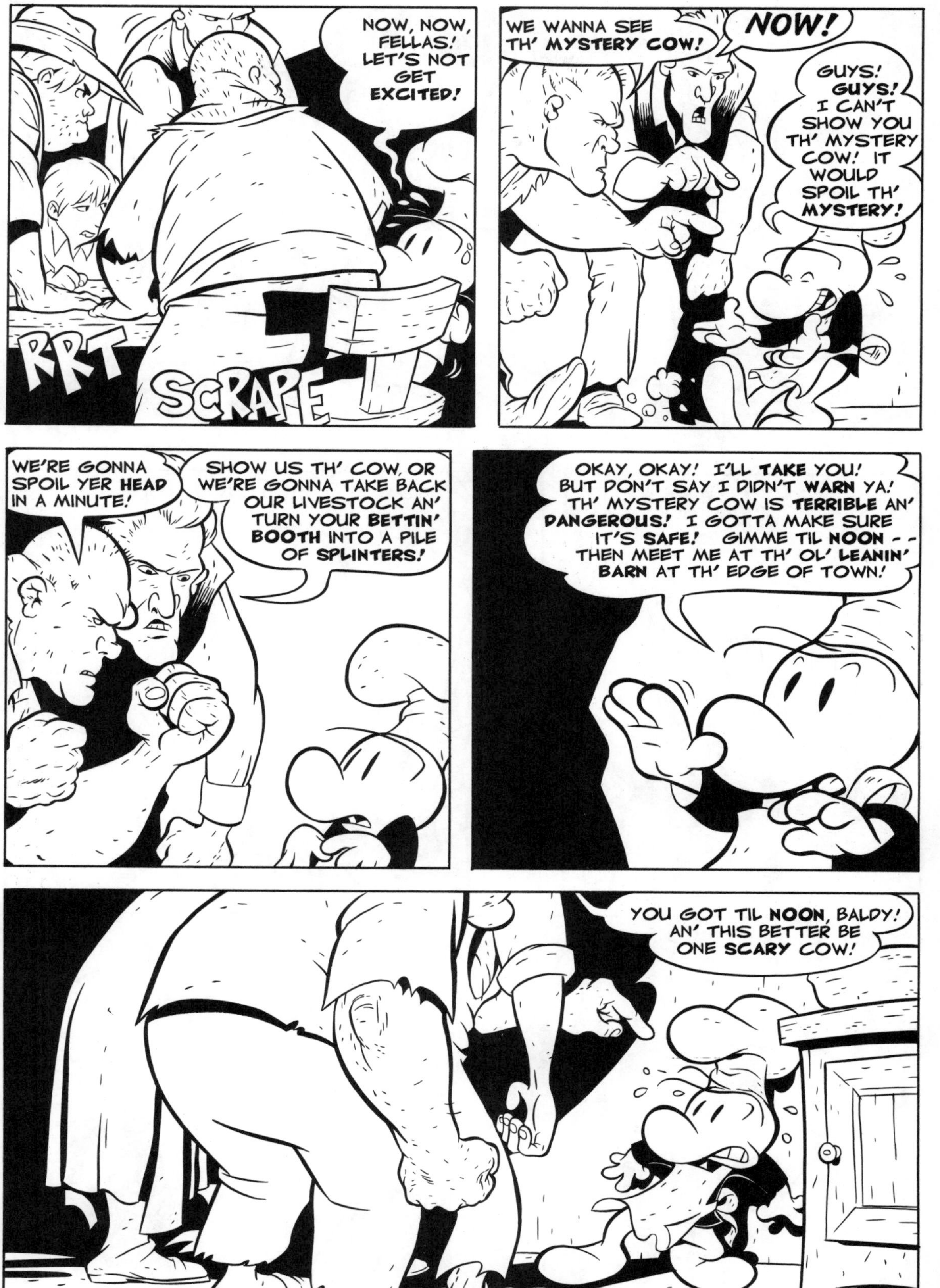
NOW, NOW, FELLAS! LET'S NOT GET EXCITED!
RRT
SCRAPE
WE WANNA SEE TH' MYSTERY COW!
NOW!
GUYS! GUYS! I CAN'T SHOW YOU TH' MYSTERY COW! IT WOULD SPOIL TH' MYSTERY!
WE'RE GONNA SPOIL YER HEAD IN A MINUTE!
SHOW US TH' COW, OR WE'RE GONNA TAKE BACK OUR LIVESTOCK AN' TURN YOUR BETTIN' BOOTH INTO A PILE OF SPLINTERS!
OKAY, OKAY! I'LL TAKE YOU! BUT DON'T SAY I DIDN'T WARN YA! TH' MYSTERY COW IS TERRIBLE AN' DANGEROUS! I GOTTA MAKE SURE IT'S SAFE! GIMME TIL NOON -- THEN MEET ME AT TH' OL' LEANIN' BARN AT TH' EDGE OF TOWN!
YOU GOT TIL NOON, BALDY! AN' THIS BETTER BE ONE SCARY COW!

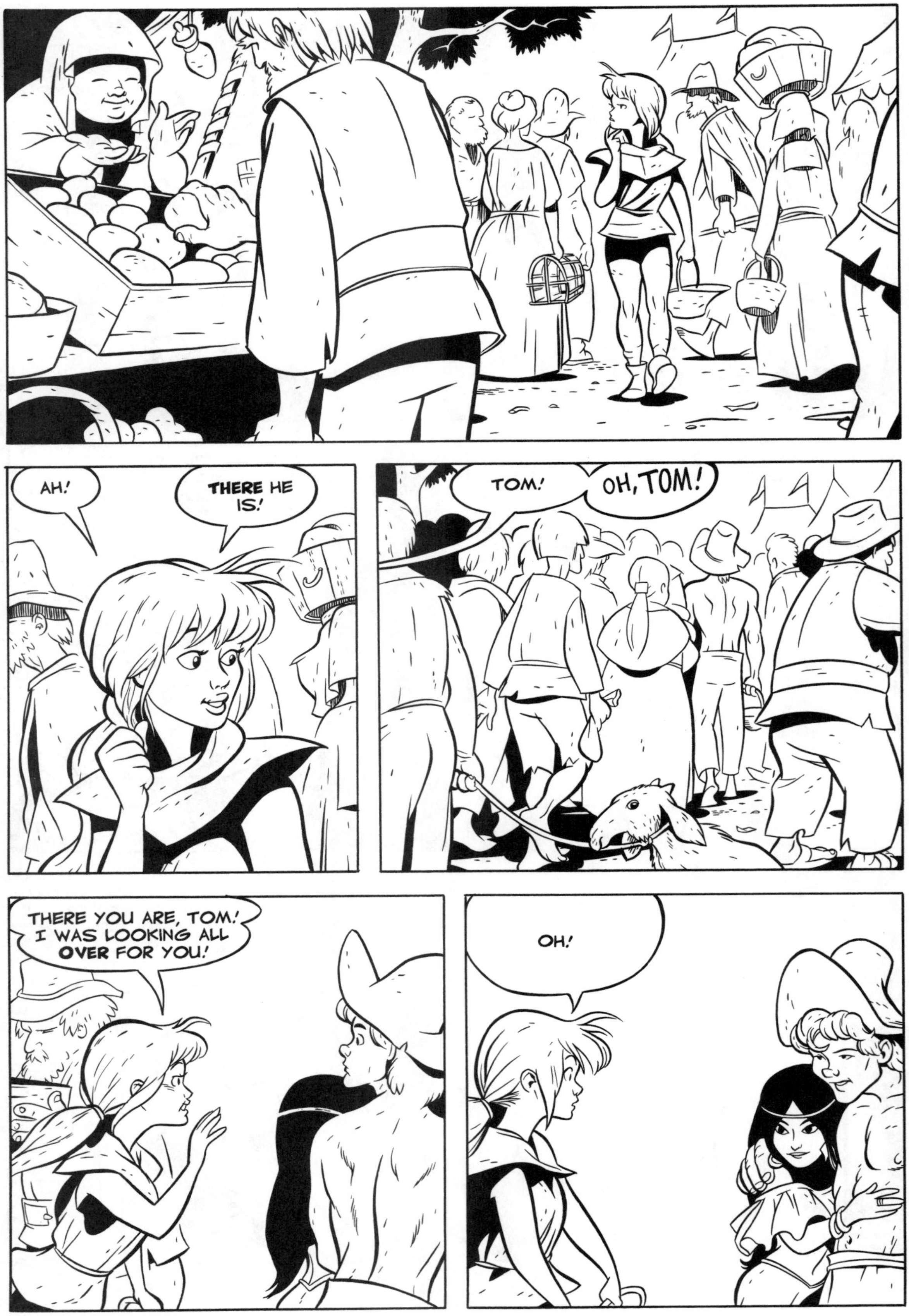
AH!
THERE HE IS!
TOM!
OH, TOM!
THERE YOU ARE, TOM! I WAS LOOKING ALL OVER FOR YOU!
OH!

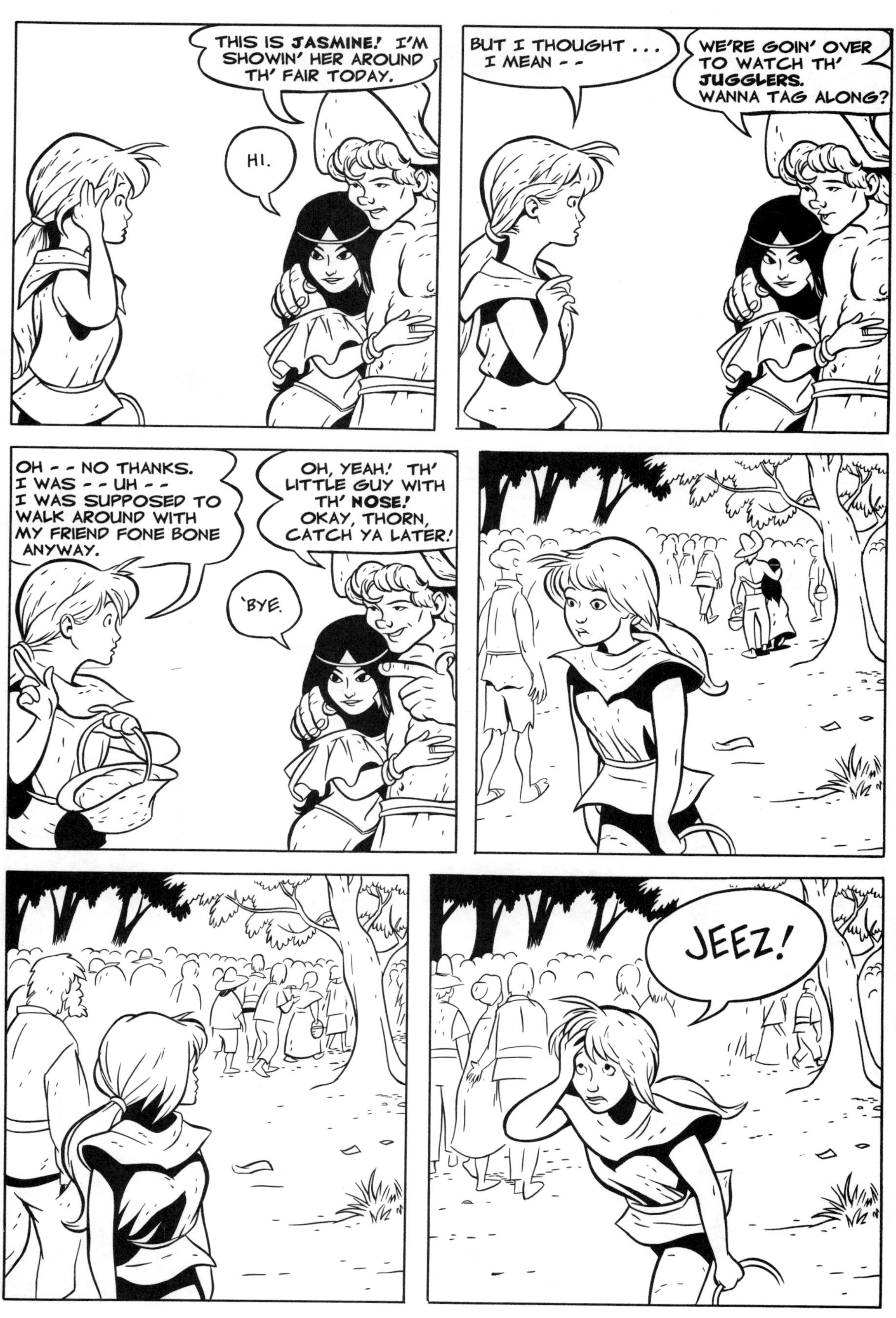
THIS IS **JASMINE!** I'M SHOWIN' HER AROUND TH' FAIR TODAY.
HI.
BUT I THOUGHT . . . I MEAN - -
WE'RE GOIN' OVER TO WATCH TH' **JUGGLERS.** WANNA TAG ALONG?
OH - - NO THANKS. I WAS - - UH - - I WAS SUPPOSED TO WALK AROUND WITH MY FRIEND FONE BONE ANYWAY.
OH, YEAH! TH' LITTLE GUY WITH TH' **NOSE!** OKAY, THORN, CATCH YA LATER!
'BYE.
JEEZ!

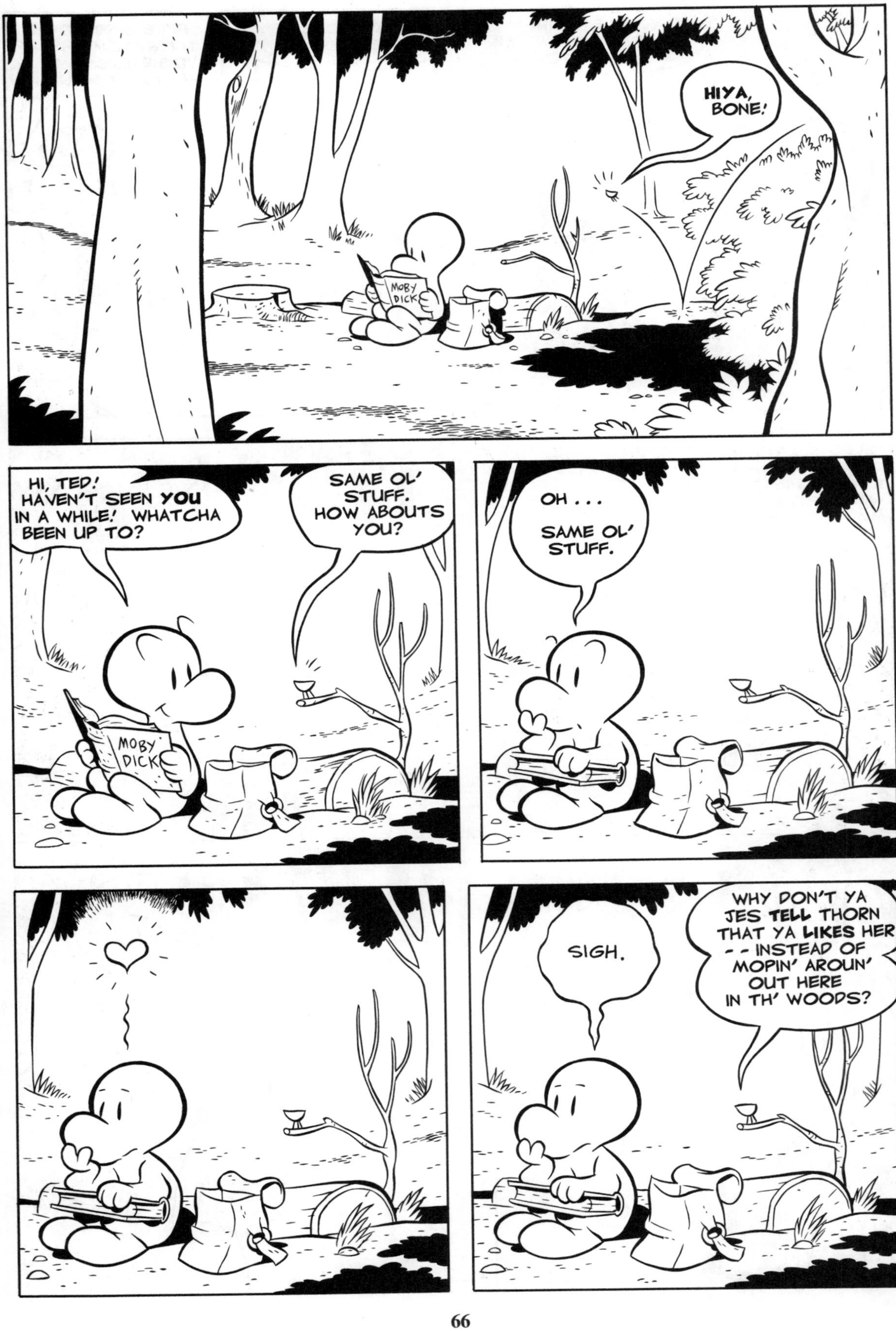
HIYA, BONE!
HI, TED! HAVEN'T SEEN YOU IN A WHILE! WHATCHA BEEN UP TO?
SAME OL' STUFF. HOW ABOUTS YOU?
MOBY DICK
OH . . .
SAME OL' STUFF.
SIGH.
WHY DON'T YA JES TELL THORN THAT YA LIKES HER - - INSTEAD OF MOPIN' AROUN' OUT HERE IN TH' WOODS?

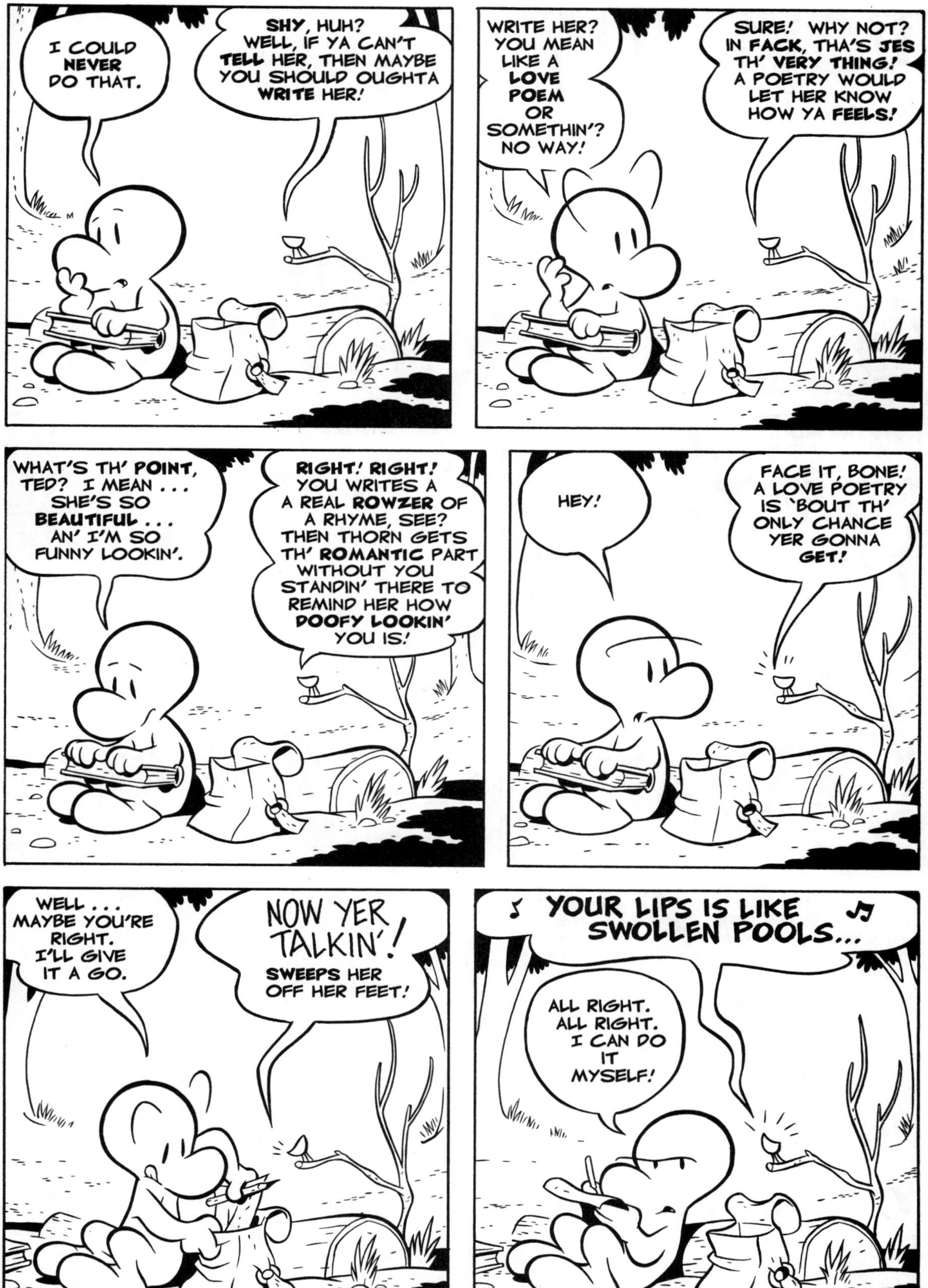
I COULD NEVER DO THAT.
SHY, HUH? WELL, IF YA CAN'T TELL HER, THEN MAYBE YOU SHOULD OUGHTA WRITE HER!
WRITE HER? YOU MEAN LIKE A LOVE POEM OR SOMETHIN'? NO WAY!
SURE! WHY NOT? IN FACK, THA'S JES TH' VERY THING! A POETRY WOULD LET HER KNOW HOW YA FEELS!
WHAT'S TH' POINT, TED? I MEAN . . . SHE'S SO BEAUTIFUL . . . AN' I'M SO FUNNY LOOKIN'.
RIGHT! RIGHT! YOU WRITES A A REAL ROWZER OF A RHYME, SEE? THEN THORN GETS TH' ROMANTIC PART WITHOUT YOU STANDIN' THERE TO REMIND HER HOW DOOFY LOOKIN' YOU IS!
HEY!
FACE IT, BONE! A LOVE POETRY IS 'BOUT TH' ONLY CHANCE YER GONNA GET!
WELL . . . MAYBE YOU'RE RIGHT. I'LL GIVE IT A GO.
NOW YER TALKIN'! SWEEPS HER OFF HER FEET!
YOUR LIPS IS LIKE SWOLLEN POOLS...
ALL RIGHT. ALL RIGHT. I CAN DO IT MYSELF!

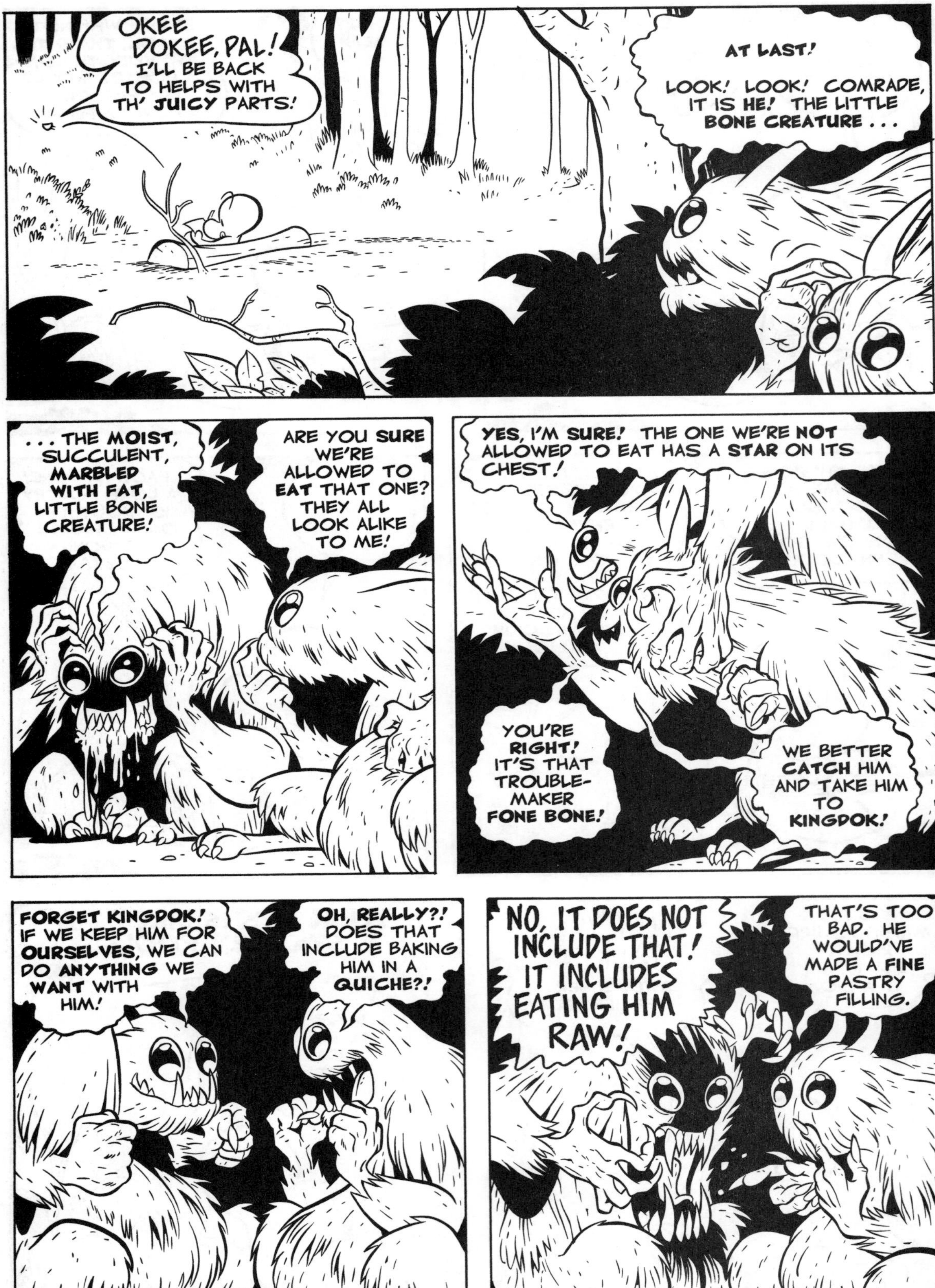
OKEE DOKEE, PAL! I'LL BE BACK TO HELPS WITH TH' JUICY PARTS!
AT LAST!
LOOK! LOOK! COMRADE, IT IS HE! THE LITTLE BONE CREATURE . . .
. . . THE MOIST, SUCCULENT, MARBLED WITH FAT, LITTLE BONE CREATURE!
ARE YOU SURE WE'RE ALLOWED TO EAT THAT ONE? THEY ALL LOOK ALIKE TO ME!
YES, I'M SURE! THE ONE WE'RE NOT ALLOWED TO EAT HAS A STAR ON ITS CHEST!
YOU'RE RIGHT! IT'S THAT TROUBLE-MAKER FONE BONE!
WE BETTER CATCH HIM AND TAKE HIM TO KINGDOK!
FORGET KINGDOK! IF WE KEEP HIM FOR OURSELVES, WE CAN DO ANYTHING WE WANT WITH HIM!
OH, REALLY?! DOES THAT INCLUDE BAKING HIM IN A QUICHE?!
NO, IT DOES NOT INCLUDE THAT! IT INCLUDES EATING HIM RAW!
THAT'S TOO BAD. HE WOULD'VE MADE A FINE PASTRY FILLING.

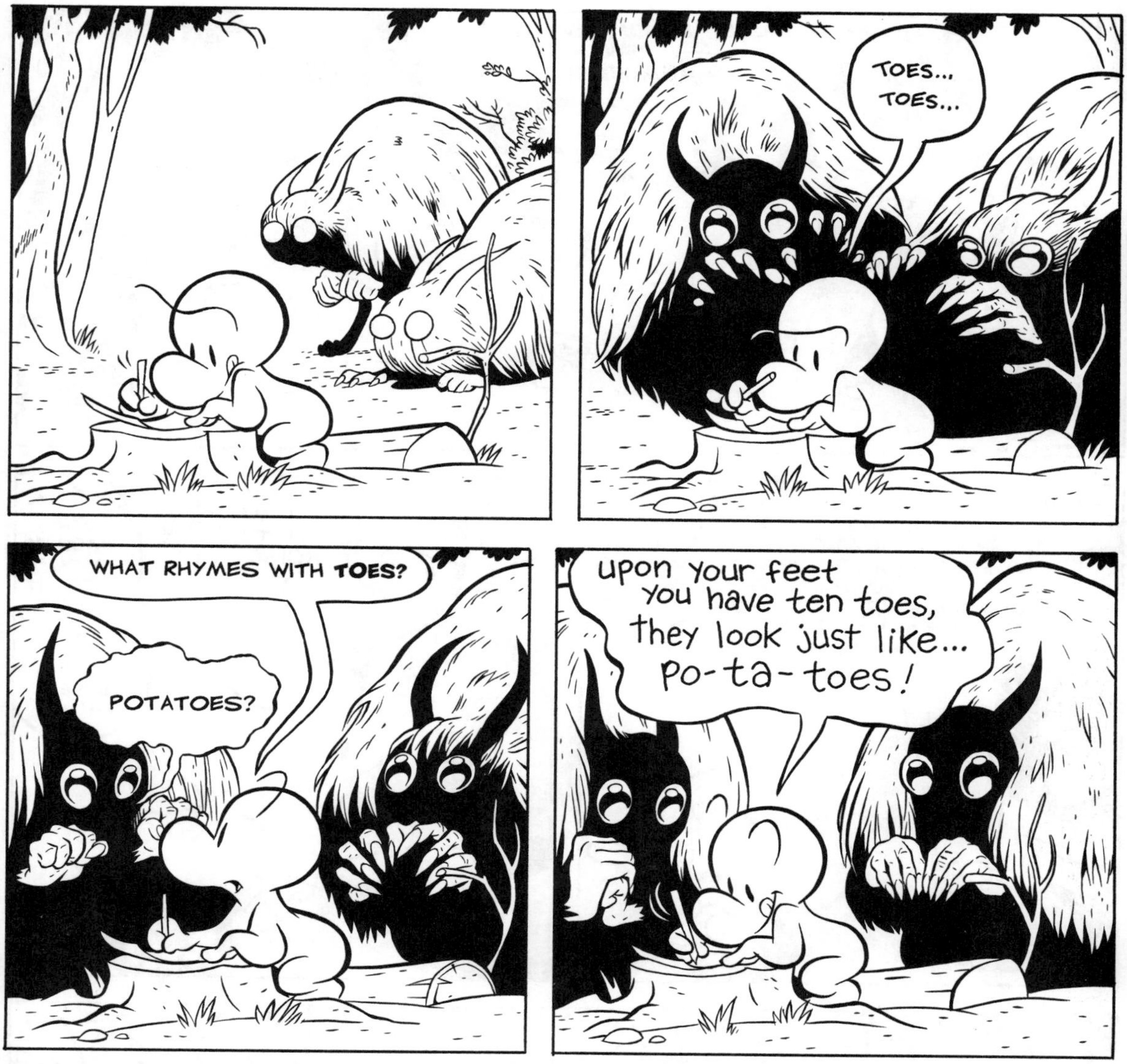
TOES... TOES...
WHAT RHYMES WITH TOES?
POTATOES?
upon your feet you have ten toes, they look just like... po-ta-toes!
WHOOOPS!
HELLO, SMALL MAMMAL.

MOO!
BAM!
BAM!
BAM!
MOO!
MOO!
BAM
BAM
WOWF!
BAM!
BAM
BAM
BAM
BAM
MOO!
MOO!
BAM
Danger
Mad cow!

72

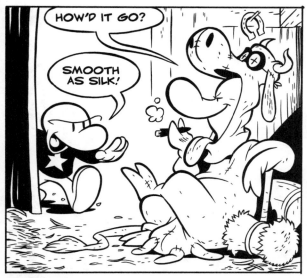

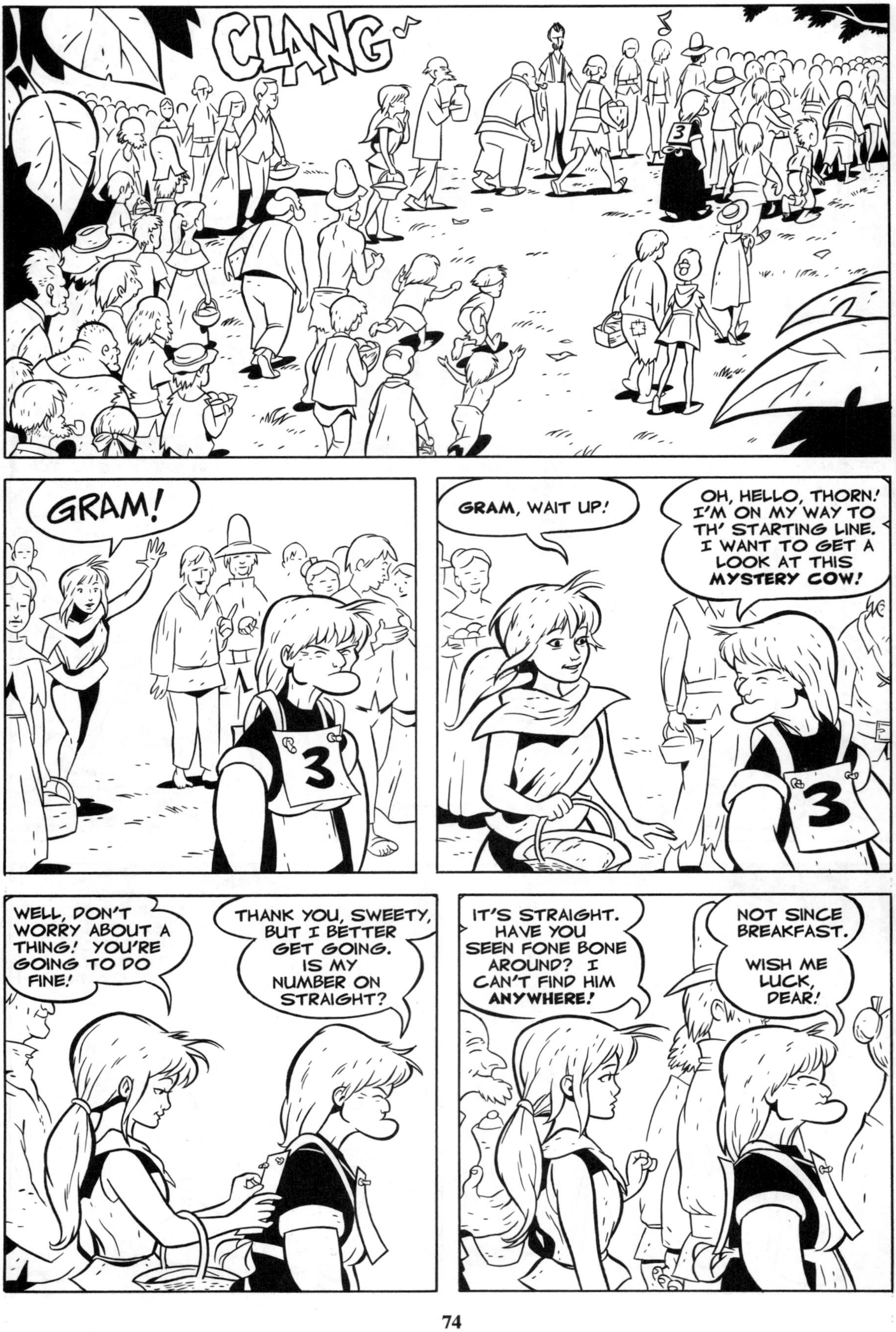
CLANG
GRAM!
GRAM, WAIT UP!
OH, HELLO, THORN! I'M ON MY WAY TO TH' STARTING LINE. I WANT TO GET A LOOK AT THIS MYSTERY COW!
WELL, DON'T WORRY ABOUT A THING! YOU'RE GOING TO DO FINE!
THANK YOU, SWEETY, BUT I BETTER GET GOING. IS MY NUMBER ON STRAIGHT?
IT'S STRAIGHT. HAVE YOU SEEN FONE BONE AROUND? I CAN'T FIND HIM ANYWHERE!
NOT SINCE BREAKFAST.
WISH ME LUCK, DEAR!

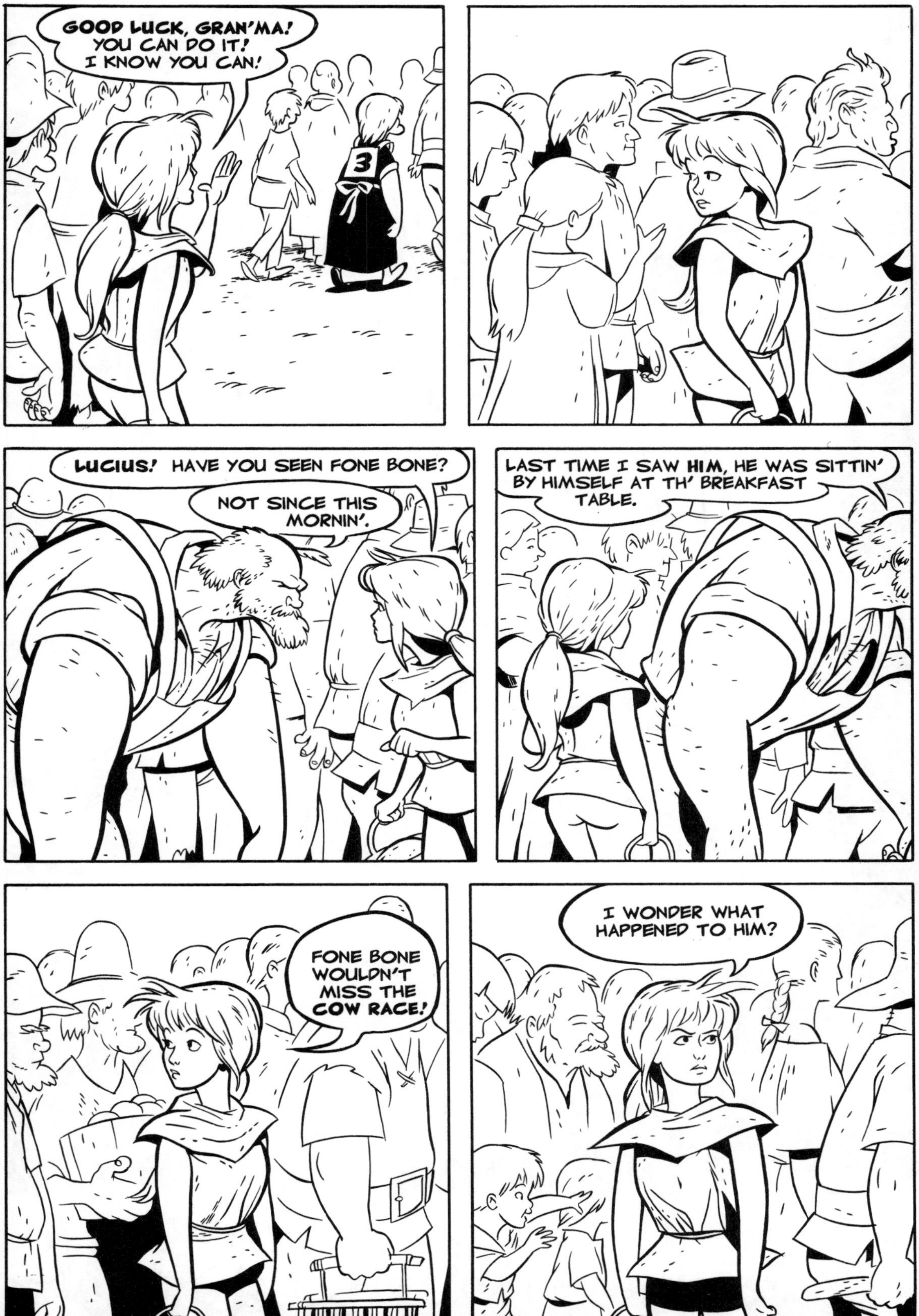
GOOD LUCK, GRAN'MA! YOU CAN DO IT! I KNOW YOU CAN!
3
LUCIUS! HAVE YOU SEEN FONE BONE?
NOT SINCE THIS MORNIN'.
LAST TIME I SAW HIM, HE WAS SITTIN' BY HIMSELF AT TH' BREAKFAST TABLE.
FONE BONE WOULDN'T MISS THE COW RACE!
I WONDER WHAT HAPPENED TO HIM?

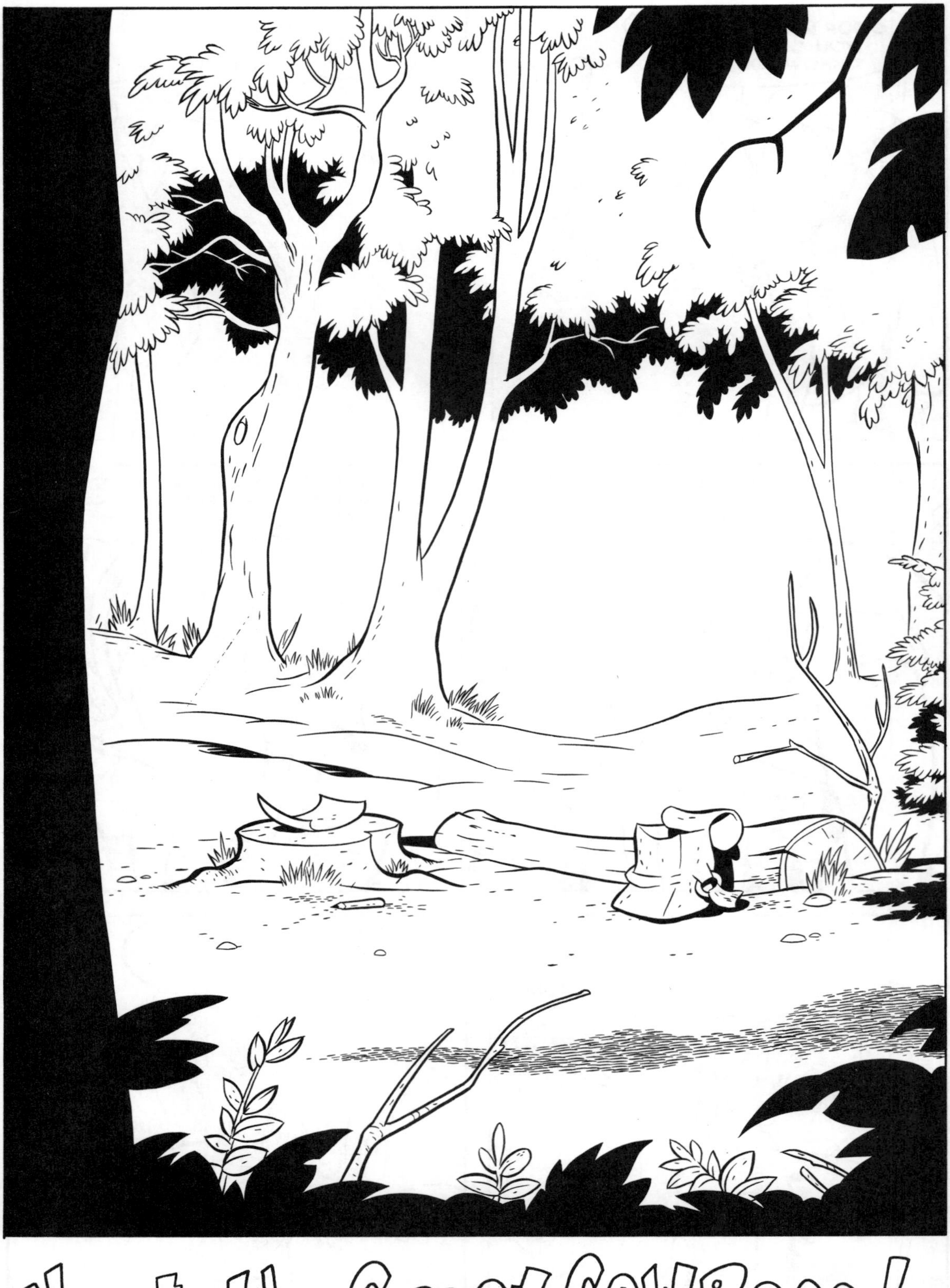

Next: the Great COW Race!

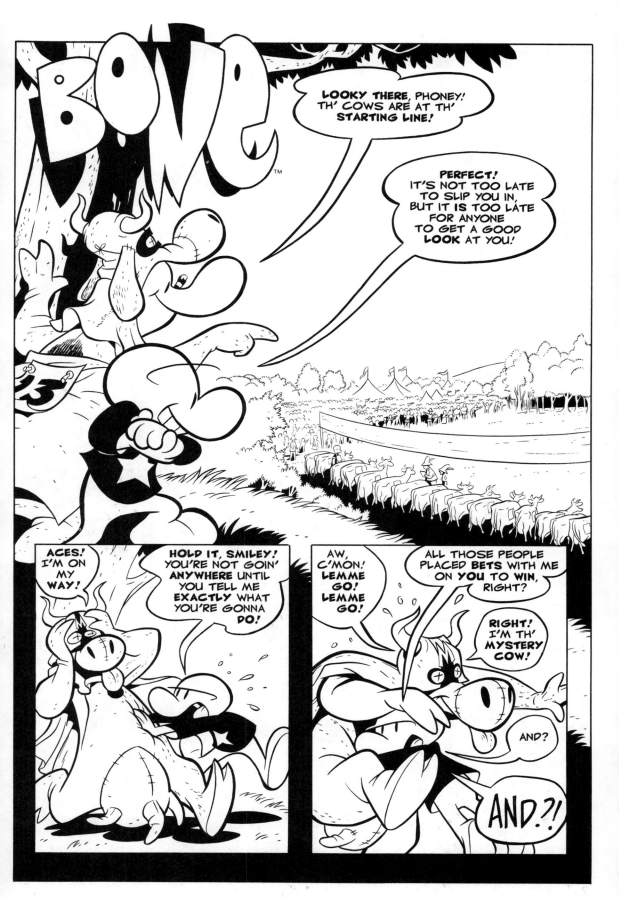

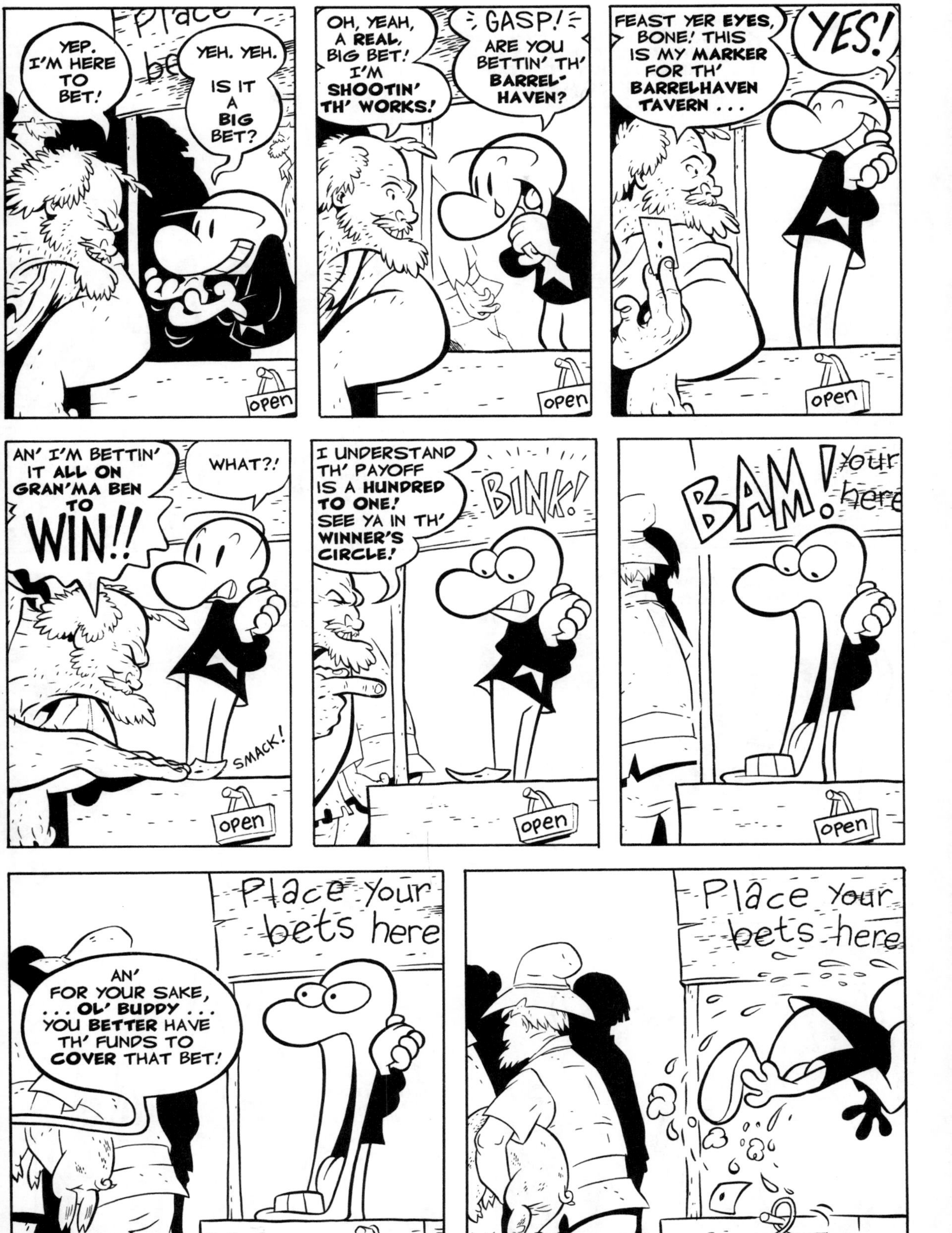
YEP. I'M HERE TO BET!
YEH. YEH. IS IT A BIG BET?
OH, YEAH, A REAL, BIG BET! I'M SHOOTIN' TH' WORKS!
GASP! ARE YOU BETTIN' TH' BARREL-HAVEN?
FEAST YER EYES, BONE! THIS IS MY MARKER FOR TH' BARRELHAVEN TAVERN . . .
YES!
open
AN' I'M BETTIN' IT ALL ON GRAN'MA BEN TO WIN!!
WHAT?!
SMACK!
I UNDERSTAND TH' PAYOFF IS A HUNDRED TO ONE! SEE YA IN TH' WINNER'S CIRCLE!
BINK!
BAM!
AN' FOR YOUR SAKE, . . . OL' BUDDY . . . YOU BETTER HAVE TH' FUNDS TO COVER THAT BET!
Place your bets here
closed

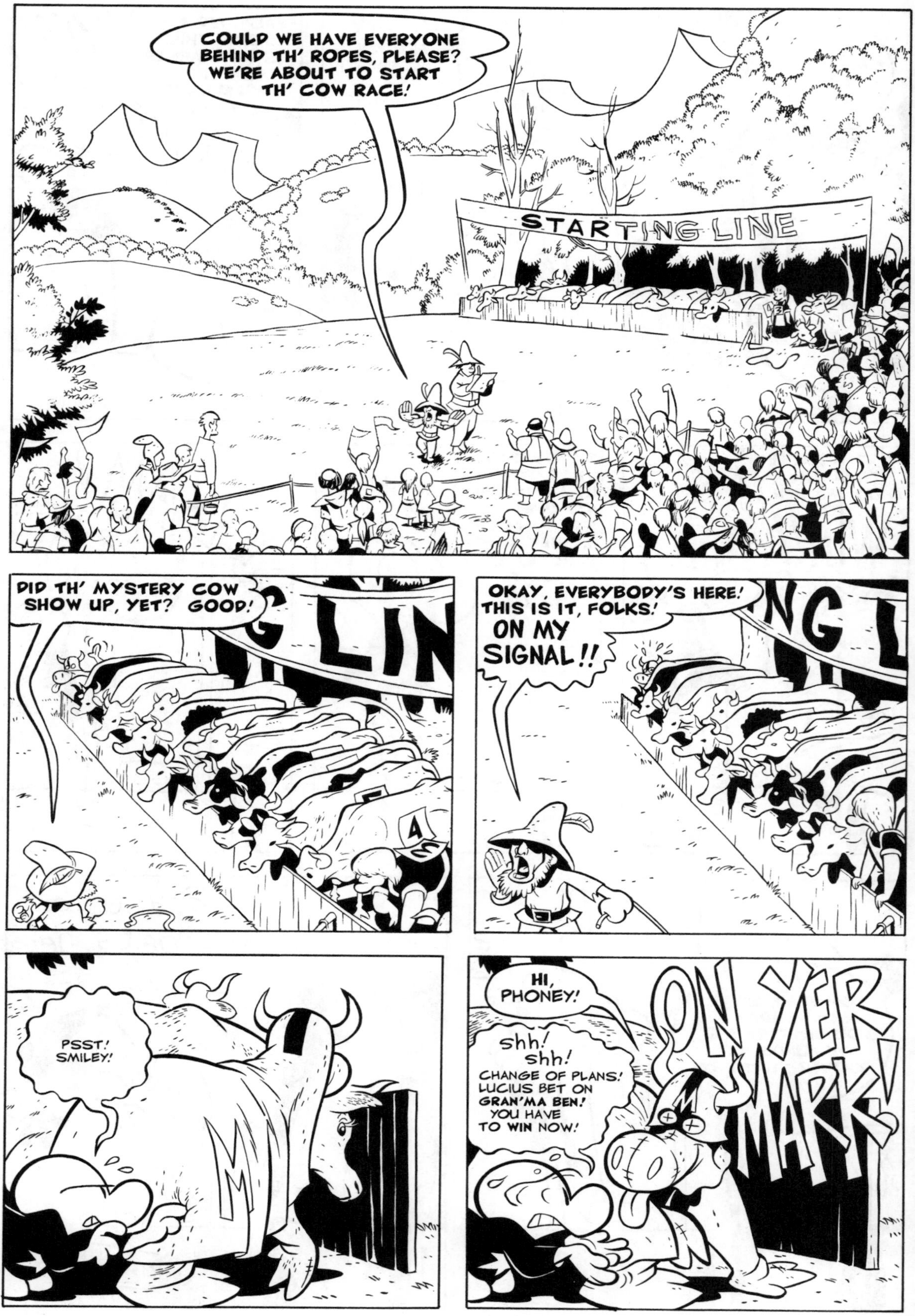
COULD WE HAVE EVERYONE BEHIND TH' ROPES, PLEASE? WE'RE ABOUT TO START TH' COW RACE!
STARTING LINE
DID TH' MYSTERY COW SHOW UP, YET? GOOD!
OKAY, EVERYBODY'S HERE! THIS IS IT, FOLKS! ON MY SIGNAL!!
PSST! SMILEY!
HI, PHONEY!
shh! shh! CHANGE OF PLANS! LUCIUS BET ON GRAN'MA BEN! YOU HAVE TO WIN NOW!
ON YER MARK!

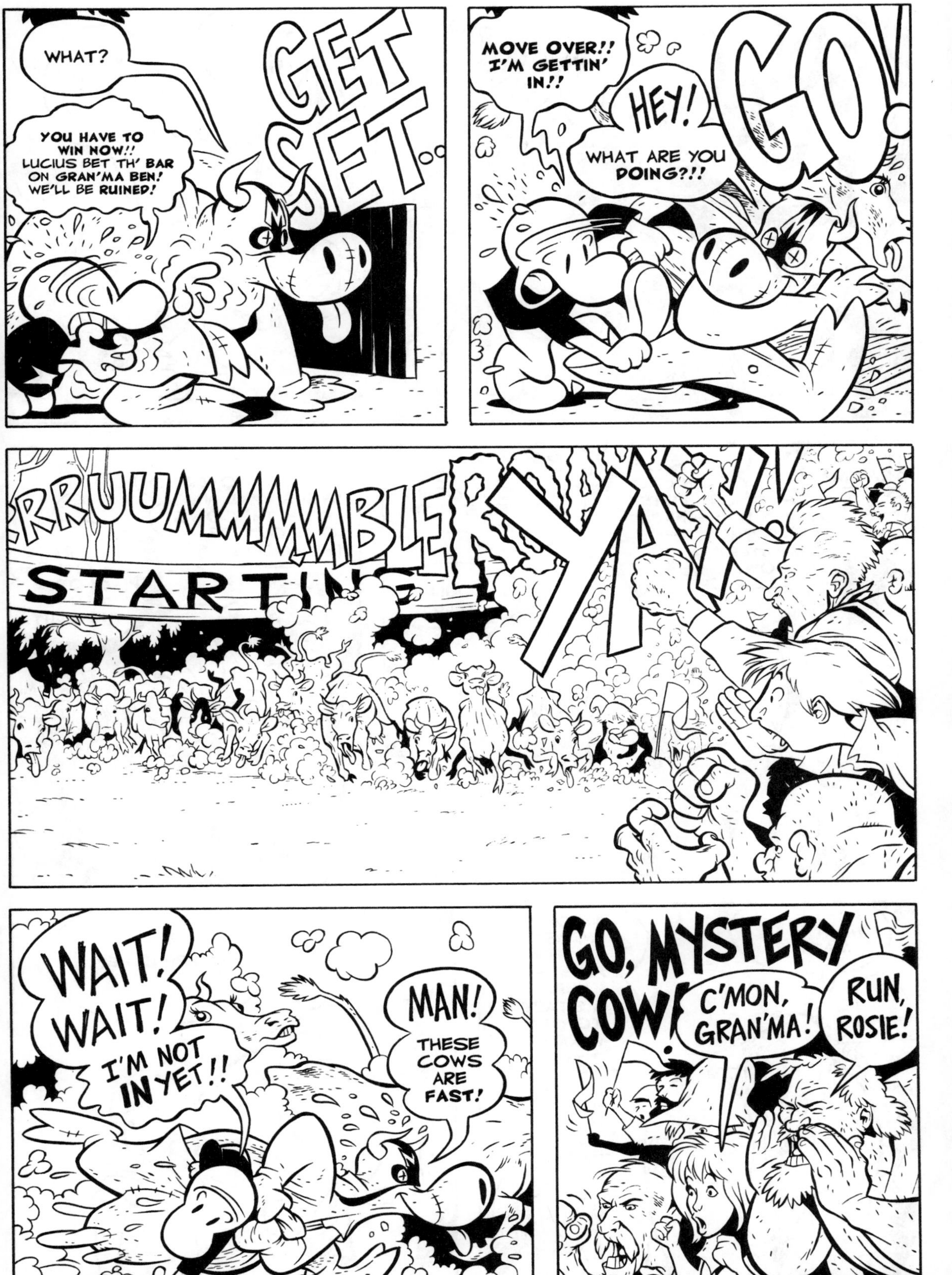
WHAT?
YOU HAVE TO WIN NOW!! LUCIUS BET TH' BAR ON GRAN'MA BEN! WE'LL BE RUINED!
GET SET..
MOVE OVER!! I'M GETTIN' IN!!
HEY!
WHAT ARE YOU DOING?!!
GO!
START
WAIT! WAIT! I'M NOT IN YET!!
MAN! THESE COWS ARE FAST!
GO, MYSTERY COW!
C'MON, GRAN'MA!
RUN, ROSIE!

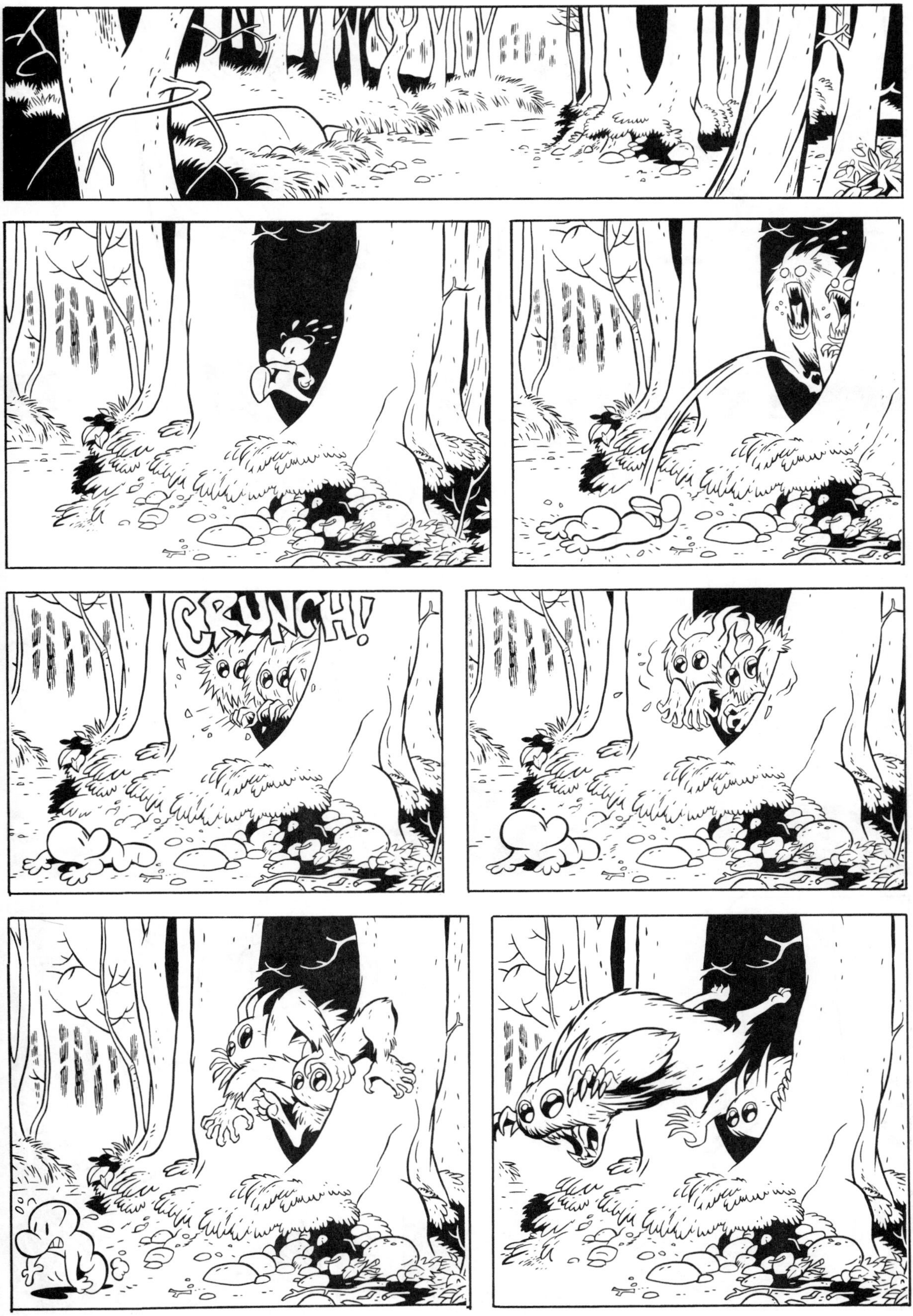
CRUNCH!

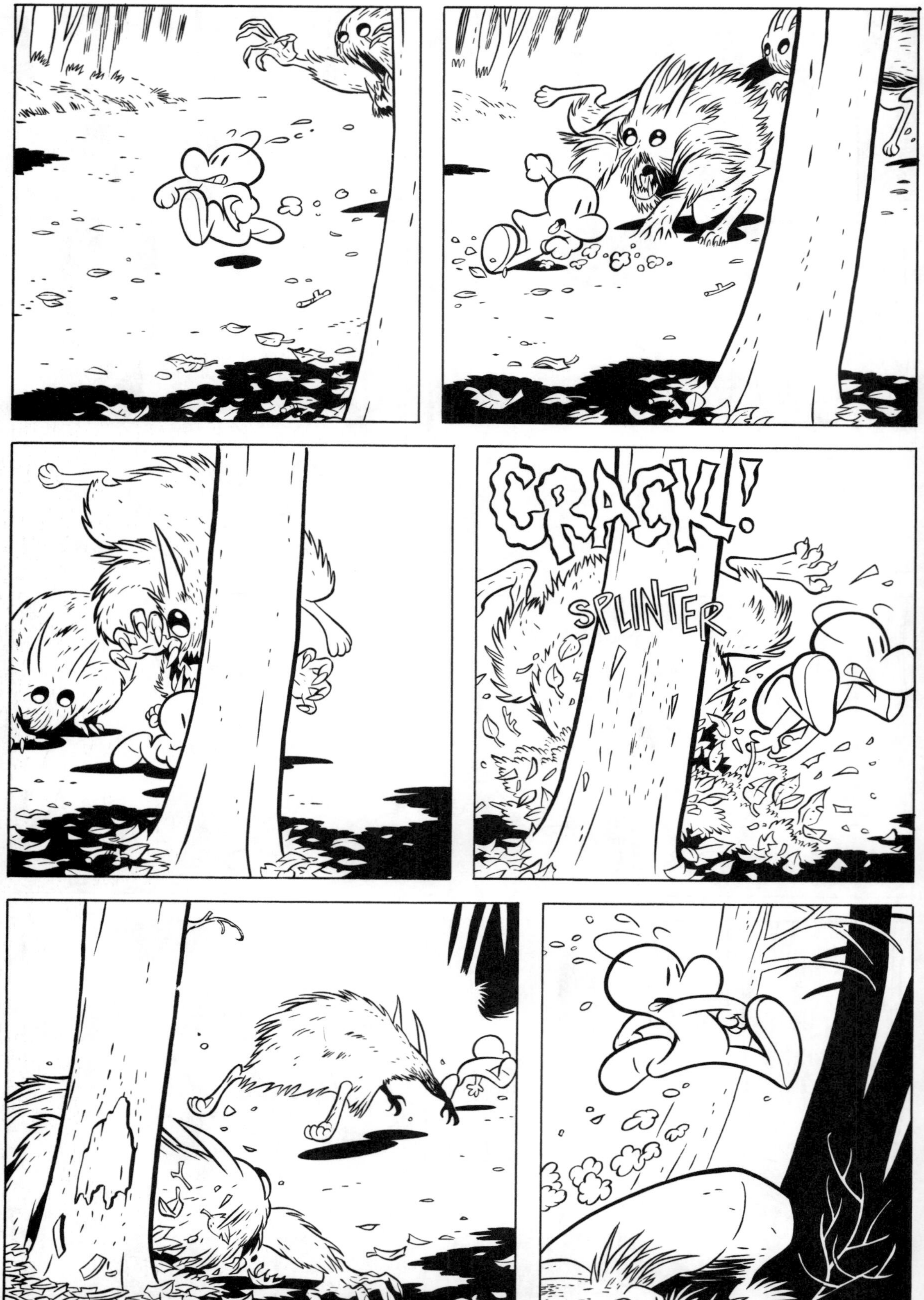
CRACK!
SPLINTER

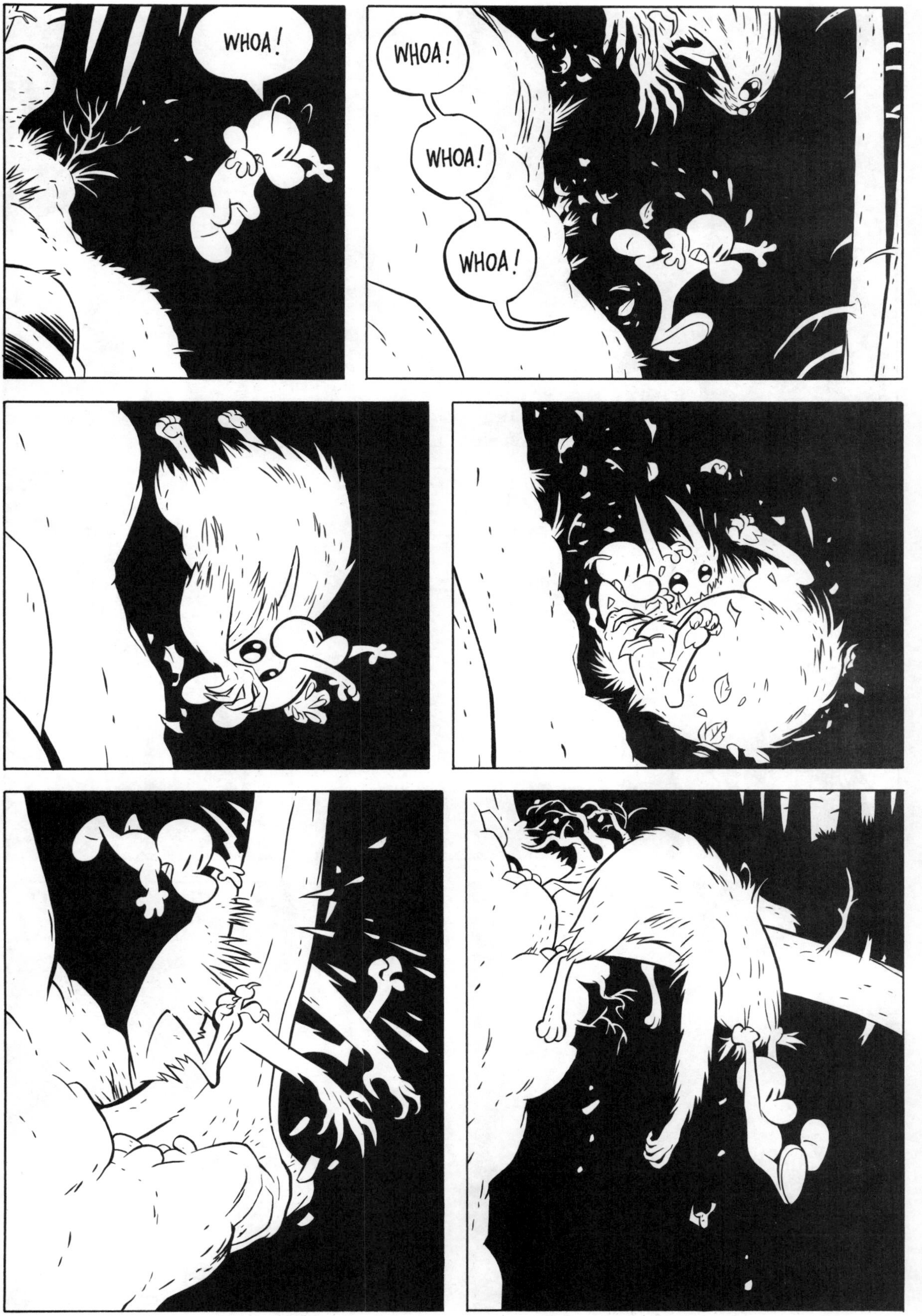
WHOA!
WHOA!
WHOA!
WHOA!

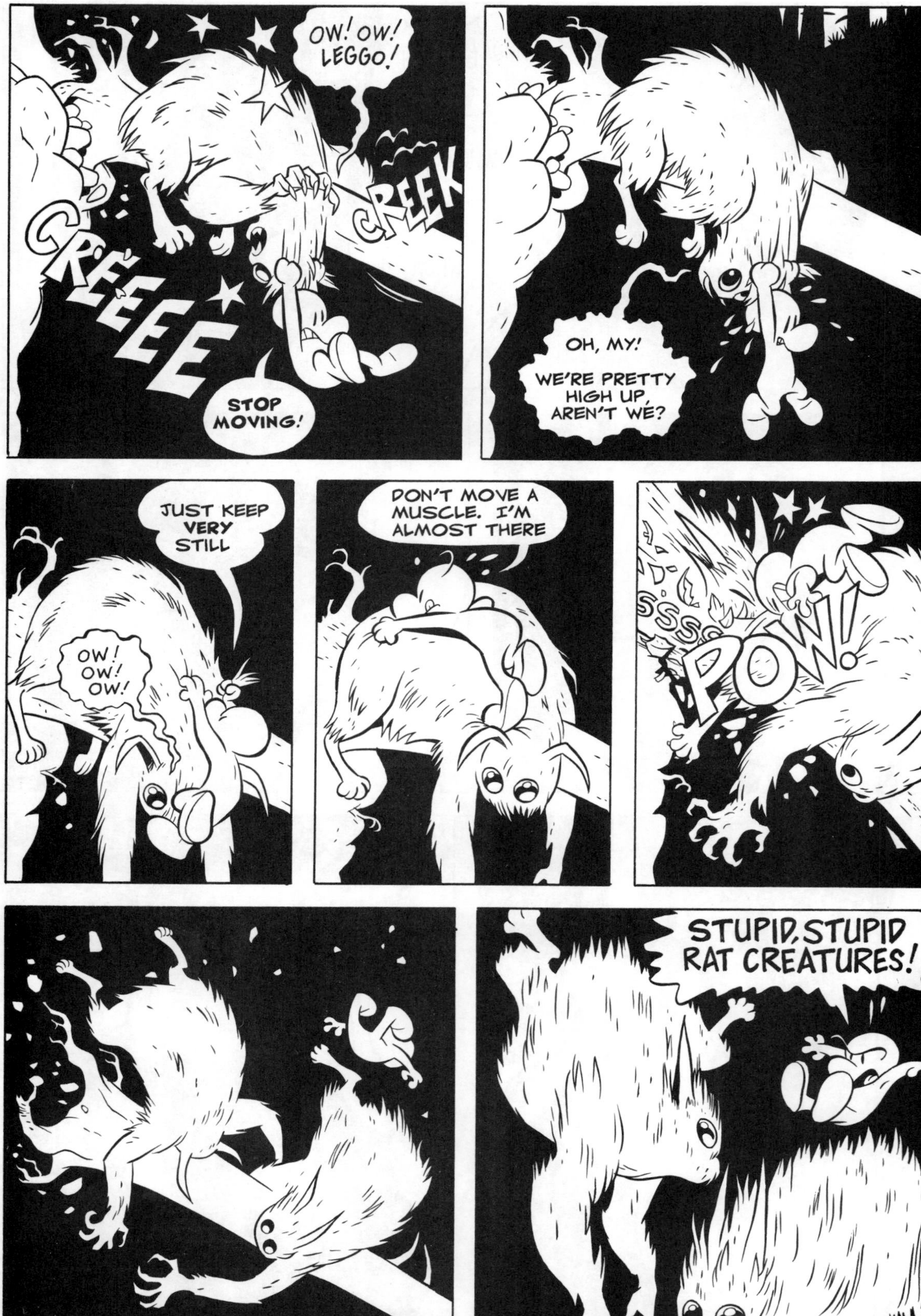
OW! OW! LEGGO!
CREEEEE
CREEK
STOP MOVING!
OH, MY!
WE'RE PRETTY HIGH UP, AREN'T WE?
JUST KEEP VERY STILL
OW! OW! OW!
DON'T MOVE A MUSCLE. I'M ALMOST THERE
POW!
STUPID, STUPID RAT CREATURES!

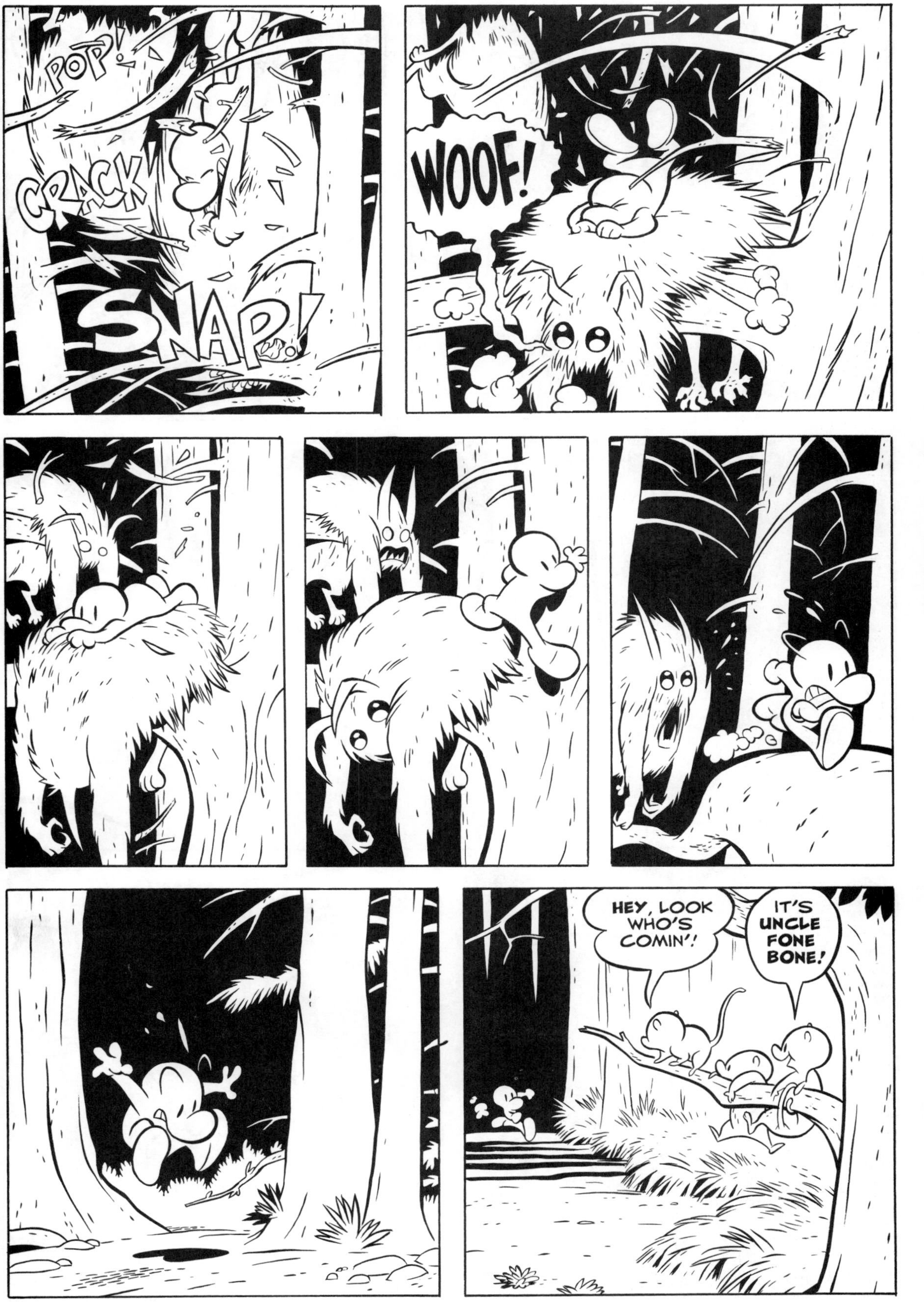
POP!
CRACK!
SNAP!
WOOF!
HEY, LOOK WHO'S COMIN'!
IT'S UNCLE FONE BONE!

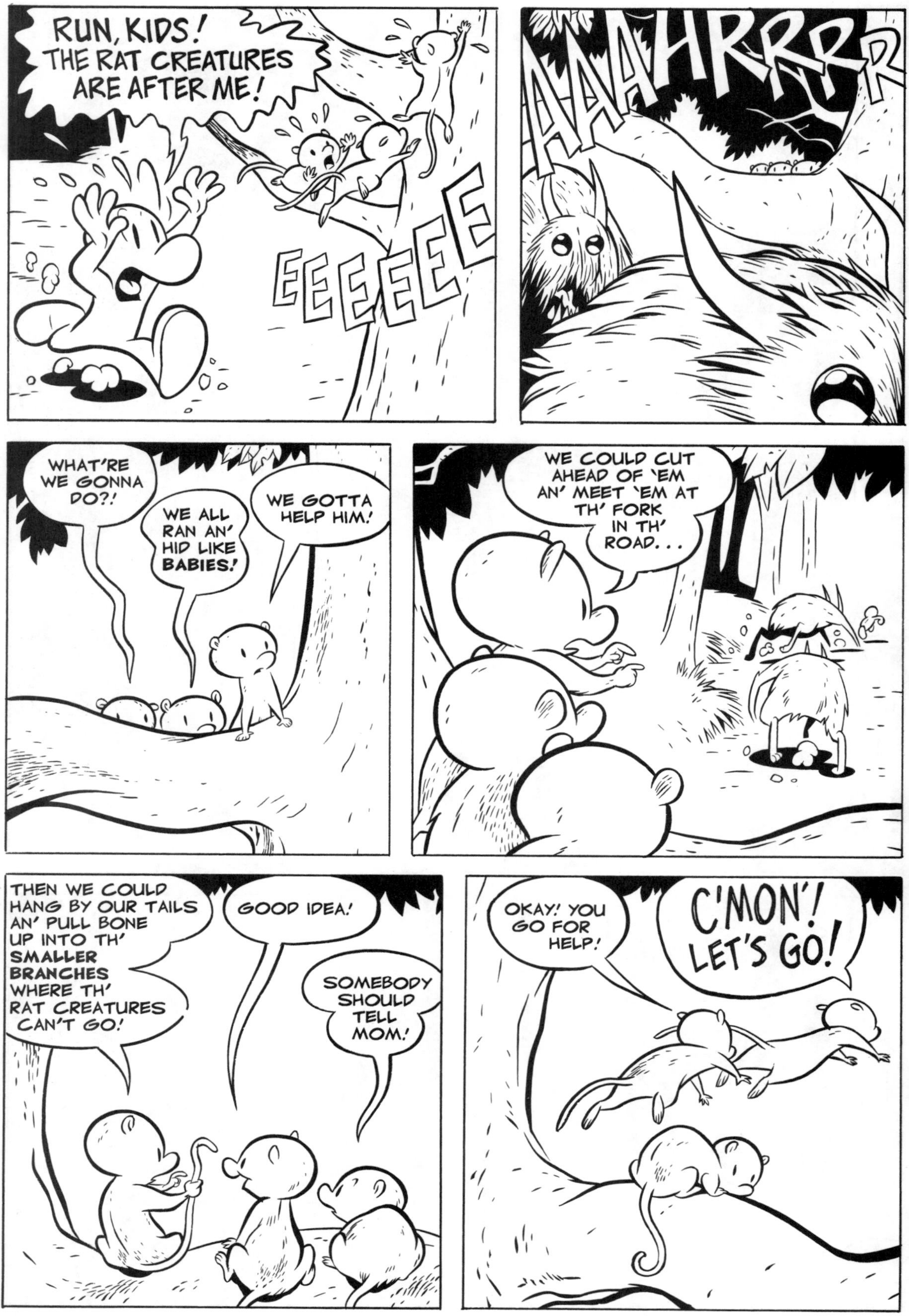

RUN, KIDS! THE RAT CREATURES ARE AFTER ME!
EEEEEEE
AAAAHRRRR
WHAT'RE WE GONNA DO?!
WE ALL RAN AN' HID LIKE BABIES!
WE GOTTA HELP HIM!
WE COULD CUT AHEAD OF 'EM AN' MEET 'EM AT TH' FORK IN TH' ROAD...
THEN WE COULD HANG BY OUR TAILS AN' PULL BONE UP INTO TH' SMALLER BRANCHES WHERE TH' RAT CREATURES CAN'T GO!
GOOD IDEA!
SOMEBODY SHOULD TELL MOM!
OKAY! YOU GO FOR HELP!
C'MON! LET'S GO!

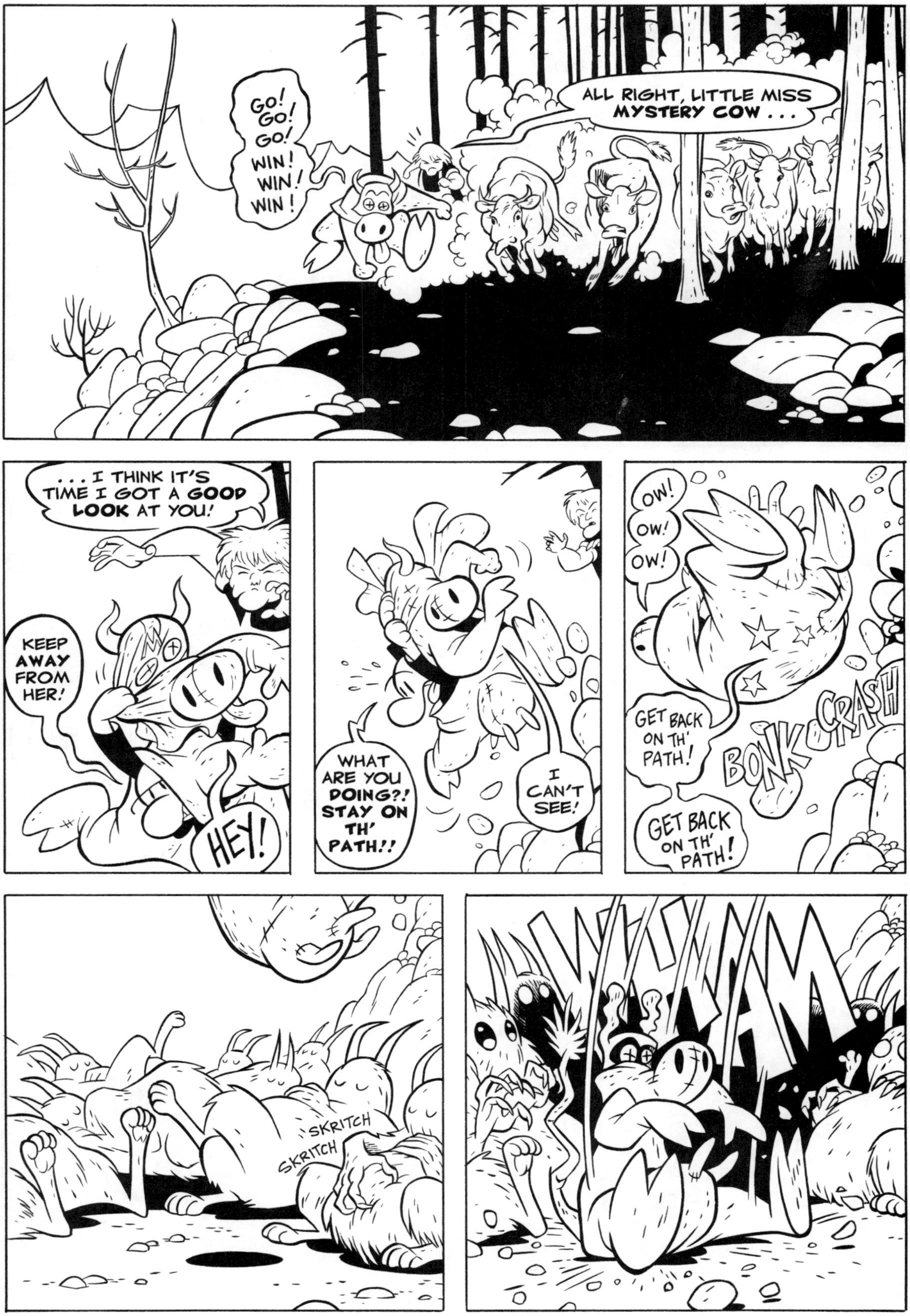
GO! GO! GO! WIN! WIN! WIN!
ALL RIGHT, LITTLE MISS MYSTERY COW . . .
. . . I THINK IT'S TIME I GOT A GOOD LOOK AT YOU!
KEEP AWAY FROM HER!
HEY!
WHAT ARE YOU DOING?! STAY ON TH' PATH!!
I CAN'T SEE!
OW! OW! OW!
GET BACK ON TH' PATH!
GET BACK ON TH' PATH!
BONK
CRASH
SKRITCH SKRITCH
WHAM

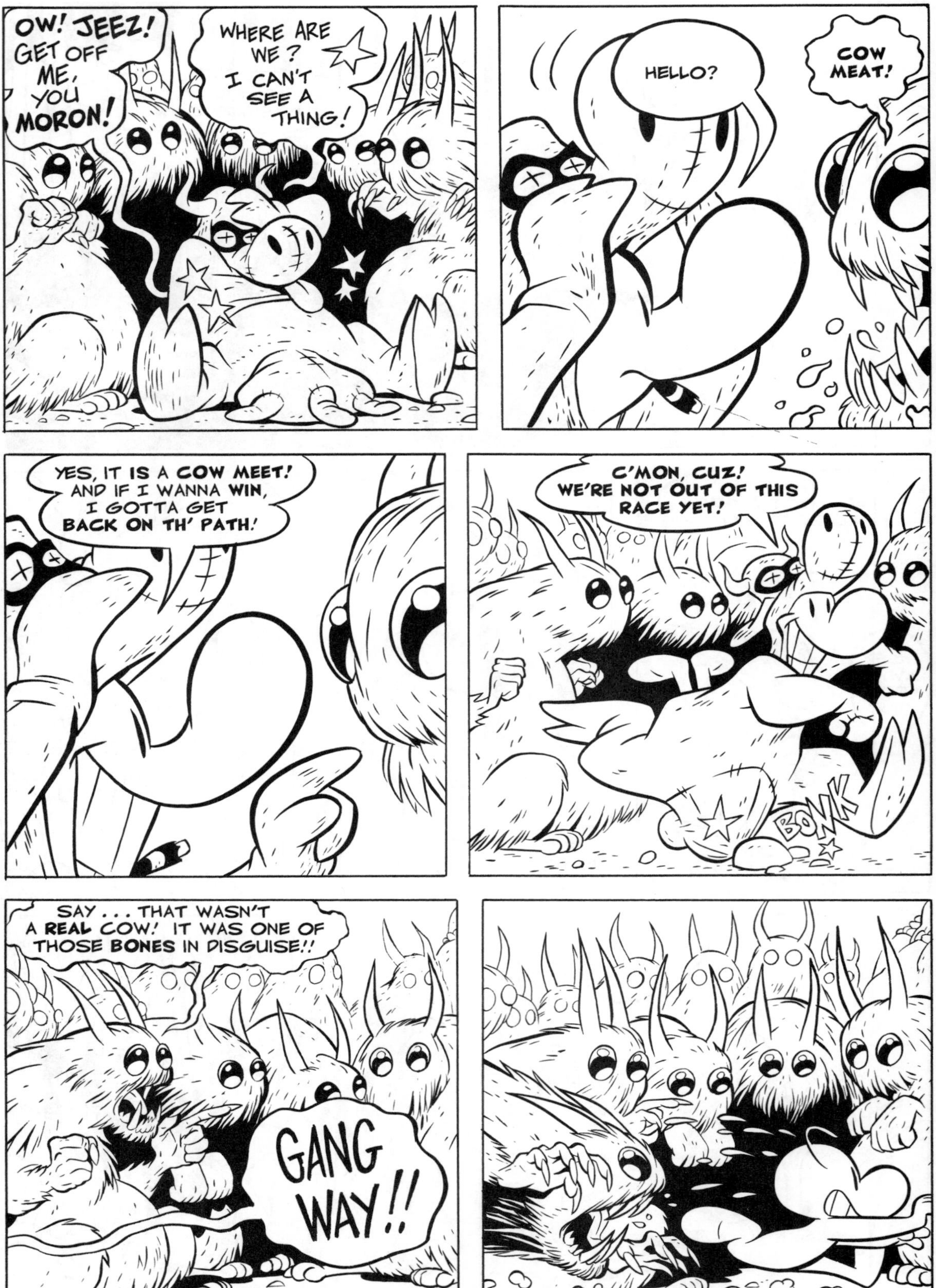
OW! JEEZ! GET OFF ME, YOU MORON!
WHERE ARE WE? I CAN'T SEE A THING!
HELLO?
COW MEAT!
YES, IT IS A COW MEET! AND IF I WANNA WIN, I GOTTA GET BACK ON TH' PATH!
C'MON, CUZ! WE'RE NOT OUT OF THIS RACE YET!
BONK
SAY . . . THAT WASN'T A REAL COW! IT WAS ONE OF THOSE BONES IN DISGUISE!!
GANG WAY!!

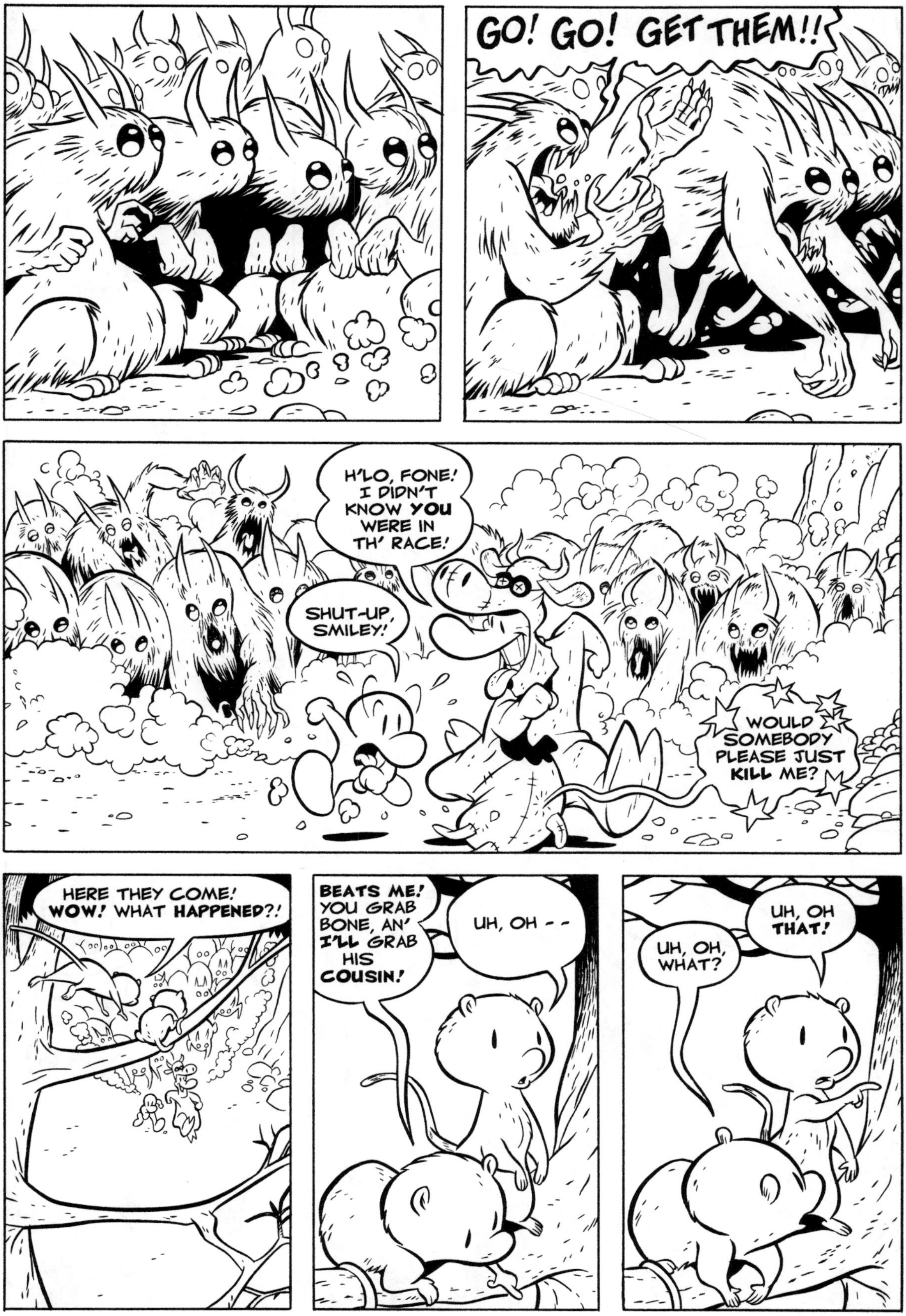

GO! GO! GET THEM!!
H'LO, FONE! I DIDN'T KNOW YOU WERE IN TH' RACE!
SHUT-UP, SMILEY!
WOULD SOMEBODY PLEASE JUST KILL ME?
HERE THEY COME! WOW! WHAT HAPPENED?!
BEATS ME! YOU GRAB BONE, AN' I'LL GRAB HIS COUSIN!
UH, OH - -
UH, OH, WHAT?
UH, OH THAT!

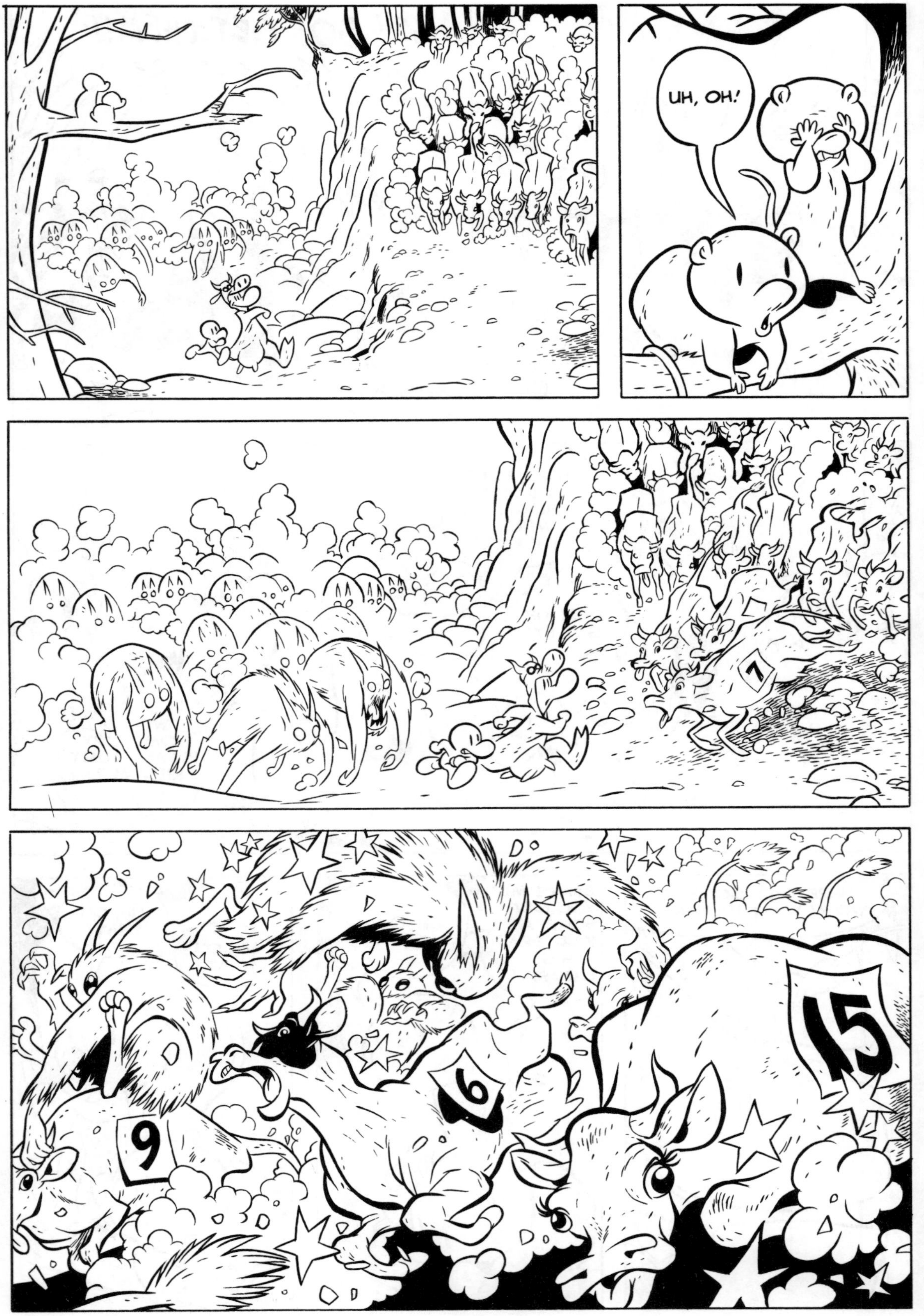
UH, OH!

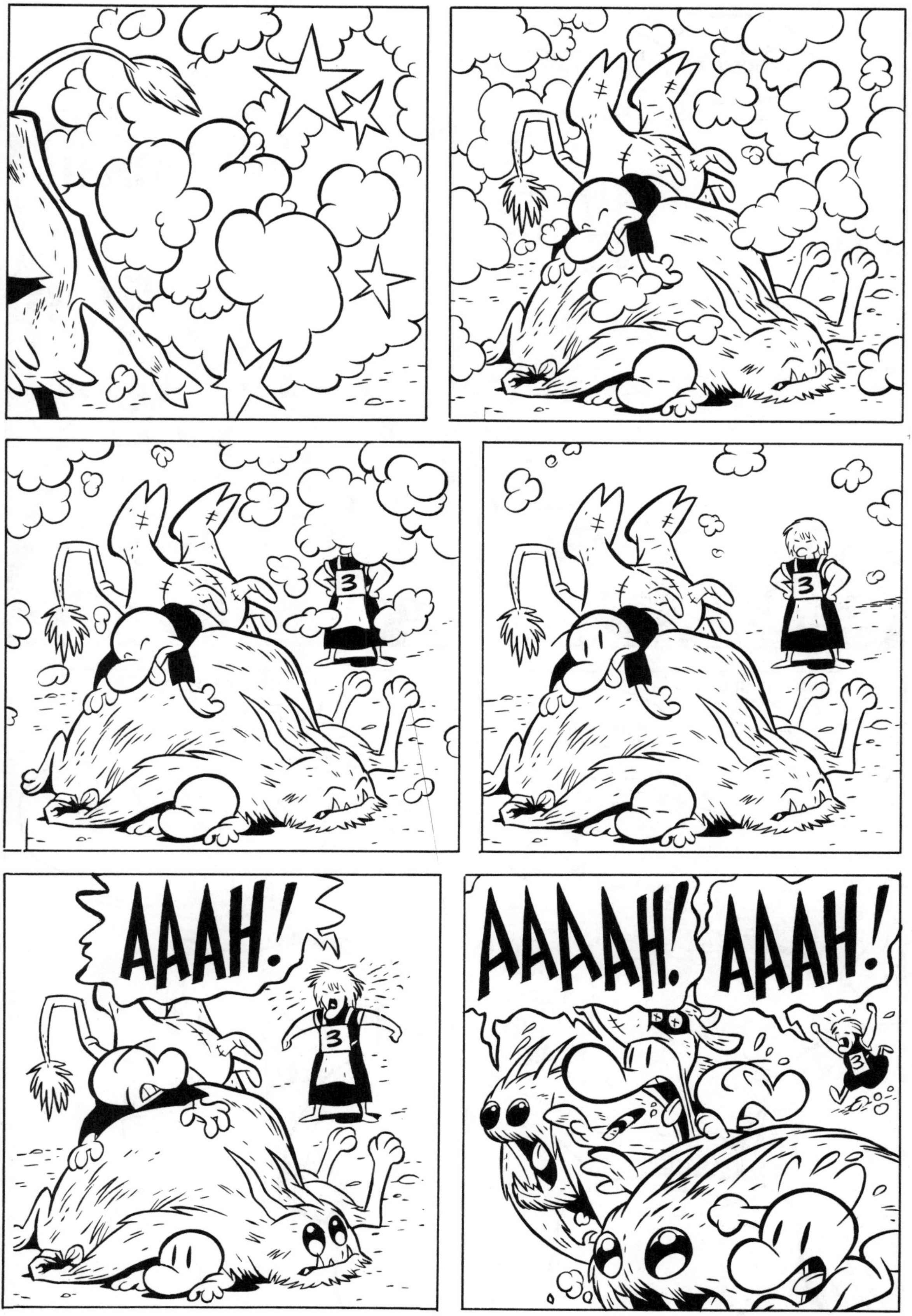
AAAH!
AAAAH!
AAAH!

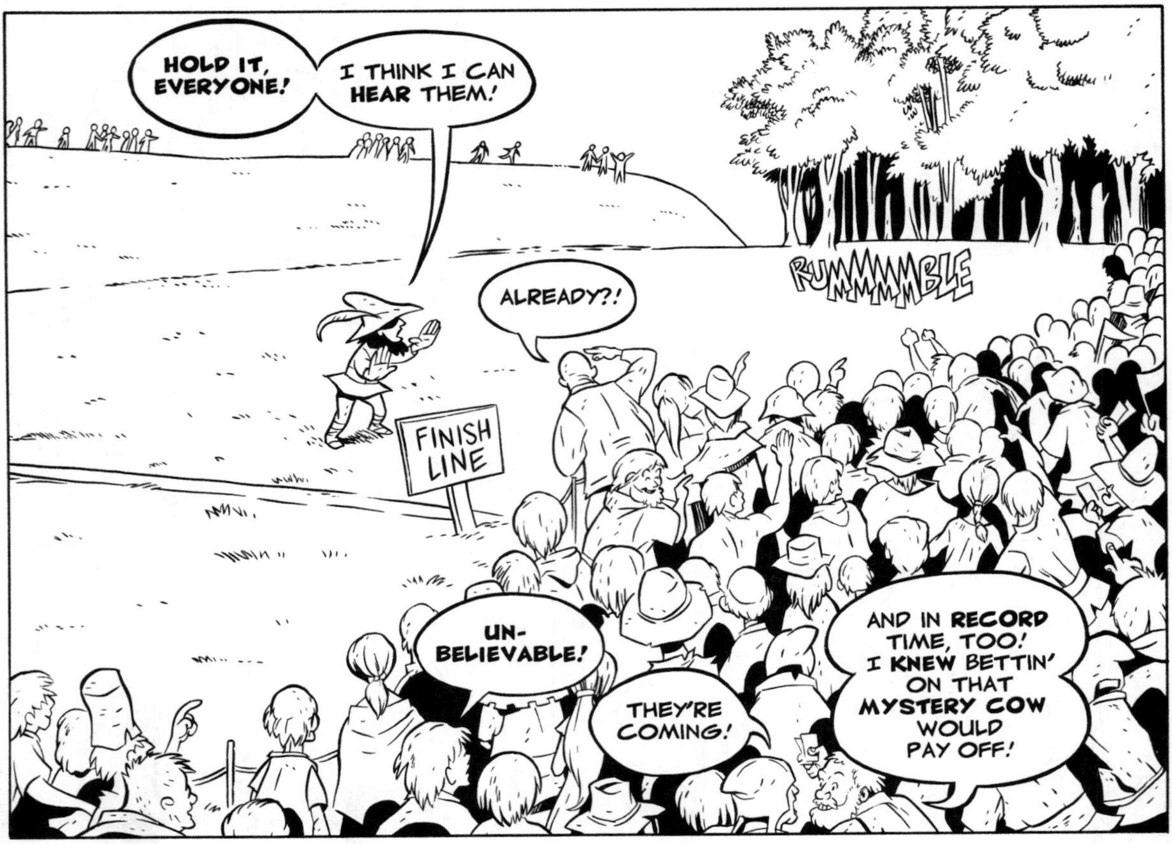
HOLD IT, EVERYONE!
I THINK I CAN HEAR THEM!
RUMMMMMBLE
ALREADY?!
FINISH LINE
UN-BELIEVABLE!
THEY'RE COMING!
AND IN RECORD TIME, TOO! I KNEW BETTIN' ON THAT MYSTERY COW WOULD PAY OFF!

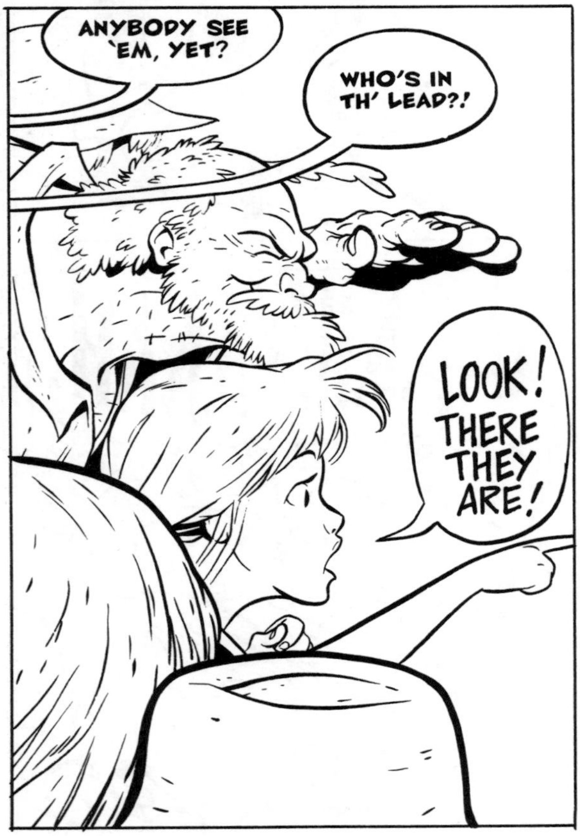
ANYBODY SEE `EM, YET?
WHO'S IN TH' LEAD?!
LOOK! THERE THEY ARE!

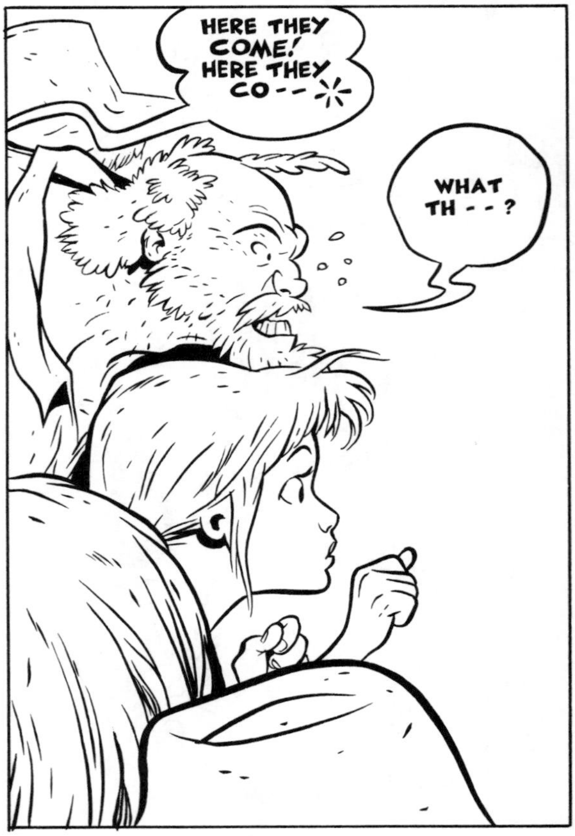
HERE THEY COME! HERE THEY CO--
WHAT TH --?

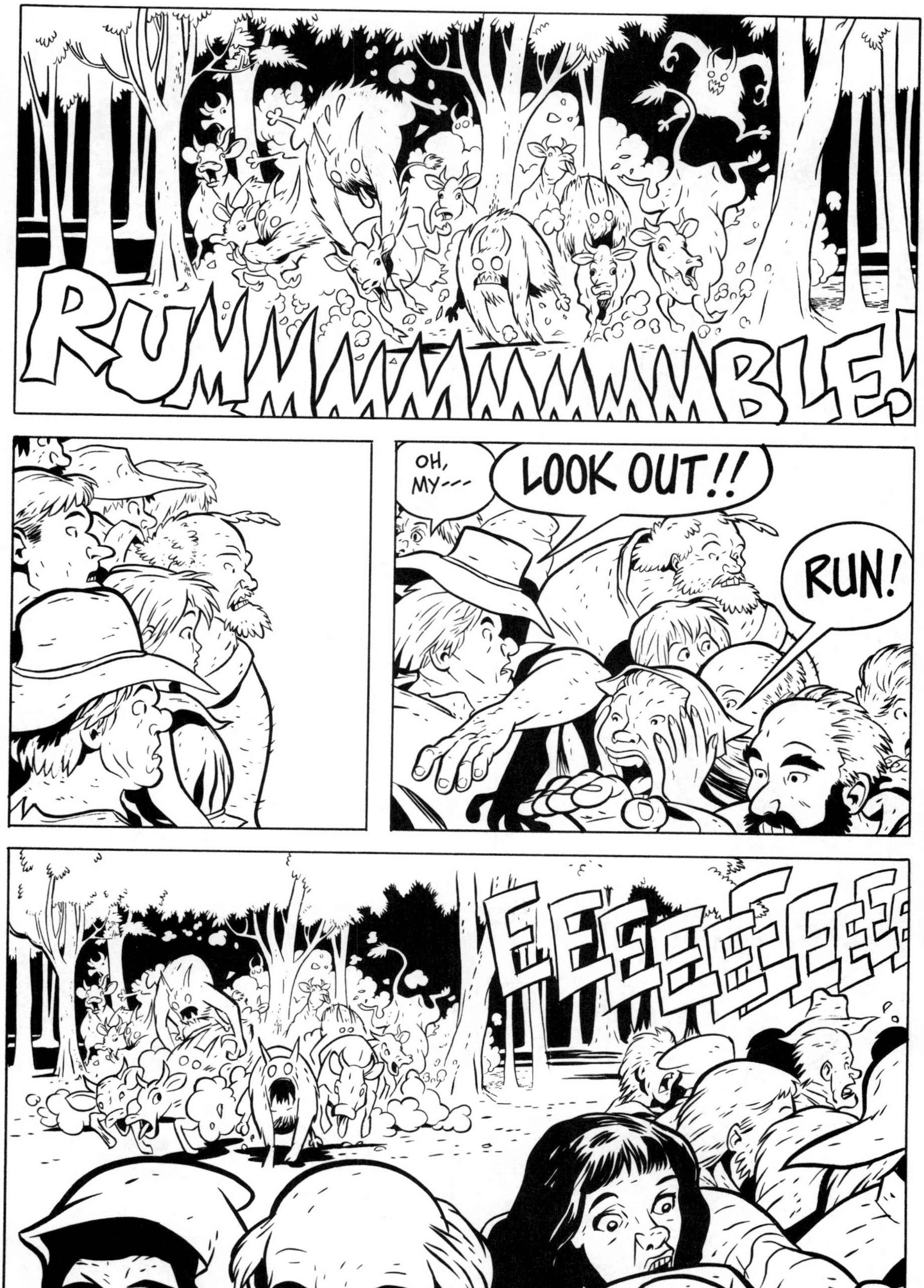
RUMMMMMMMMMBLE!
OH, MY---
LOOK OUT!!
RUN!
EEEEEEEEE

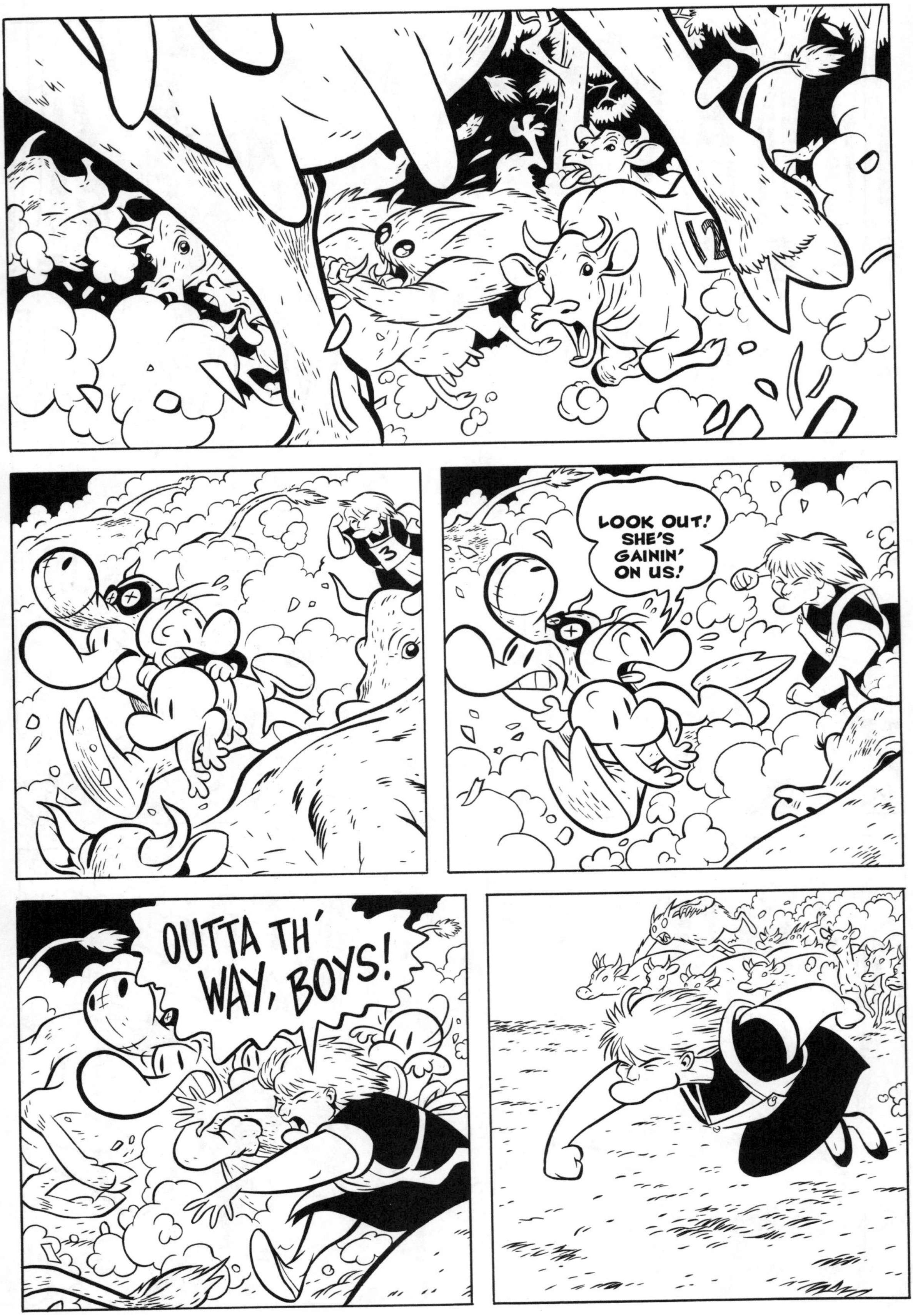
LOOK OUT! SHE'S GAININ' ON US!
OUTTA TH' WAY, BOYS!

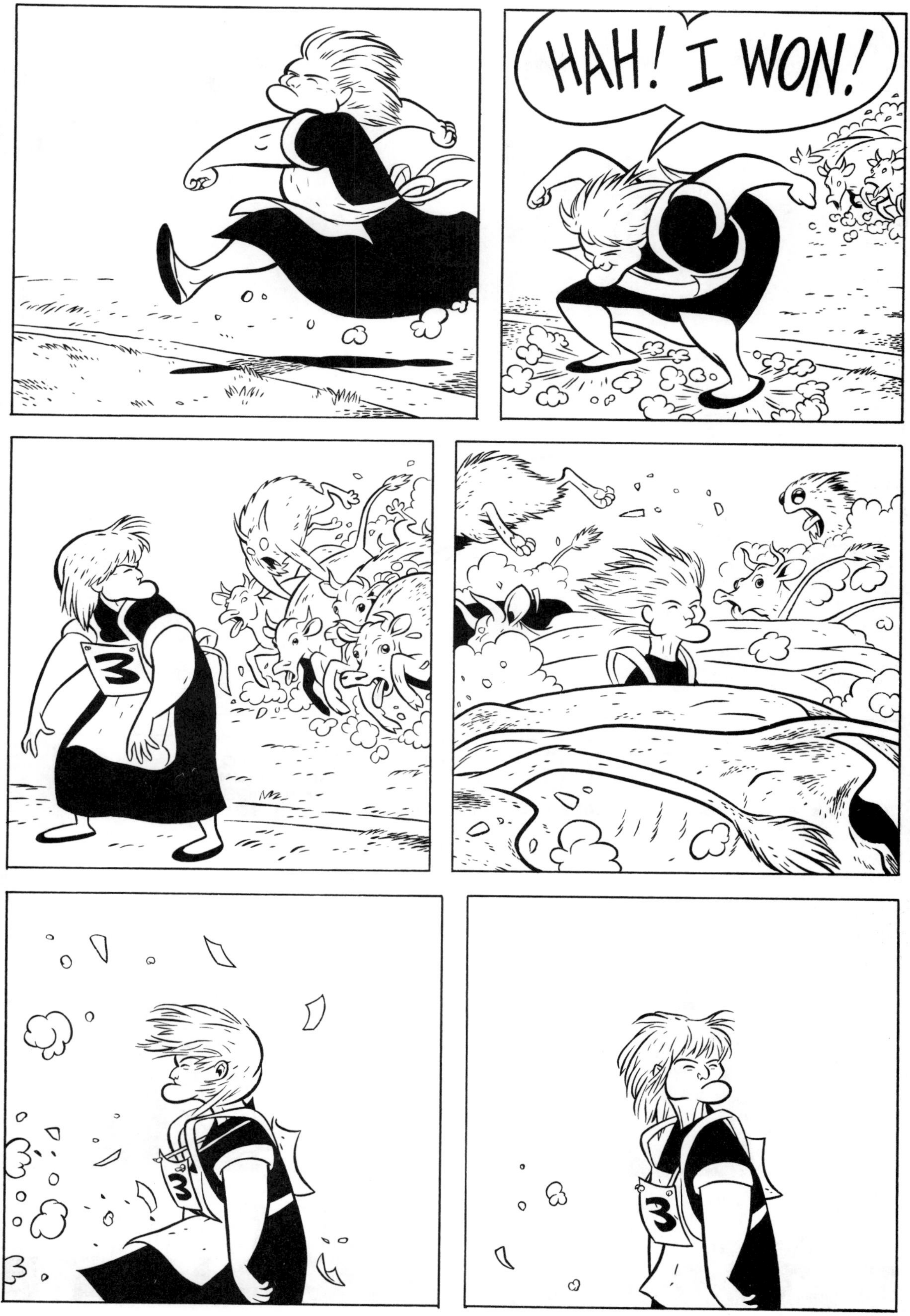
HAH! I WON!

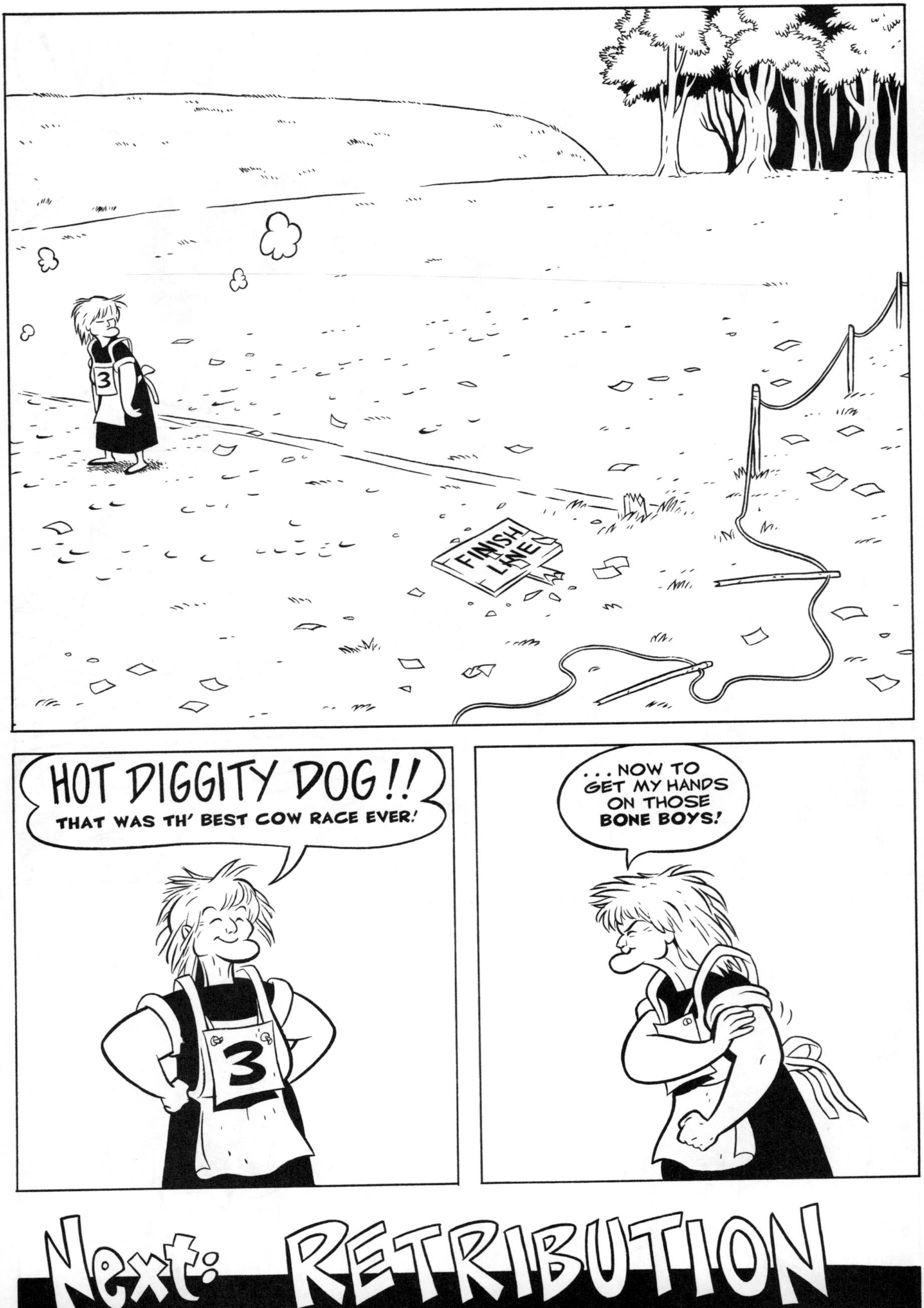
FINISH LINE
HOT DIGGITY DOG!! THAT WAS TH' BEST COW RACE EVER!
...NOW TO GET MY HANDS ON THOSE BONE BOYS!
Next: RETRIBUTION

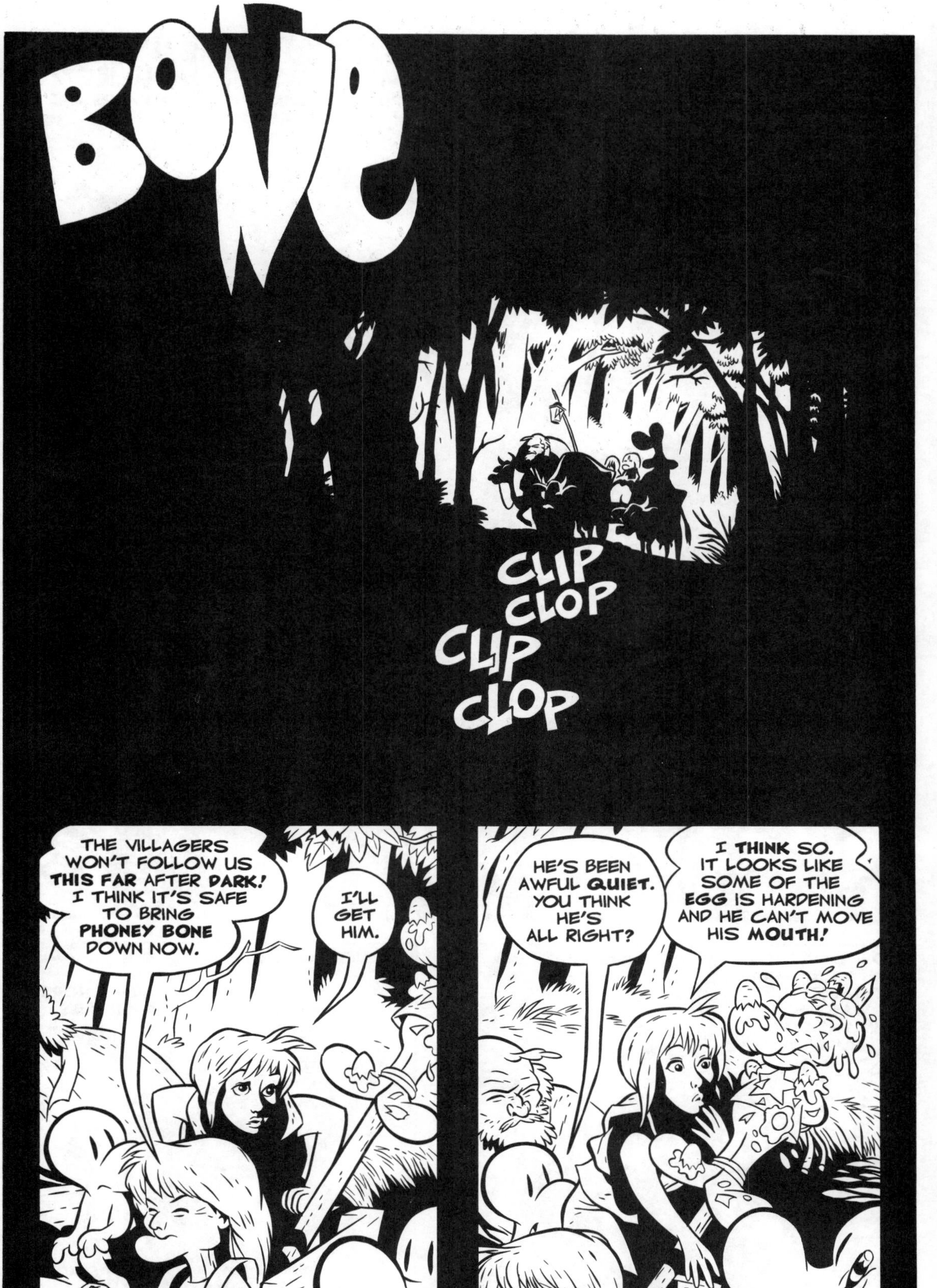
BONE
CLIP CLOP CLIP CLOP
THE VILLAGERS WON'T FOLLOW US THIS FAR AFTER DARK! I THINK IT'S SAFE TO BRING PHONEY BONE DOWN NOW.
I'LL GET HIM.
HE'S BEEN AWFUL QUIET. YOU THINK HE'S ALL RIGHT?
I THINK SO. IT LOOKS LIKE SOME OF THE EGG IS HARDENING AND HE CAN'T MOVE HIS MOUTH!

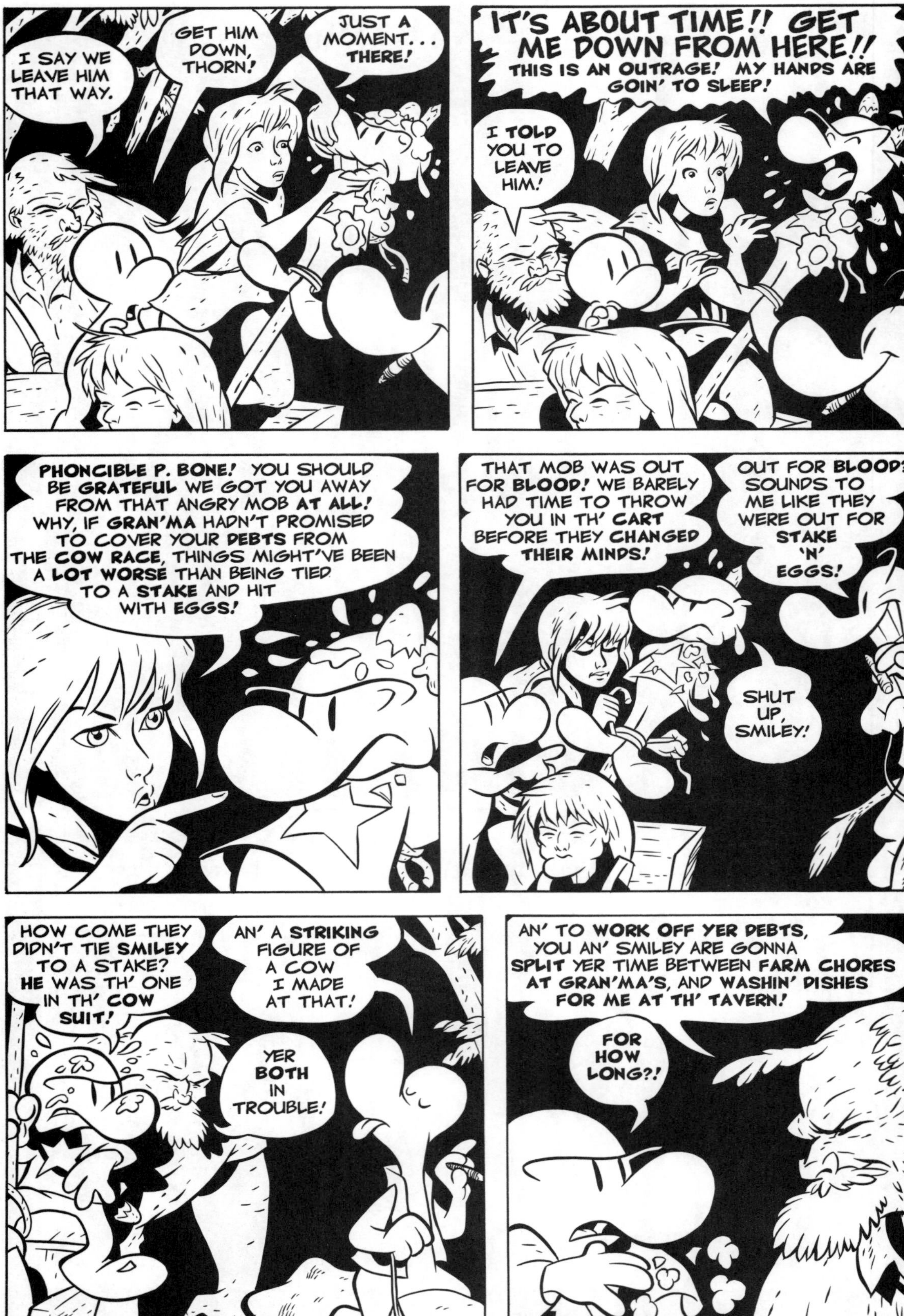
I SAY WE LEAVE HIM THAT WAY.
GET HIM DOWN, THORN!
JUST A MOMENT... THERE!
IT'S ABOUT TIME!! GET ME DOWN FROM HERE!! THIS IS AN OUTRAGE! MY HANDS ARE GOIN' TO SLEEP!
I TOLD YOU TO LEAVE HIM!
PHONCIBLE P. BONE! YOU SHOULD BE GRATEFUL WE GOT YOU AWAY FROM THAT ANGRY MOB AT ALL! WHY, IF GRAN'MA HADN'T PROMISED TO COVER YOUR DEBTS FROM THE COW RACE, THINGS MIGHT'VE BEEN A LOT WORSE THAN BEING TIED TO A STAKE AND HIT WITH EGGS!
THAT MOB WAS OUT FOR BLOOD! WE BARELY HAD TIME TO THROW YOU IN TH' CART BEFORE THEY CHANGED THEIR MINDS!
OUT FOR BLOOD? SOUNDS TO ME LIKE THEY WERE OUT FOR STAKE 'N' EGGS!
SHUT UP, SMILEY!
HOW COME THEY DIDN'T TIE SMILEY TO A STAKE? HE WAS TH' ONE IN TH' COW SUIT!
AN' A STRIKING FIGURE OF A COW I MADE AT THAT!
YER BOTH IN TROUBLE!
AN' TO WORK OFF YER DEBTS, YOU AN' SMILEY ARE GONNA SPLIT YER TIME BETWEEN FARM CHORES AT GRAN'MA'S, AND WASHIN' DISHES FOR ME AT TH' TAVERN!
FOR HOW LONG?!

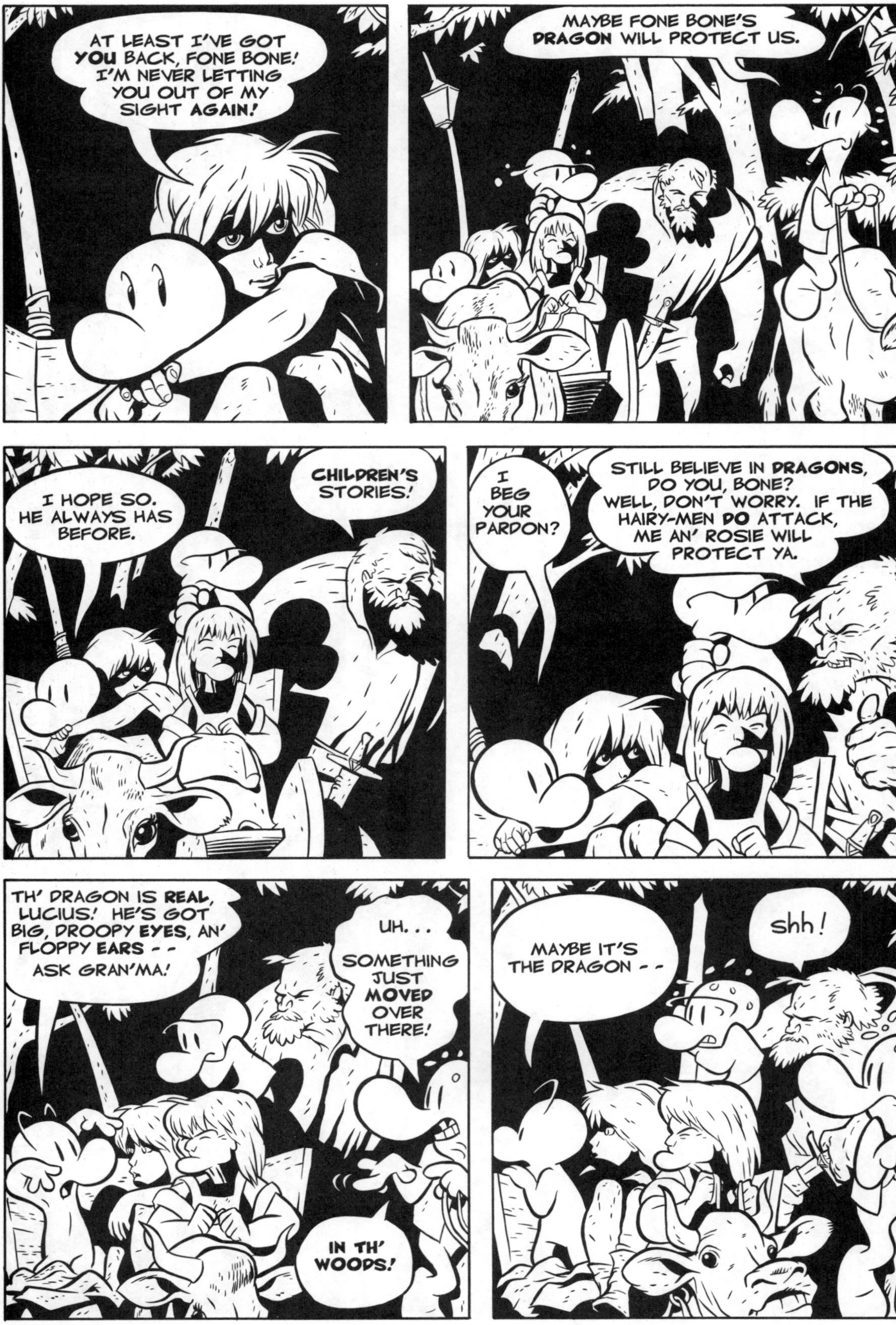
AT LEAST I'VE GOT YOU BACK, FONE BONE! I'M NEVER LETTING YOU OUT OF MY SIGHT AGAIN!
MAYBE FONE BONE'S DRAGON WILL PROTECT US.
I HOPE SO. HE ALWAYS HAS BEFORE.
CHILDREN'S STORIES!
I BEG YOUR PARDON?
STILL BELIEVE IN DRAGONS, DO YOU, BONE? WELL, DON'T WORRY. IF THE HAIRY-MEN DO ATTACK, ME AN' ROSIE WILL PROTECT YA.
TH' DRAGON IS REAL, LUCIUS! HE'S GOT BIG, DROOPY EYES, AN' FLOPPY EARS - - ASK GRAN'MA!
UH. . .
SOMETHING JUST MOVED OVER THERE!
IN TH' WOODS!
MAYBE IT'S THE DRAGON - -
shh!

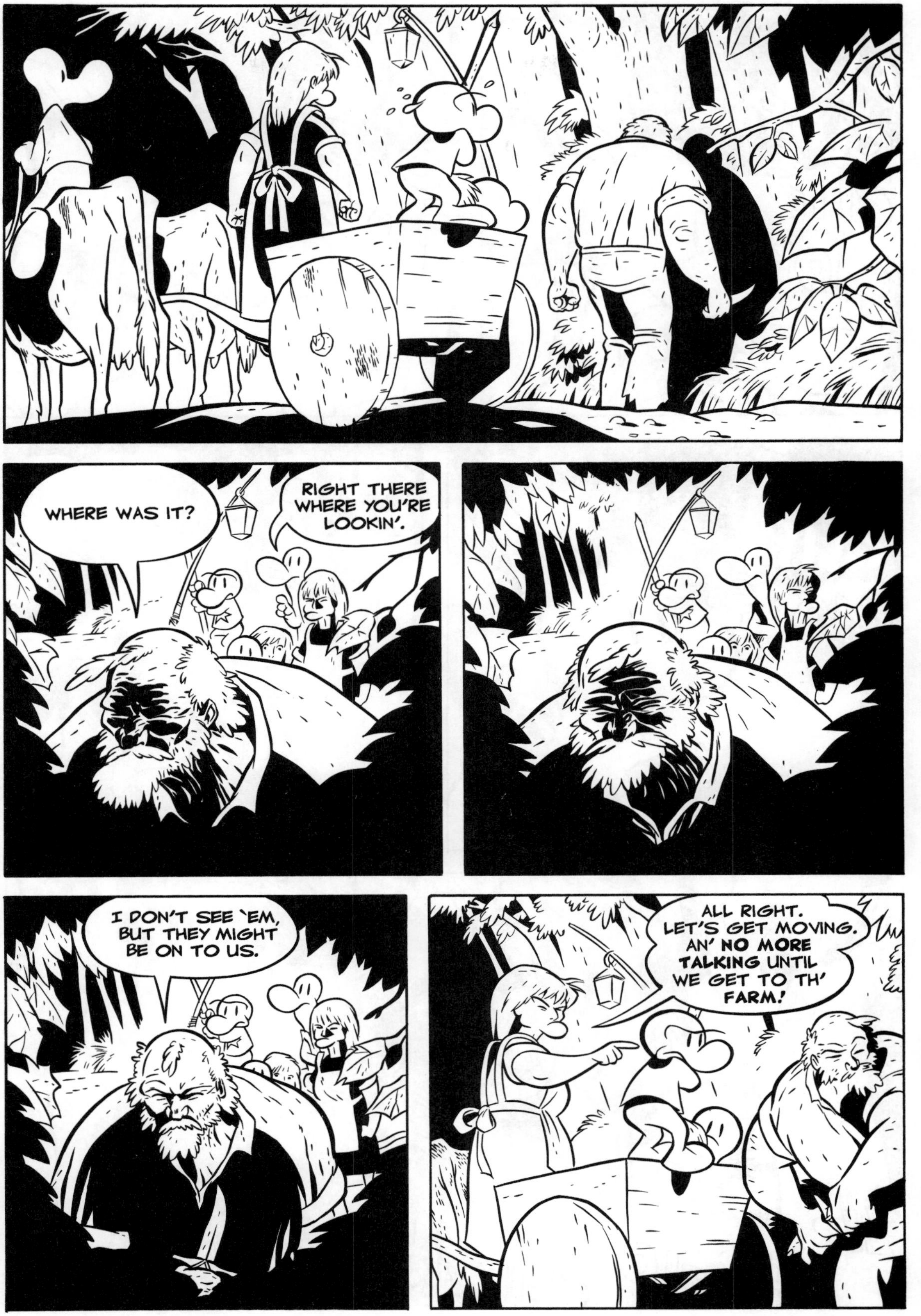
WHERE WAS IT?
RIGHT THERE WHERE YOU'RE LOOKIN'.
I DON'T SEE 'EM, BUT THEY MIGHT BE ON TO US.
ALL RIGHT. LET'S GET MOVING. AN' NO MORE TALKING UNTIL WE GET TO TH' FARM!

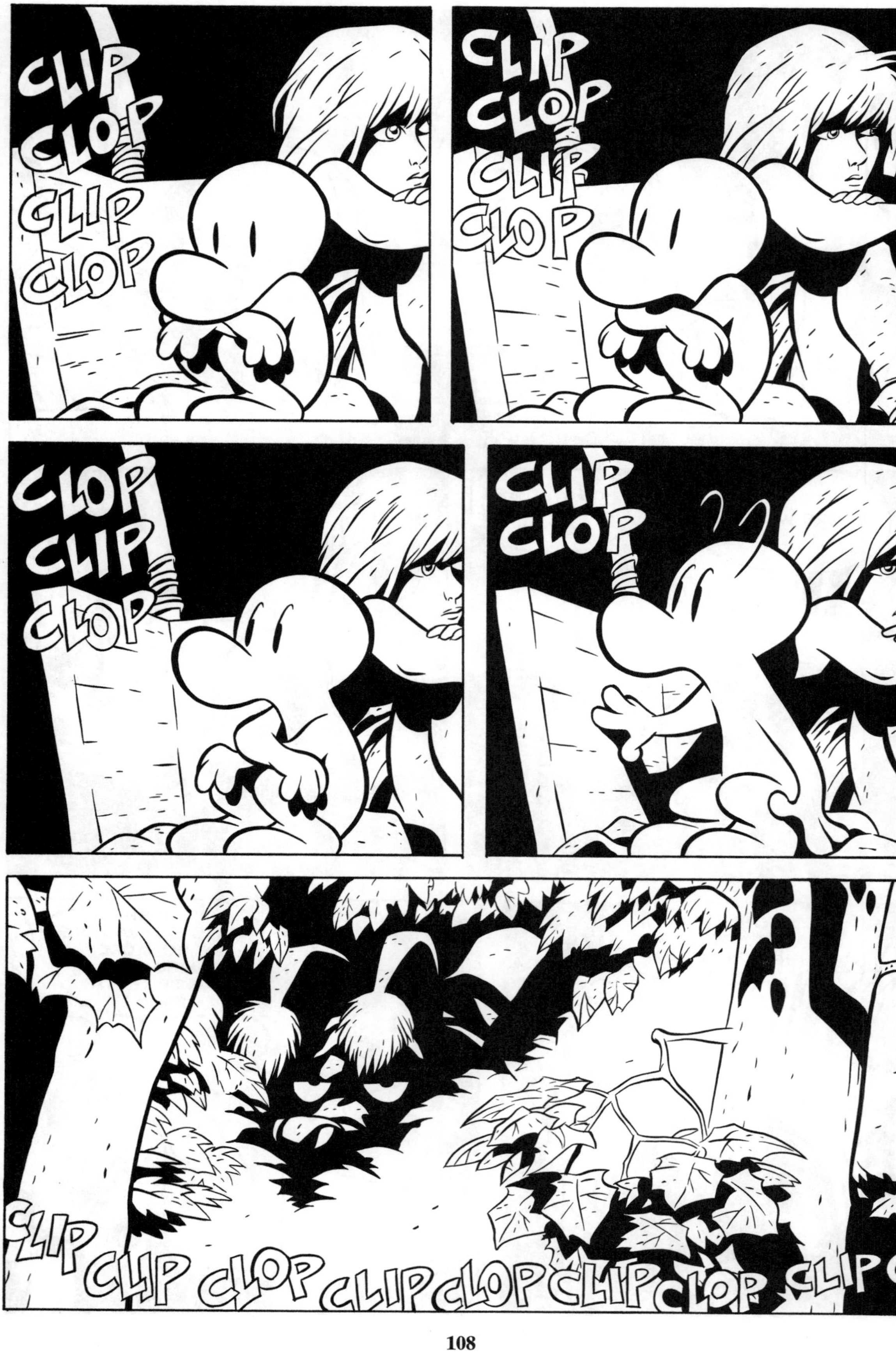
CLIP
CLOP
CLIP
CLOP
CLIP
CLOP
CLIP
CLOP
CLOP
CLIP
CLOP
CLIP
CLOP
CLIP
CLIP
CLOP
CLIP
CLOP
CLIP
CLOP
CLIP

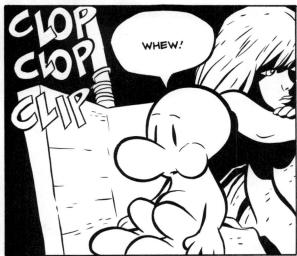

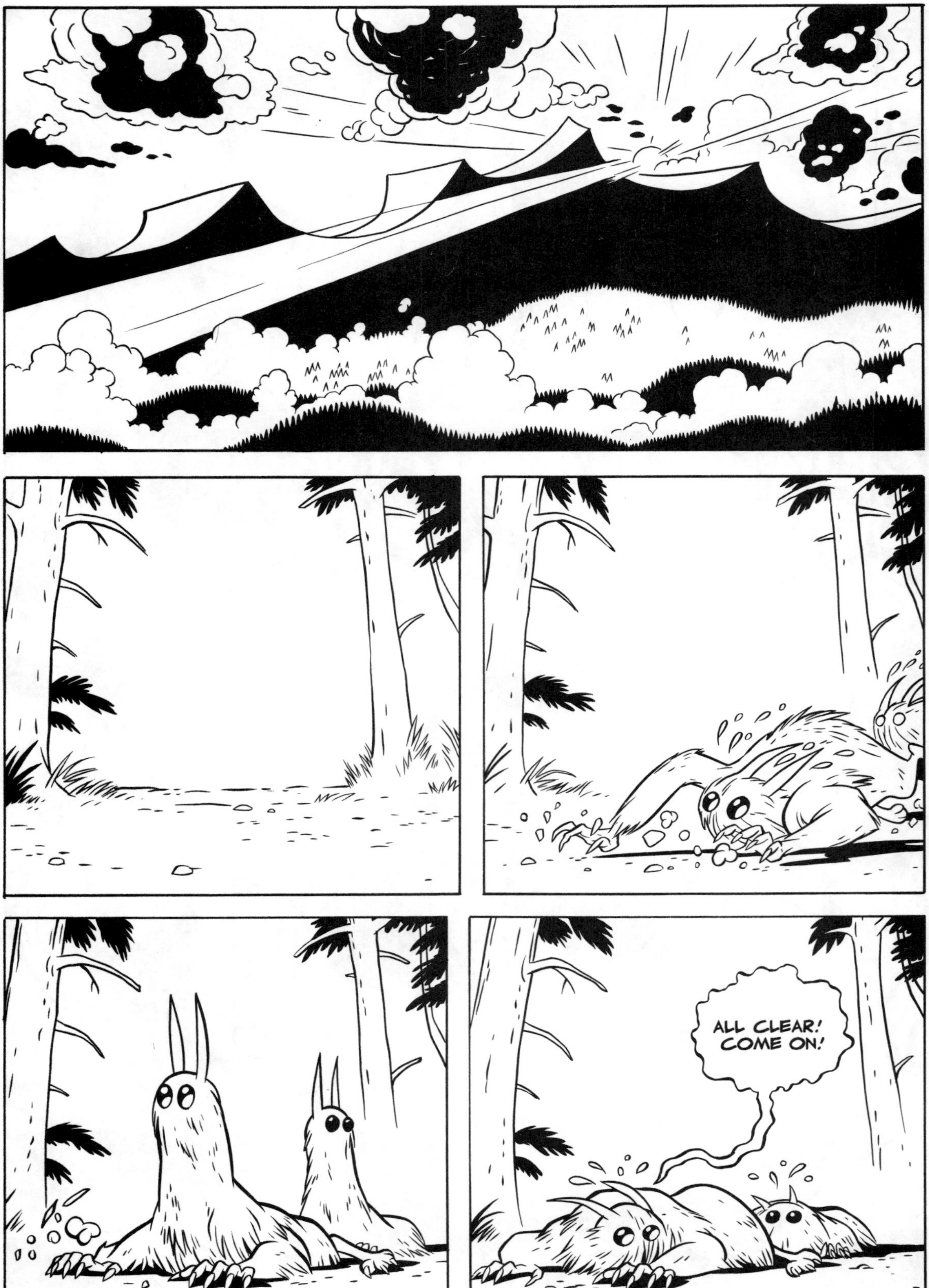
ALL CLEAR! COME ON!

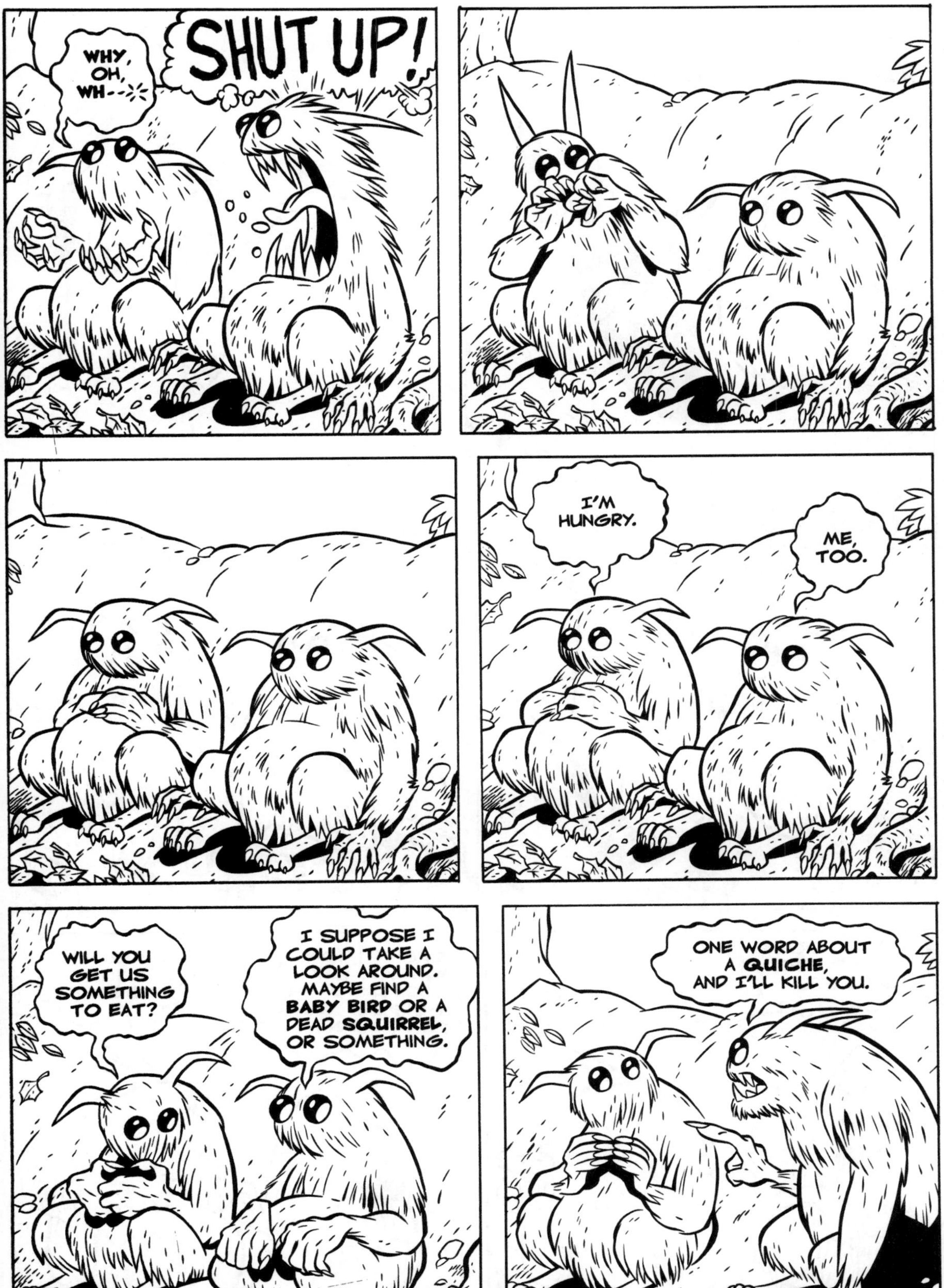

WHY, OH, WH--
SHUT UP!
I'M HUNGRY.
ME, TOO.
WILL YOU GET US SOMETHING TO EAT?
I SUPPOSE I COULD TAKE A LOOK AROUND. MAYBE FIND A **BABY BIRD** OR A DEAD **SQUIRREL**, OR SOMETHING.
ONE WORD ABOUT A **QUICHE**, AND I'LL KILL YOU.

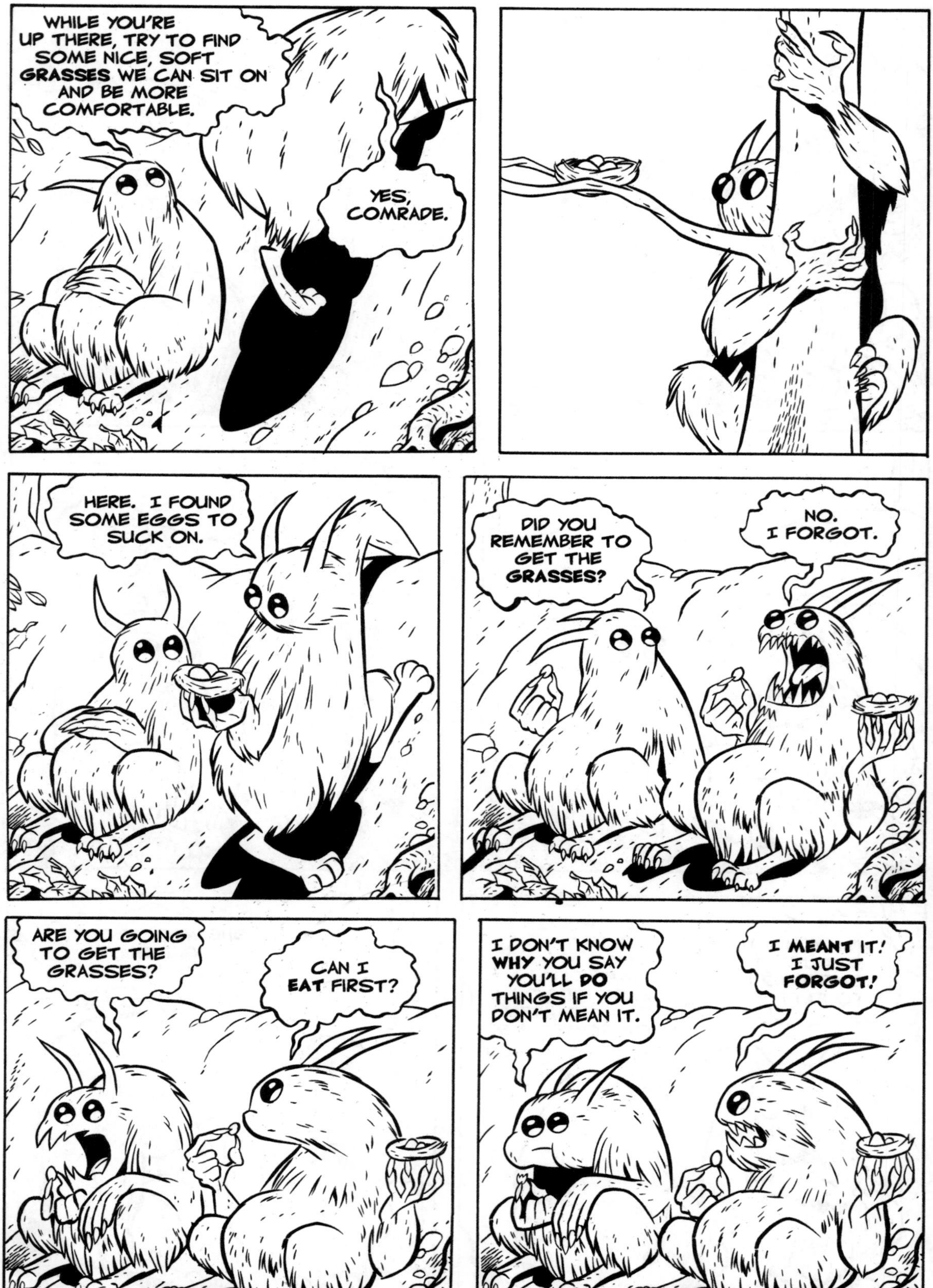
WHILE YOU'RE UP THERE, TRY TO FIND SOME NICE, SOFT GRASSES WE CAN SIT ON AND BE MORE COMFORTABLE.
YES, COMRADE.
HERE. I FOUND SOME EGGS TO SUCK ON.
DID YOU REMEMBER TO GET THE GRASSES?
NO. I FORGOT.
ARE YOU GOING TO GET THE GRASSES?
CAN I EAT FIRST?
I DON'T KNOW WHY YOU SAY YOU'LL DO THINGS IF YOU DON'T MEAN IT.
I MEANT IT! I JUST FORGOT!

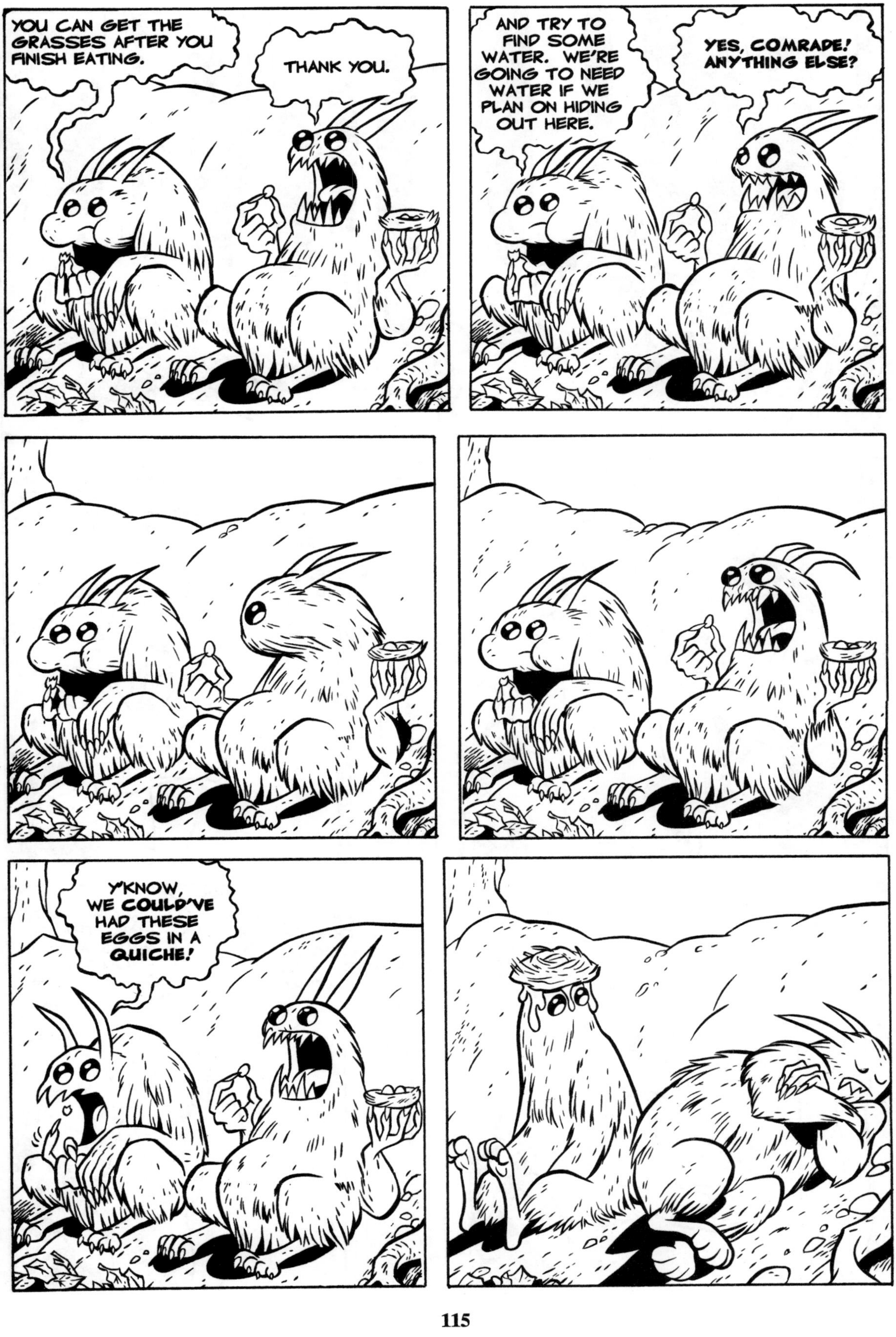
YOU CAN GET THE GRASSES AFTER YOU FINISH EATING.
THANK YOU.
AND TRY TO FIND SOME WATER. WE'RE GOING TO NEED WATER IF WE PLAN ON HIDING OUT HERE.
YES, COMRADE! ANYTHING ELSE?
Y'KNOW, WE COULD'VE HAD THESE EGGS IN A QUICHE!

WELL... THE BEAMS ARE SOUND. MOST OF TH' DAMAGE IS TO TH' ROOF.

AND, OF COURSE, THERE'S A GIANT **HOLE** IN TH' WALL. WHAT TH' **HECK** DID YOU **DO** TO THOSE POOR MONSTERS, ROSIE?

THE RAT CREATURES HAD US **SURROUNDED**, DEAR. I HAD TO GET A LITTLE **ROUGH.**

THIS PLACE LOOKS LIKE A **BATTLEFIELD!** YOU'RE LUCKY YOU ESCAPED WITH YOUR **LIVES!**

IT WAS A BIT SCARY, BUT DON'T FORGET I FOUGHT TH' **RATS** BACK IN TH' BIG WAR!

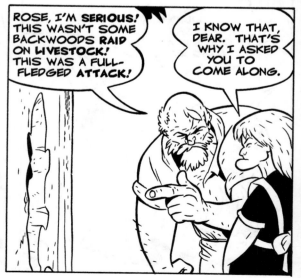

ROSE, I'M **SERIOUS!** THIS WASN'T SOME BACKWOODS RAID ON **LIVESTOCK!** THIS WAS A FULL-FLEDGED ATTACK!

I KNOW THAT, DEAR. THAT'S WHY I ASKED YOU TO COME ALONG.

116

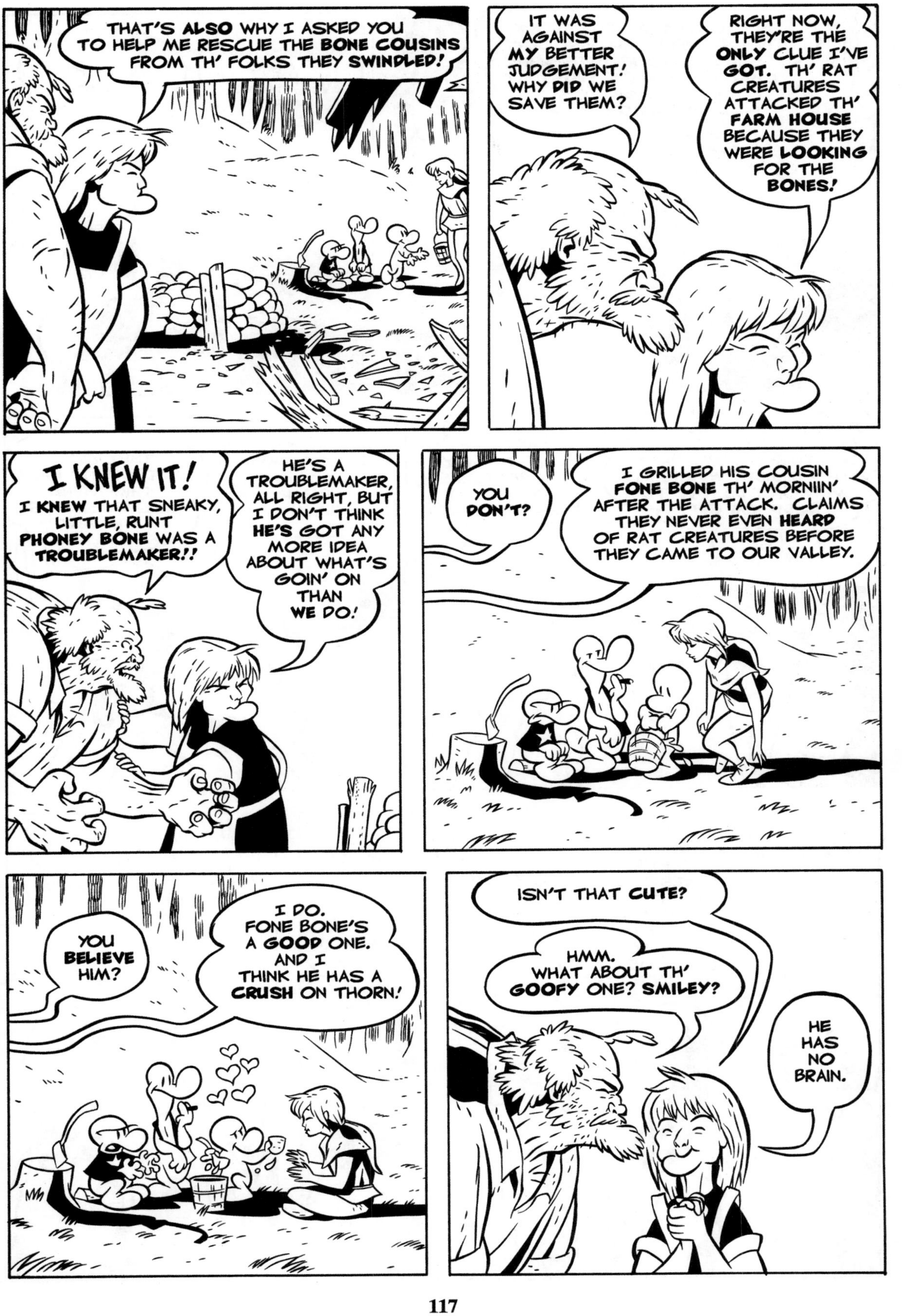
THAT'S ALSO WHY I ASKED YOU TO HELP ME RESCUE THE BONE COUSINS FROM TH' FOLKS THEY SWINDLED!
IT WAS AGAINST MY BETTER JUDGEMENT! WHY DID WE SAVE THEM?
RIGHT NOW, THEY'RE THE ONLY CLUE I'VE GOT. TH' RAT CREATURES ATTACKED TH' FARM HOUSE BECAUSE THEY WERE LOOKING FOR THE BONES!
I KNEW IT! I KNEW THAT SNEAKY, LITTLE, RUNT PHONEY BONE WAS A TROUBLEMAKER!!
HE'S A TROUBLEMAKER, ALL RIGHT, BUT I DON'T THINK HE'S GOT ANY MORE IDEA ABOUT WHAT'S GOIN' ON THAN WE DO!
YOU DON'T?
I GRILLED HIS COUSIN FONE BONE TH' MORNIIN' AFTER THE ATTACK. CLAIMS THEY NEVER EVEN HEARD OF RAT CREATURES BEFORE THEY CAME TO OUR VALLEY.
YOU BELIEVE HIM?
I DO. FONE BONE'S A GOOD ONE. AND I THINK HE HAS A CRUSH ON THORN!
ISN'T THAT CUTE?
HMM. WHAT ABOUT TH' GOOFY ONE? SMILEY?
HE HAS NO BRAIN.

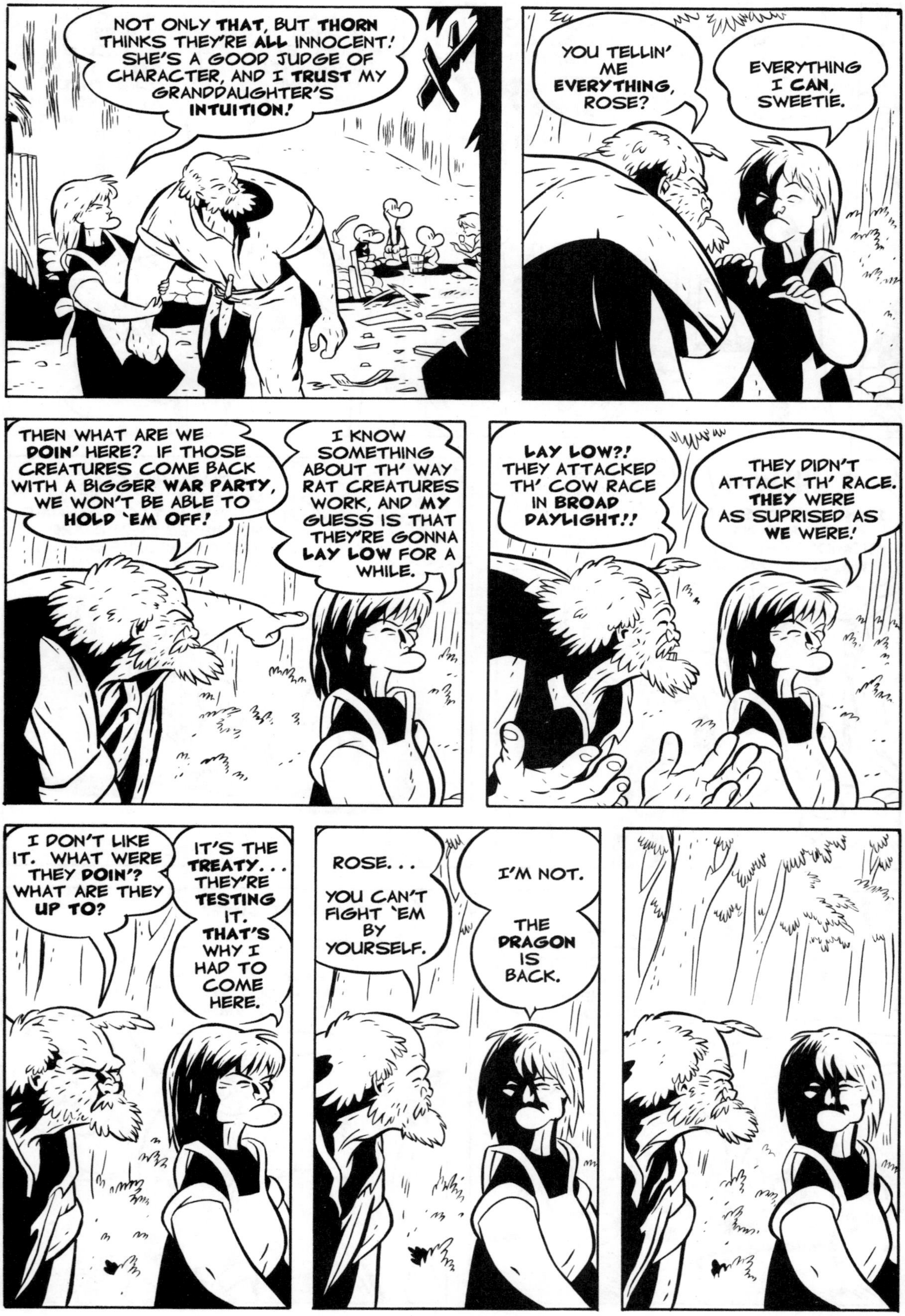
NOT ONLY THAT, BUT THORN THINKS THEY'RE ALL INNOCENT! SHE'S A GOOD JUDGE OF CHARACTER, AND I TRUST MY GRANDDAUGHTER'S INTUITION!
YOU TELLIN' ME EVERYTHING, ROSE?
EVERYTHING I CAN, SWEETIE.
THEN WHAT ARE WE DOIN' HERE? IF THOSE CREATURES COME BACK WITH A BIGGER WAR PARTY, WE WON'T BE ABLE TO HOLD 'EM OFF!
I KNOW SOMETHING ABOUT TH' WAY RAT CREATURES WORK, AND MY GUESS IS THAT THEY'RE GONNA LAY LOW FOR A WHILE.
LAY LOW?! THEY ATTACKED TH' COW RACE IN BROAD DAYLIGHT!!
THEY DIDN'T ATTACK TH' RACE. THEY WERE AS SUPRISED AS WE WERE!
I DON'T LIKE IT. WHAT WERE THEY DOIN'? WHAT ARE THEY UP TO?
IT'S THE TREATY... THEY'RE TESTING IT. THAT'S WHY I HAD TO COME HERE.
ROSE...
YOU CAN'T FIGHT 'EM BY YOURSELF.
I'M NOT.
THE DRAGON IS BACK.

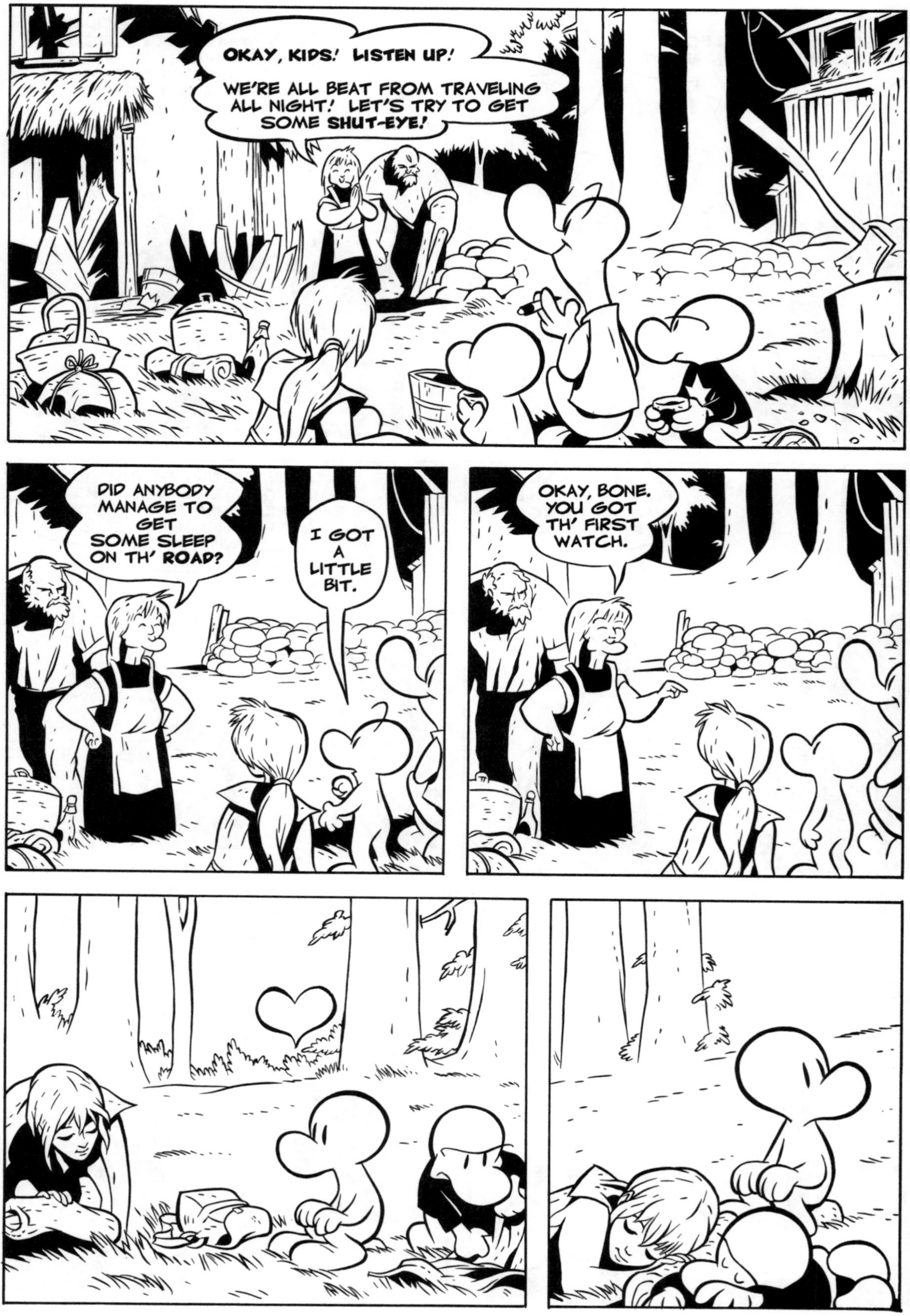
OKAY, KIDS! LISTEN UP!
WE'RE ALL BEAT FROM TRAVELING ALL NIGHT! LET'S TRY TO GET SOME SHUT-EYE!
DID ANYBODY MANAGE TO GET SOME SLEEP ON TH' ROAD?
I GOT A LITTLE BIT.
OKAY, BONE. YOU GOT TH' FIRST WATCH.

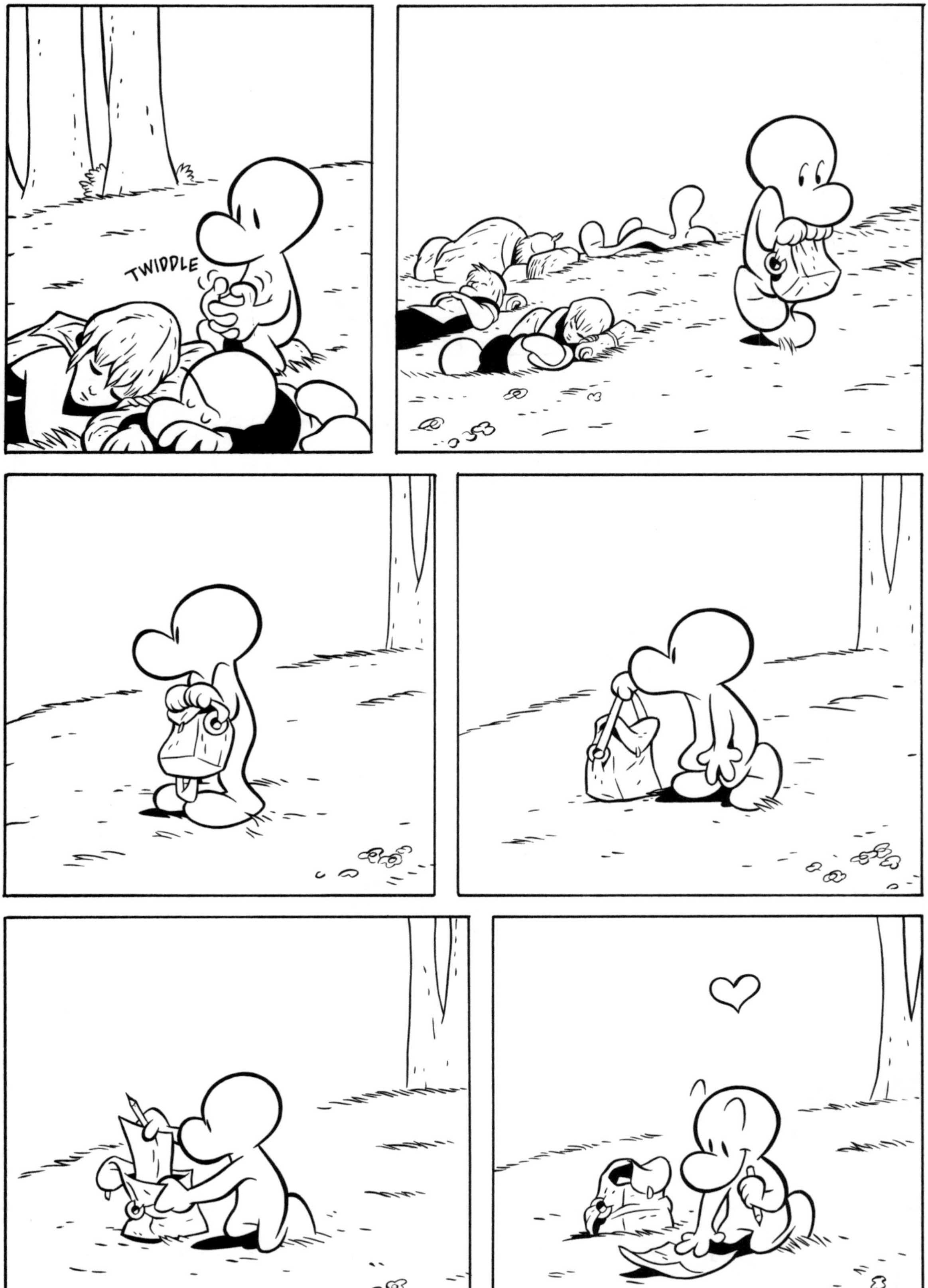
TWIDDLE

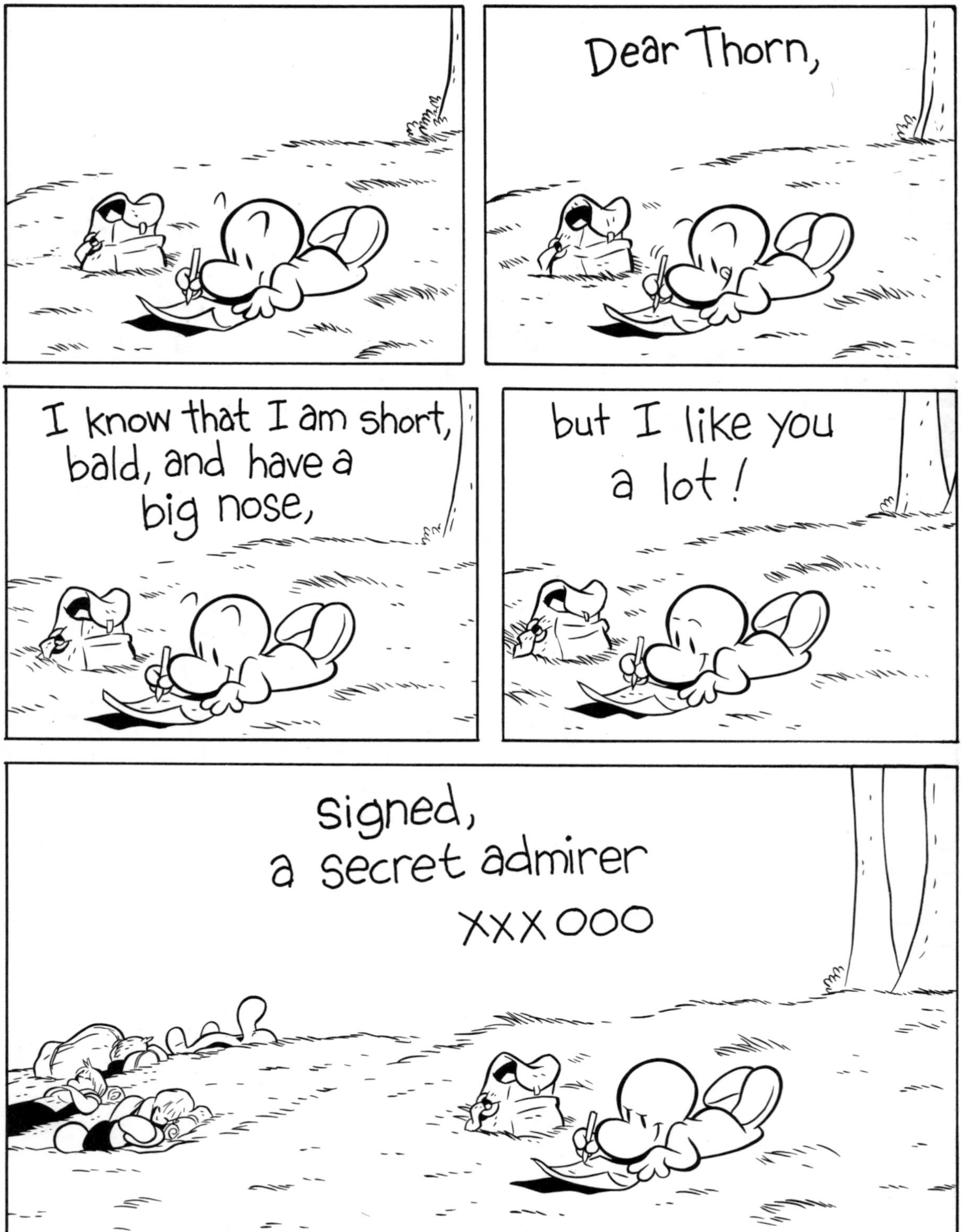
Dear Thorn,
I know that I am short, bald, and have a big nose,
but I like you a lot!
signed, a secret admirer
XXX OOO

NEXT: UP ON THE ROOF

'ROUND AND 'ROUND
  OUR BUSY FEET GO

HURRY AND FURY
  AND APPLE-RED GLOW...

The sights and sounds of places to do . . .

THE LAUGHING AND SHOUTING WILL NEVER BE THROUGH!

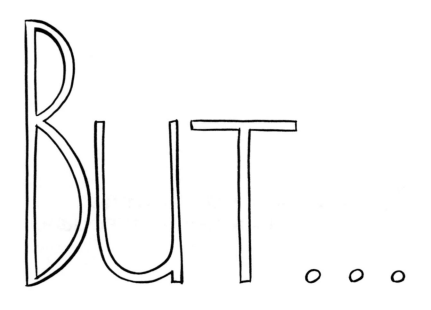

BUT...

AFTER ALL THAT RUNNING,
THE REST IS BEST

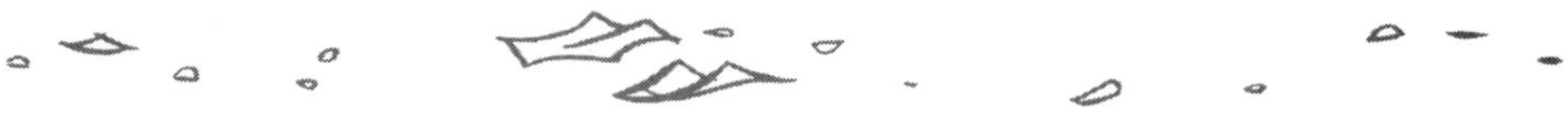

AND THE BEST TO REST WITH
IS YOU.

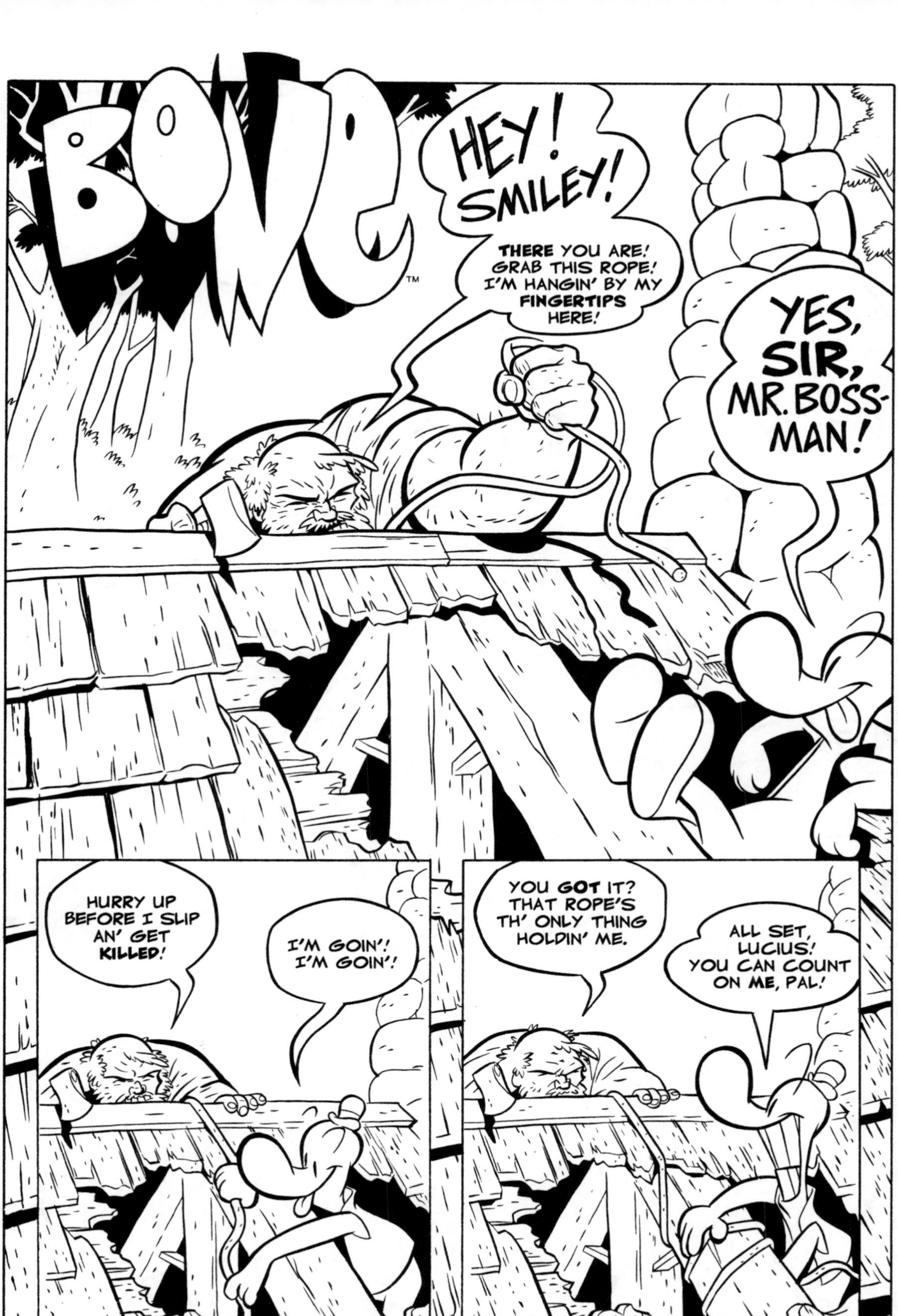
BONE™
HEY! SMILEY!
THERE YOU ARE! GRAB THIS ROPE! I'M HANGIN' BY MY FINGERTIPS HERE!
YES, SIR, MR. BOSS-MAN!
HURRY UP BEFORE I SLIP AN' GET KILLED!
I'M GOIN'! I'M GOIN'!
YOU GOT IT? THAT ROPE'S TH' ONLY THING HOLDIN' ME.
ALL SET, LUCIUS! YOU CAN COUNT ON ME, PAL!

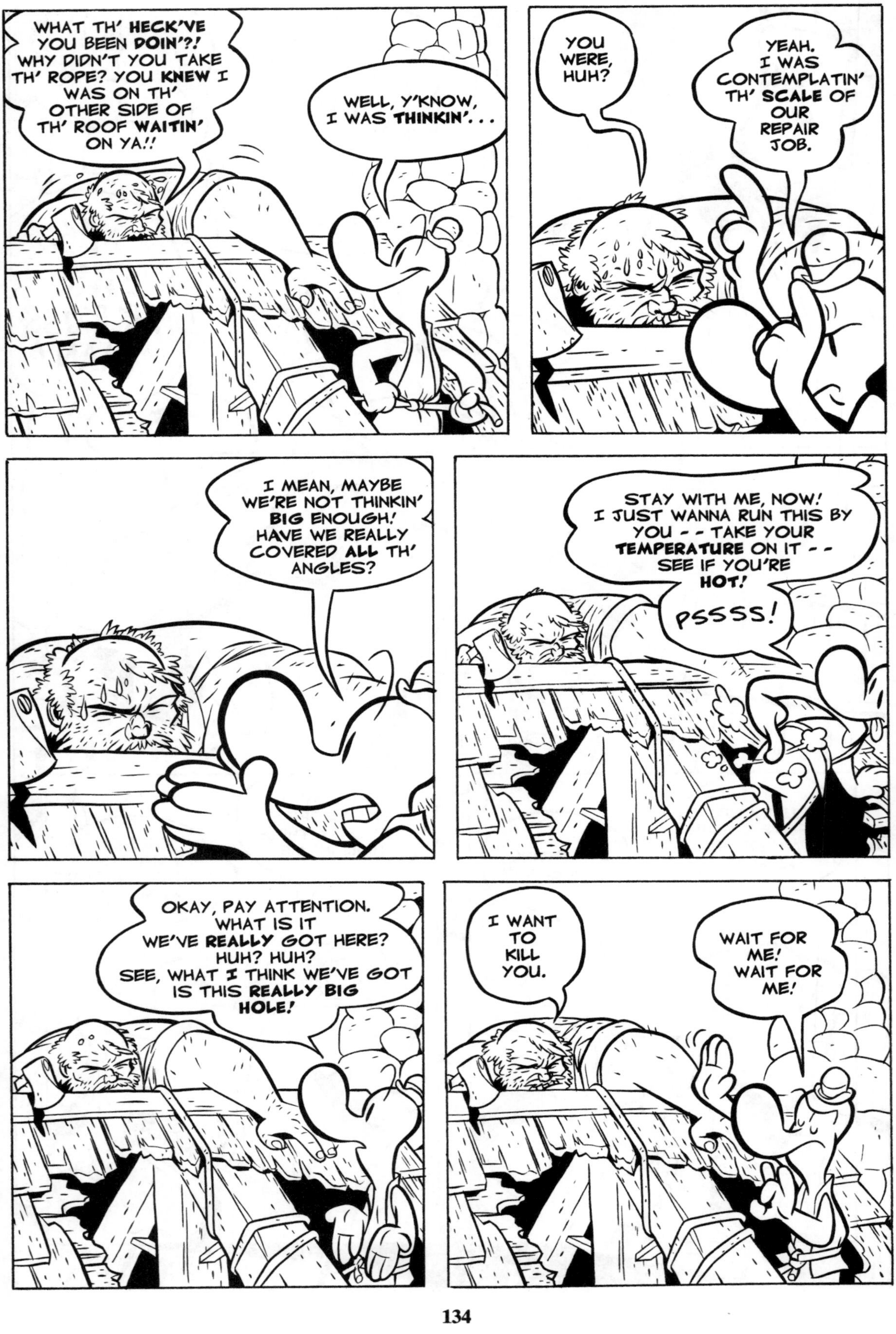
WHAT TH' HECK'VE YOU BEEN DOIN'?! WHY DIDN'T YOU TAKE TH' ROPE? YOU KNEW I WAS ON TH' OTHER SIDE OF TH' ROOF WAITIN' ON YA!!
WELL, Y'KNOW, I WAS THINKIN'. . .
YOU WERE, HUH?
YEAH. I WAS CONTEMPLATIN' TH' SCALE OF OUR REPAIR JOB.
I MEAN, MAYBE WE'RE NOT THINKIN' BIG ENOUGH! HAVE WE REALLY COVERED ALL TH' ANGLES?
STAY WITH ME, NOW! I JUST WANNA RUN THIS BY YOU - - TAKE YOUR TEMPERATURE ON IT - - SEE IF YOU'RE HOT!
PSSSS!
OKAY, PAY ATTENTION. WHAT IS IT WE'VE REALLY GOT HERE? HUH? HUH? SEE, WHAT I THINK WE'VE GOT IS THIS REALLY BIG HOLE!
I WANT TO KILL YOU.
WAIT FOR ME! WAIT FOR ME!

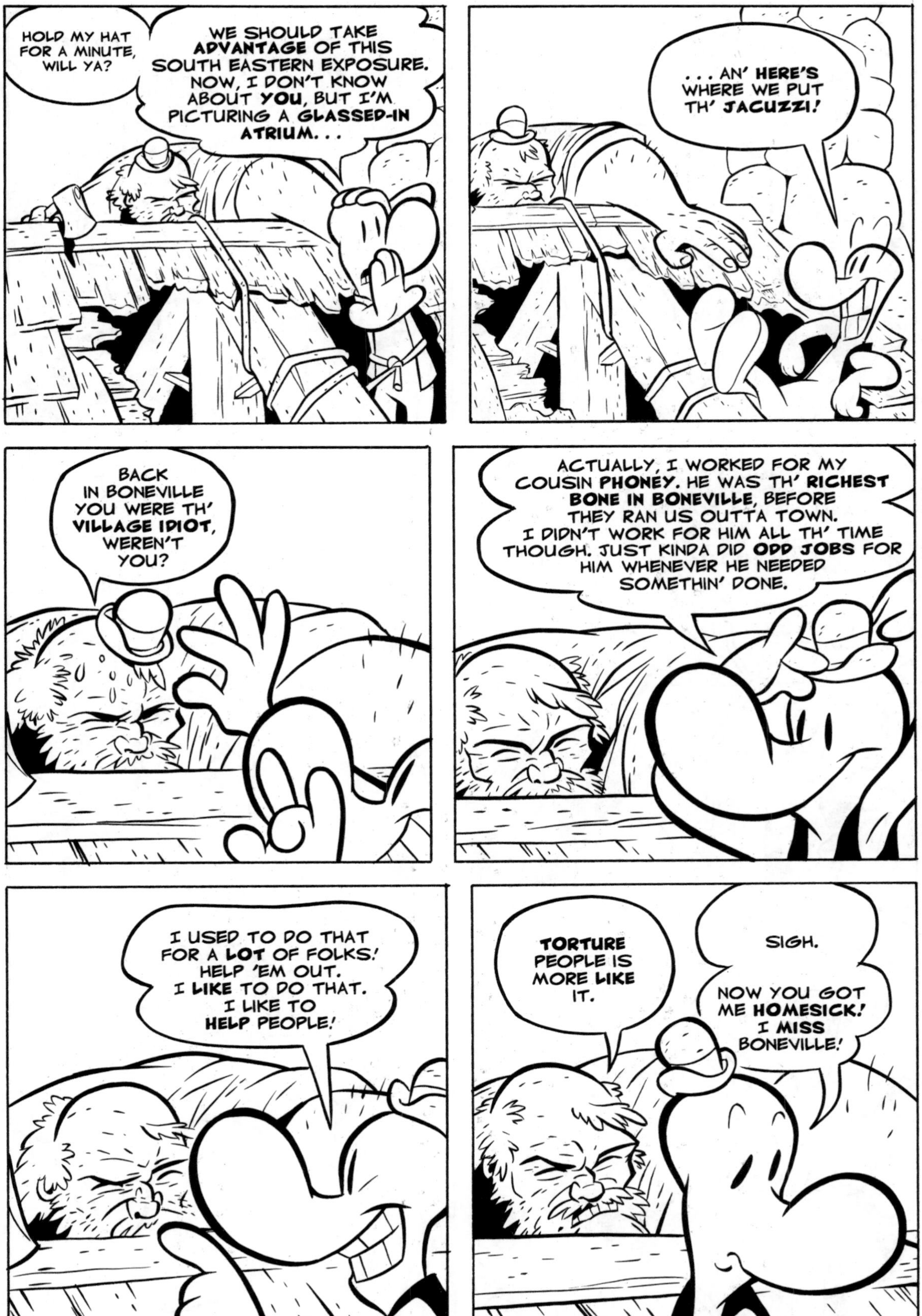
HOLD MY HAT FOR A MINUTE, WILL YA?
WE SHOULD TAKE ADVANTAGE OF THIS SOUTH EASTERN EXPOSURE. NOW, I DON'T KNOW ABOUT YOU, BUT I'M PICTURING A GLASSED-IN ATRIUM. . .
. . . AN' HERE'S WHERE WE PUT TH' JACUZZI!
BACK IN BONEVILLE YOU WERE TH' VILLAGE IDIOT, WEREN'T YOU?
ACTUALLY, I WORKED FOR MY COUSIN PHONEY. HE WAS TH' RICHEST BONE IN BONEVILLE, BEFORE THEY RAN US OUTTA TOWN. I DIDN'T WORK FOR HIM ALL TH' TIME THOUGH. JUST KINDA DID ODD JOBS FOR HIM WHENEVER HE NEEDED SOMETHIN' DONE.
I USED TO DO THAT FOR A LOT OF FOLKS! HELP 'EM OUT. I LIKE TO DO THAT. I LIKE TO HELP PEOPLE!
TORTURE PEOPLE IS MORE LIKE IT.
SIGH.
NOW YOU GOT ME HOMESICK! I MISS BONEVILLE!

SMILEY.

THERE WAS THIS **GREAT** PLACE DOWN IN TH' PARK BY THE OL' STATUE OF **BIG JOHNSON BONE** WHERE YOU COULD SIT AN' FEED TH' BIRDS....

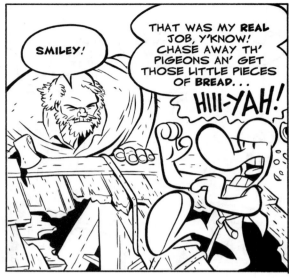

SMILEY!

THAT WAS MY **REAL** JOB, Y'KNOW! CHASE AWAY TH' PIGEONS AN' GET THOSE LITTLE PIECES OF **BREAD**...

HIII-YAH!

SMILEY! I'M NOT HANGIN' AROUND HERE FOR MY HEALTH! I'M TRYIN' TO FIX TH' ROOF!!

ANYTHING I CAN DO TO HELP?

HAND ME SOME OF THOSE SHAKES SO I CAN START SHINGLING!

YOU MEAN **THESE**?

YES. GIMME ENOUGH FOR MY SIDE.

HOW MANY IS **THAT**? THERE'S A WHOLE **PILE** UNDER HERE.

WELL, IF **HALF** OF TH' PILE IS FOR **YOUR** SIDE OF TH' ROOF, AN' **HALF** IS FOR MY SIDE, **YOU FIGURE IT OUT!**

137

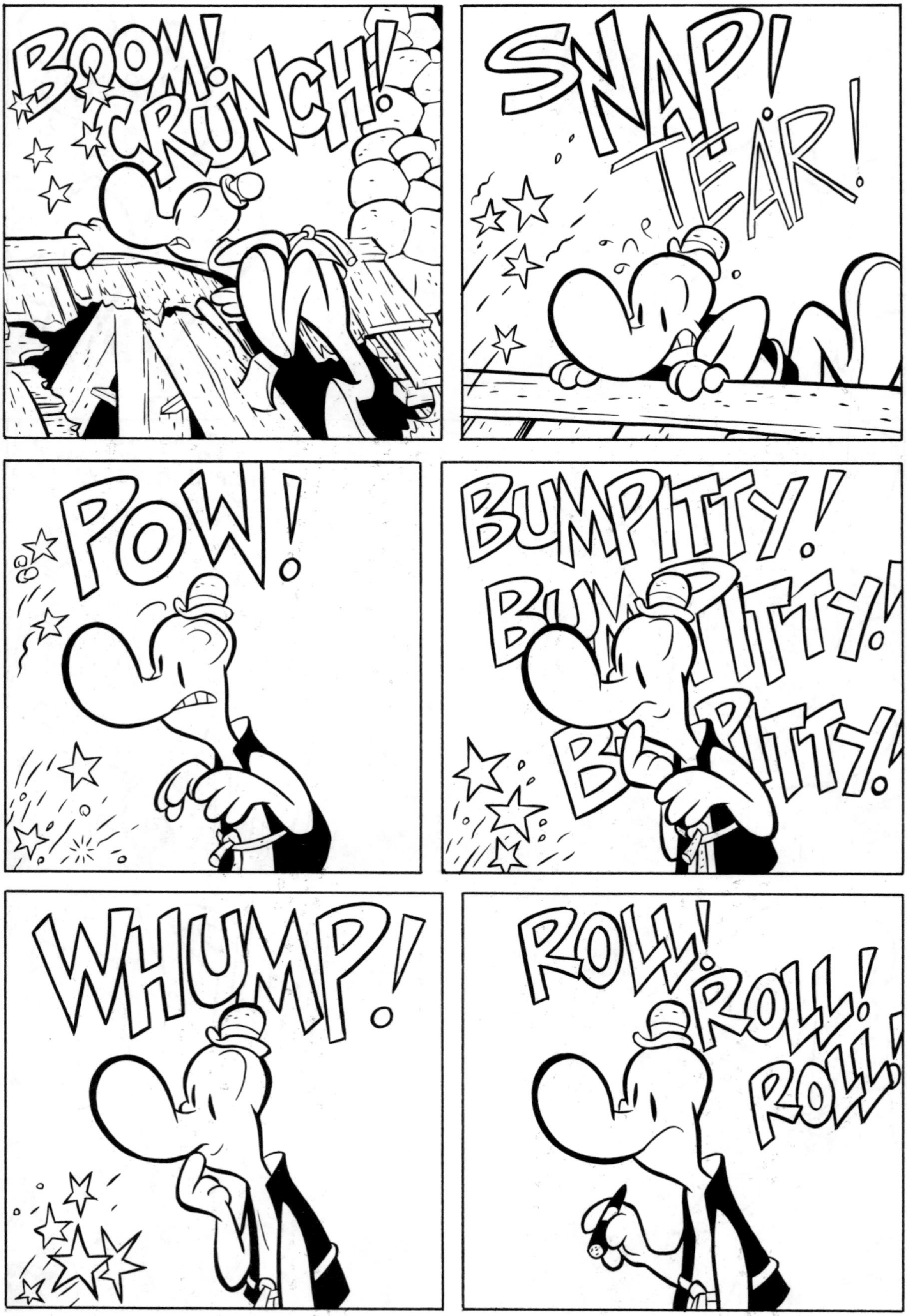
BOOM!
CRUNCH!
SNAP!
TEAR!
POW!
BUMPITTY!
BUMPITTY!
BUMPITTY!
WHUMP!
ROLL!
ROLL!
ROLL!

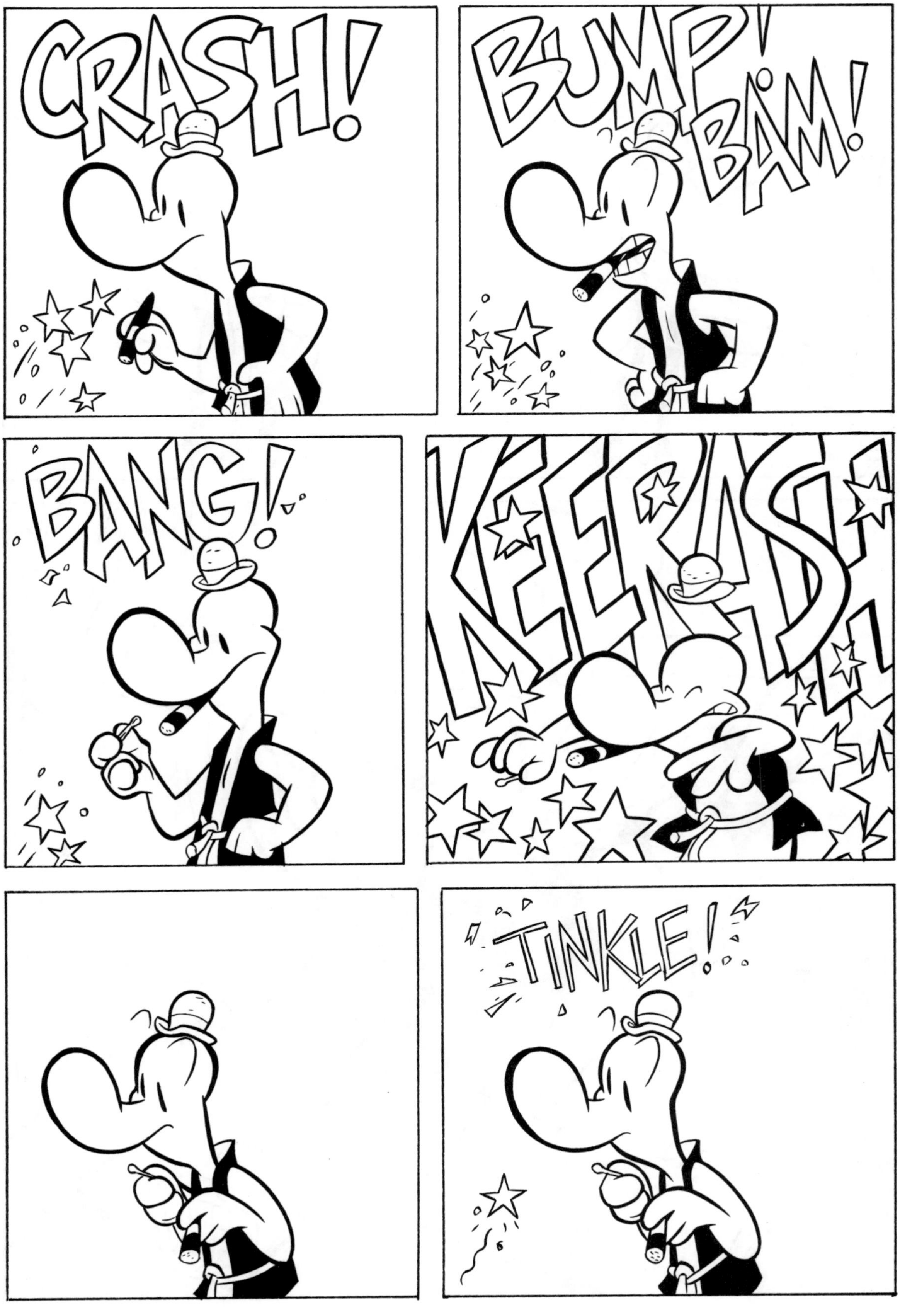
CRASH!
BUMP!
BAM!
BANG!
KEERASH
TINKLE!

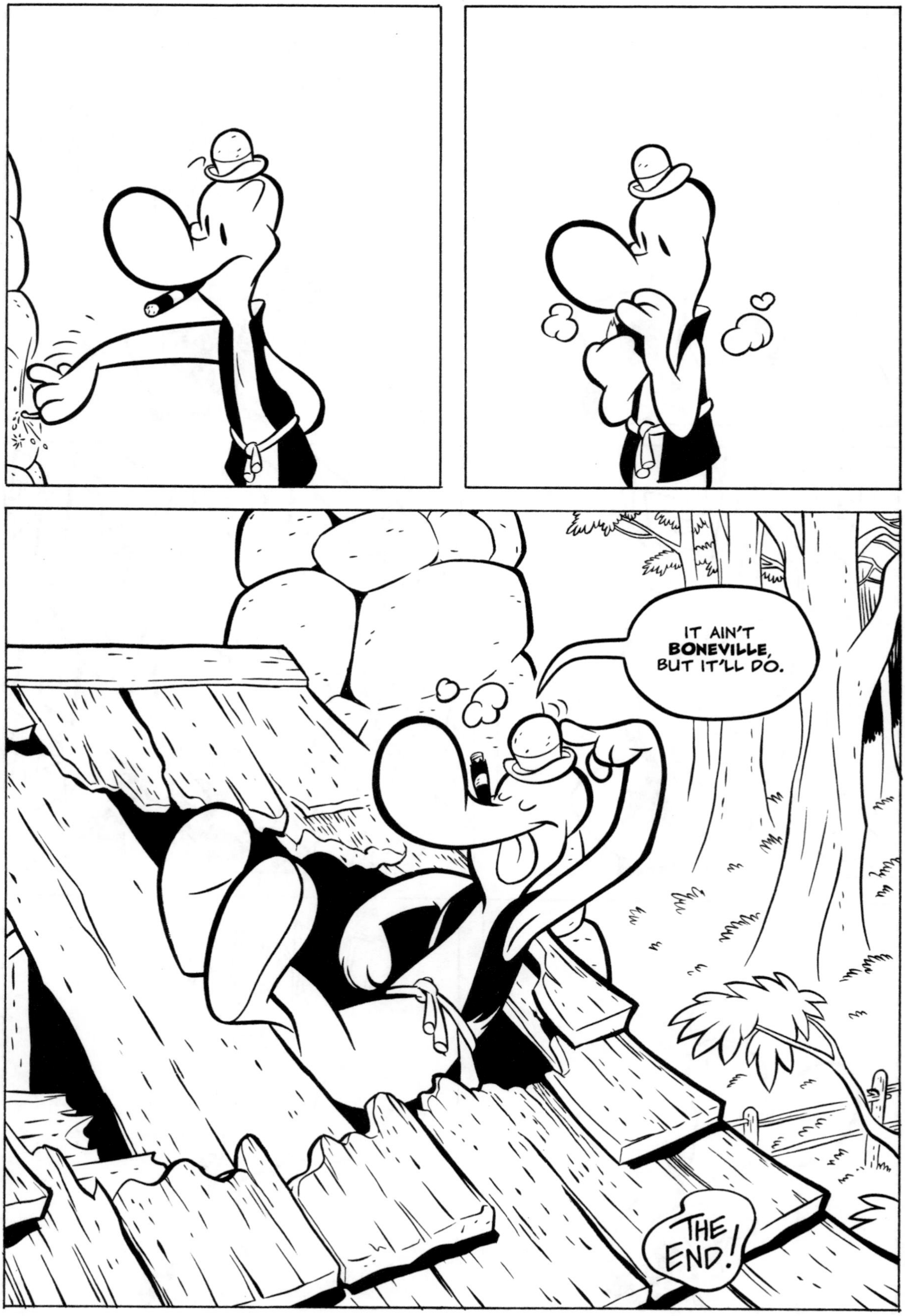
IT AIN'T BONEVILLE, BUT IT'LL DO.
THE END!

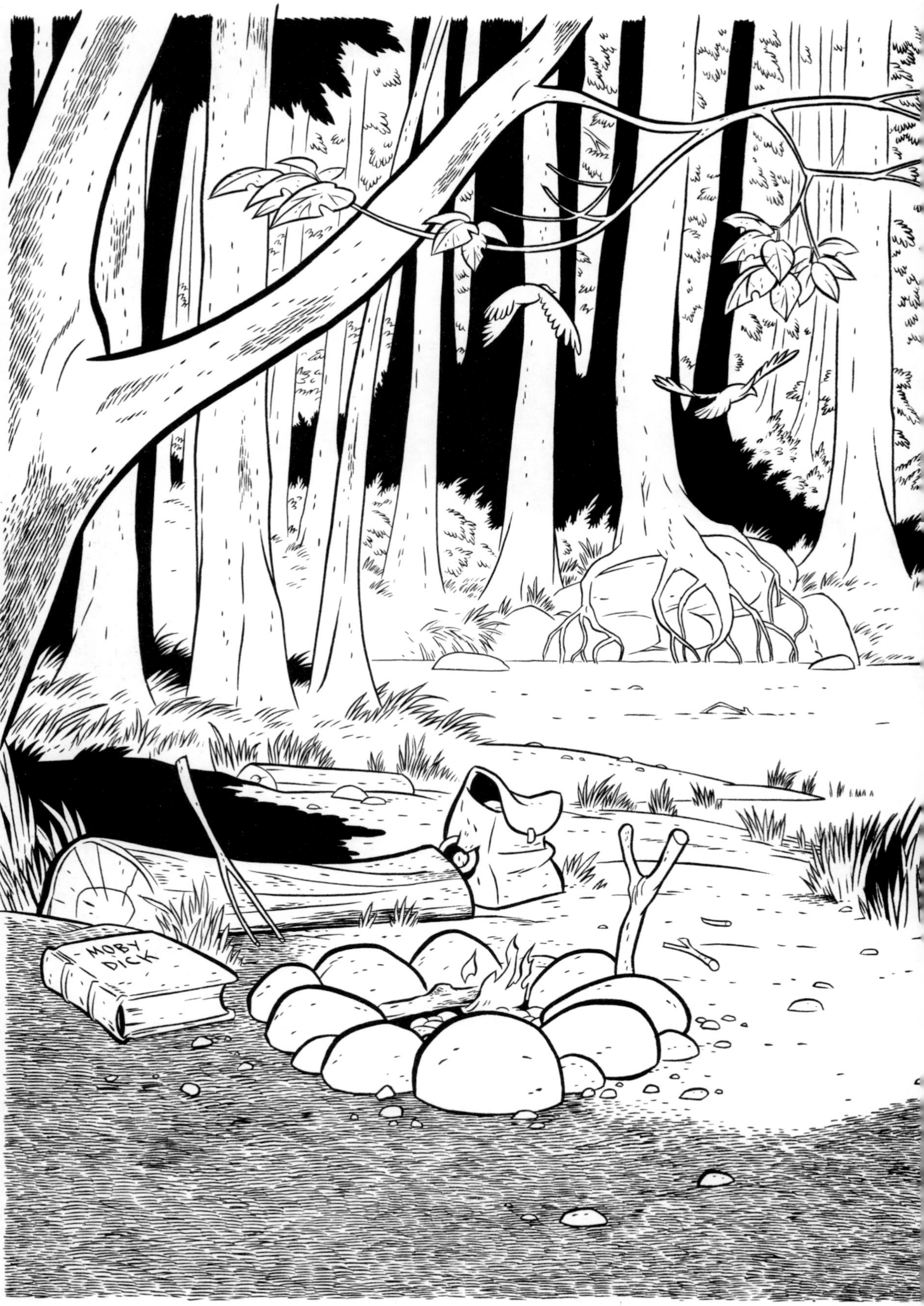
MOBY DICK

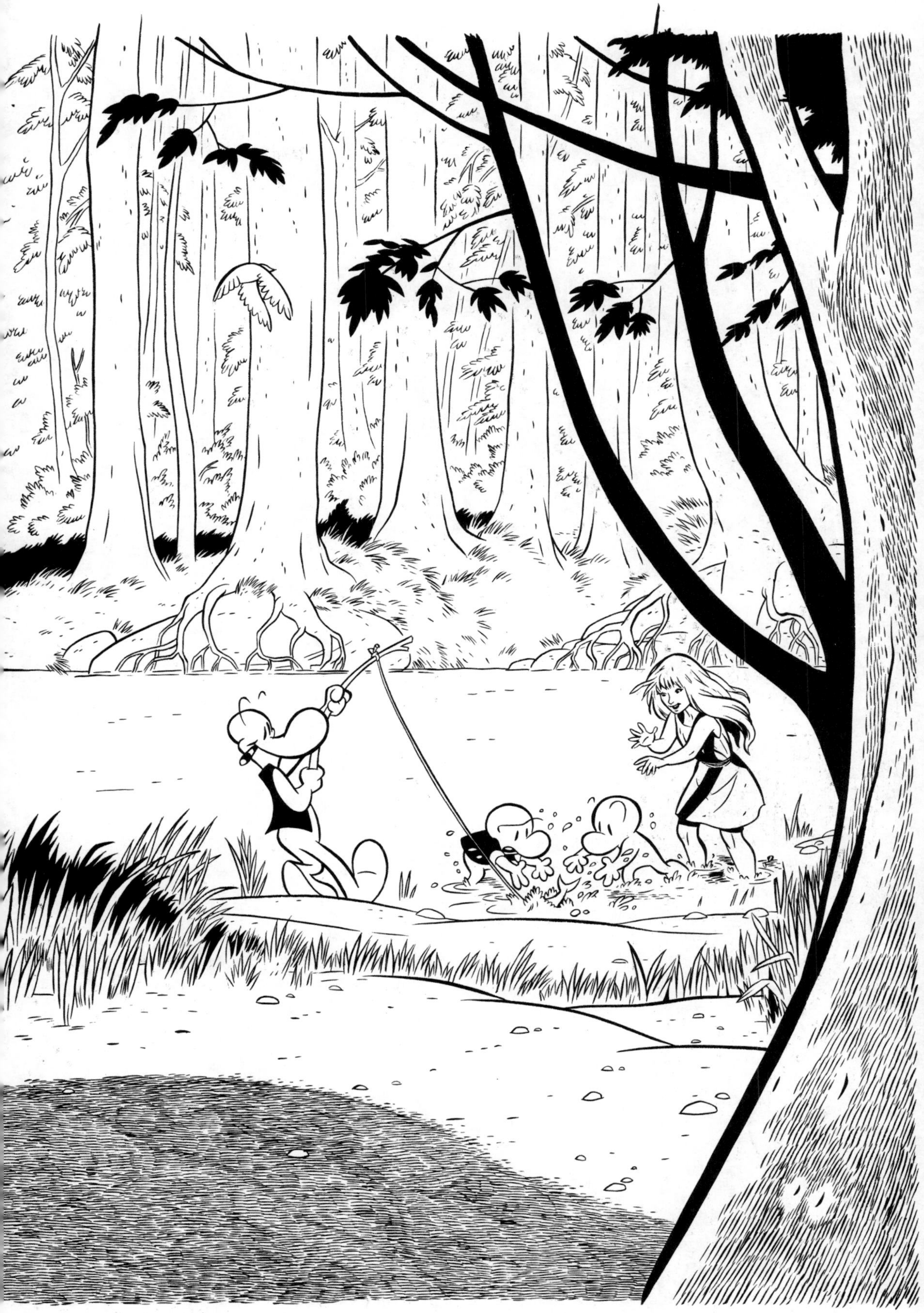

JEFF SMITH
BONE
1
OUT FROM BONEVILLE
JEFF
BONE
THE GREAT COW RACE